Adobe® Photoshop® CS6

ILLUSTRATED

Adobe® Photoshop® CS6

ILLUSTRATED

Chris Botello

COURSE TECHNOLOGY
CENGAGE Learning

Australia • Brazil • Japan • Korea • Mexico • Singapore • Spain • United Kingdom • United States

Adobe® Photoshop® CS6—Illustrated, International Edition
Chris Botello

Editor-in-Chief: Marie Lee

Executive Editor: Marjorie Hunt

Senior Product Manager: Christina Kling-Garrett

Product Manager: Kim Klasner

Associate Acquisitions Editor: Amanda Lyons

Editorial Assistant: Brandelynn Perry

Developmental Editor: Ann Fisher

Content Project Manager: Jennifer Feltri-George

Art Director: GEX Publishing Services

Print Buyer: Fola Orekoya

Text Designer: GEX Publishing Services

Proofreader: Harold Johnson

Indexer: BIM Indexing

QA Reviewers: Jeff Schwartz, John Freitas, Susan
    Whalen, Ashlee Welz Smith

Cover Designer: GEX Publishing Services

Cover Artist: Mark Hunt

Composition: GEX Publishing Services

For product information and technology assistance, contact us at
Cengage Learning Customer & Sales Support, 1-800-354-9706

For permission to use material from this text or product, submit all requests online at **www.cengage.com/permissions**
Further permissions questions can be emailed to
permissionrequest@cengage.com

International Edition:

ISBN-13: 978-1-133-52598-1

ISBN-10: 1-133-52598-9

Cengage Learning International Offices

Asia
www.cengageasia.com
tel: (65) 6410 1200

Australia/New Zealand
www.cengage.com.au
tel: (61) 3 9685 4111

Brazil
www.cengage.com.br
tel: (55) 11 3665 9900

India
www.cengage.co.in
tel: (91) 11 4364 1111

Latin America
www.cengage.com.mx
tel: (52) 55 1500 6000

UK/Europe/Middle East/Africa
www.cengage.co.uk
tel: (44) 0 1264 332 424

**Represented in Canada by
Nelson Education, Ltd.**
tel: (416) 752 9100 / (800) 668 0671
www.nelson.com

Cengage Learning is a leading provider of customized learning solutions with office locations around the globe, including Singapore, the United Kingdom, Australia, Mexico, Brazil, and Japan. Locate your local office at: **www.cengage.com/global**

For product information: **www.cengage.com/international**
Visit your local office: **www.cengage.com/global**
Visit our corporate website: **www.cengage.com**

Adobe product screen shot(s) reprinted with permission from Adobe Systems Incorporated

Adobe®, Dreamweaver®, Flash®, InDesign®, Illustrator®, and Photoshop® are either registered trademarks or trademarks of Adobe Systems Incorporated in the United States and/or other countries. THIS PRODUCT IS NOT ENDORSED OR SPONSORED BY ADOBE SYSTEMS INCORPORATED, PUBLISHER OF ADOBE® DREAMWEAVER®, FLASH®, INDESIGN®, ILLUSTRATOR®, AND PHOTOSHOP®.

AVAILABILITY OF RESOURCES MAY DIFFER BY REGION. Check with your local Cengage Learning representative for details.

Printed in the United States of America
1 2 3 4 5 6 7 18 17 16 15 14 13 12

Brief Contents

Contents

Preface

Welcome to *Adobe® Photoshop® CS6—Illustrated*. The unique page design of the book makes it a great learning tool for both new and experienced users. Each skill is presented on two facing pages so that you don't have to turn the page to find a screen shot or finish a paragraph. See the illustration on the right to learn more about the pedagogical and design elements of a typical lesson.

This book is an ideal learning tool for a wide range of learners—the "rookies" will find the clean design easy to follow and focused with only essential information presented, and the "hot shots" will appreciate being able to move quickly through the lessons to find the information they need without reading a lot of text. The design also makes this a great reference after the course is over!

Coverage

Eight units offer thorough coverage of essential skills for working with Adobe Photoshop from both the design and production perspective, including creating and managing layer masks, creating color effects and improving images with adjustment layers, working with text and combining text and imagery, and using filters and layer styles to create eye-popping special effects.

Written by Chris Botello, a professional designer who works on movie posters and theatrical campaigns for the entertainment industry, Photoshop CS6 Illustrated offers a real-world perspective with exercises designed to develop the practical skills and techniques necessary to work effectively in a professional graphic arts environment.

Each two-page spread focuses on a single skill.

Introduction briefly explains why the lesson skill is important.

A case scenario motivates the the steps and puts learning in context.

Tips and troubleshooting advice, right where you need it—next to the step itself.

Sidebars provide useful information related to the lesson skill.

Large screen shots keep students on track as they complete steps.

Brightly colored tabs indicate which section of the book you are in.

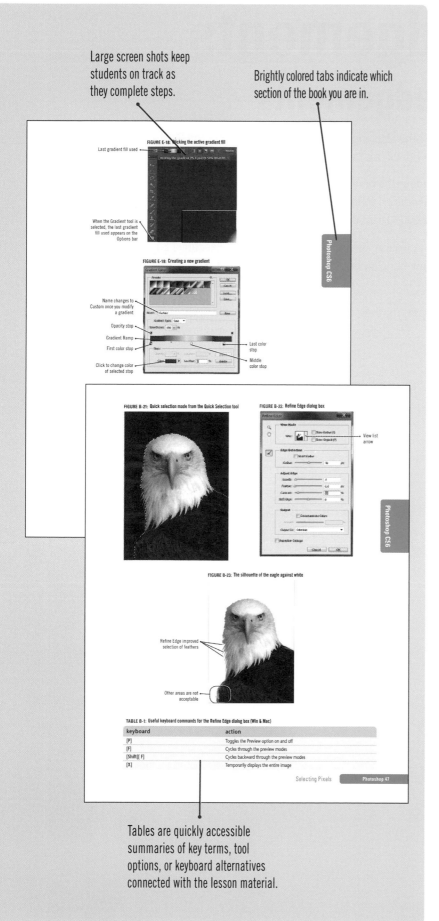

Tables are quickly accessible summaries of key terms, tool options, or keyboard alternatives connected with the lesson material.

Assignments

The lessons use MegaPixel, a graphic arts design agency, as the case study. The assignments on the light yellow pages at the end of each unit increase in difficulty. Additional case studies provide a variety of interesting and relevant exercises for students to practice skills.

Assignments include:

- **Concepts Reviews** consist of multiple choice, matching, and screen identification questions.

- **Skills Reviews** provide additional hands-on, step-by-step reinforcement.

- **Independent Challenges** are case projects requiring critical thinking and application of the unit skills. The Independent Challenges increase in difficulty, with the first one in each unit being the easiest. Independent Challenges 2 and 3 become increasingly open-ended, requiring more independent problem solving.

- **Real Life Independent Challenges** are practical exercises to help students with their everyday lives by focusing on important and useful essential skills, including creating photo montages for scrapbooks and photo albums, retouching and color-correcting family photos, applying layer styles and getting Photoshop Help online.

- **Advanced Challenge Exercises** set within the Independent Challenges provide optional steps for more advanced students.

- **Visual Workshops** are practical, self-graded capstone projects that require independent problem solving.

Acknowledgements

Author Acknowledgements

This book is one of my favorites—I was so excited by the challenge of teaching Photoshop in the Illustrated book format, and even more excited that we made it work. This is the book I use to teach my Photoshop 1 class at Tabor Academy.

Thank you to development editor Ann Fisher for guiding the book through to completion (and for all the extra work she does and never mentions). Special thanks to the technical editors, John Freitas, Ashlee Welz-Smith, Danielle Shaw, and Susan Whalen, who took great care to be sure that the exercises all worked. Thank you guys for having my back.

I would also like to thank Marie Lee, Editor-in-Chief at Course Technology, Marjorie Hunt, Executive Editor, and Amanda Lyons, Associate Acquisitions Editor. I would also like to thank our Content Project Manager, Jennifer Feltri-George, and Christina Kling-Garrett, our Product Manager.

Finally, thank you to the production and editorial teams for their hard work in putting it all together.

Chris Botello

Advisory Board Acknowledgements

We would like to thank our Advisory Board for their honest feedback and suggestions that helped guide our development decisions for this edition. They are as follows:

Rich Barnett, Wadsworth High School

Lisa Cogley, James A. Rhodes State College

Trudy Lund, Smoke Valley School District

Diane Miller, James A. Rhodes State College

Charles Schneider, Red Clay Consolidated School District

Read This Before You Begin

This book assumes the following:

1. The software has been registered properly. If the product is not registered, students must respond to registration and dialog boxes each time they start the software.
2. Default tools in the Tools panel might differ, but tool options and other settings do not carry over to the End-of-Unit exercises or between units.
3. Students know how to create a folder using a file management utility.
4. After introduction and reinforcement in initial units, the student will be able to respond to the dialog boxes that open when saving a file. Later units do not provide step-by-step guidance.
5. Panels, windows, and dialog boxes have default settings when opened. Exceptions may occur when students open these elements repeatedly in a lesson or in the unit.
6. Students will be instructed in the early units on how to update missing links. Later units do not provide step-by-step guidance.
7. The few exercises that do contain live type were created using commonly available fonts. Nevertheless, it is possible, that students may run into a missing font issue when opening a data file. In that case, students should use an available font that is similar to the size and weight of the type shown in the lesson.

Frequently Asked Questions

What are the Minimum System Requirements (Windows)?

- Intel® Pentium® 4 or AMD Athlon® 64 or faster processor with 1GB RAM (2GB recommended)

- Microsoft® Windows Vista or Windows 7

- 1.6GB of available hard disk space (2 GB recommended)

- Color monitor with 16-bit color video card

- DVD-ROM

- Adobe Flash Player 10 (for exporting SWF files)

What are Data Files and where are they located?

Your instructor will provide the Data Files to you or direct you to a location on a network drive from which you can download them. As you download the files, select where to store them, such as a hard drive, a network server, or a USB drive. The instructions in the lessons refer to "the drive and folder where your Data Files are stored" when referring to the Data Files for the book.

What software was used to write and test this book?

This book was written and tested with Adobe Photoshop CS6 using a typical installation of Microsoft Windows 7 with Aero turned on.

Do I need to be connected to the Internet to complete the steps and exercises in this book?

Some of the exercises in this book assume that your computer is connected to the Internet. If you are not connected to the Internet, see your instructor for information on how to complete the exercises.

What do I do if my screen is different from the figures shown in this book?

This book was written and tested on computers with monitors set at a resolution of 1280 × 1024. If your screen shows more or less information than the figures in the book, your monitor is probably set at a higher or lower resolution. If you don't see something on your screen, you might have to scroll down or up to see the object identified in the figures.

CourseMate

ENGAGING. TRACKABLE. AFFORDABLE

Cengage Learning's CourseMate for Adobe Photoshop CS6 Illustrated brings course concepts to life with interactive learning, study, and exam preparation tools that support the printed textbook. Watch student comprehension soar as your class works with the printed textbook and the textbook-specific website. CourseMate goes beyond the book to deliver what you need!

FOR STUDENTS:

Interactive eBook that you can read, highlight, or annotate on your computer.

Total Training videos with audio-visual, step-by-step instructions reinforce concepts you learn about Adobe Photoshop.

Glossary and Flashcards to help you master key terms.

Interactive exercises give you immediate feedback to help you learn.

FOR INSTRUCTORS:

Engagement Tracker, a first-of-its-kind tool that monitors student engagement in the course.

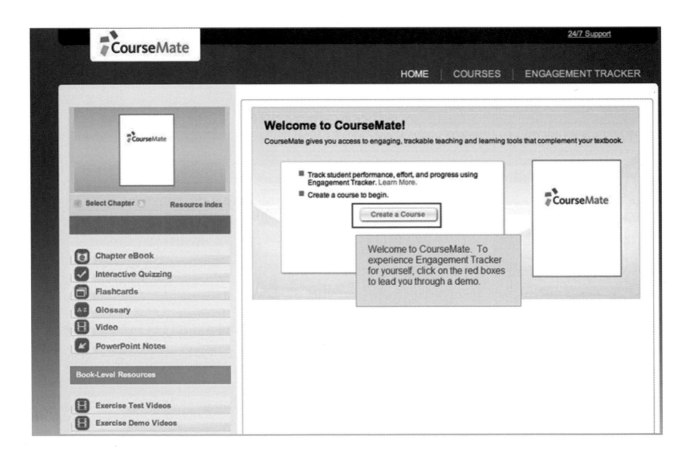

Instructor Resources

The Instructor Resources CD is Course Technology's way of putting the resources and information needed to teach and learn effectively into your hands. With an integrated array of teaching and learning tools that offer you and your students a broad range of technology-based instructional options, we believe this CD represents the highest quality and most cutting edge resources available to instructors today. The resources available with this book are:

• **Instructor's Manual**—Available as an electronic file, the Instructor's Manual includes detailed lecture topics with teaching tips for each unit.

• **Sample Syllabus**—Prepare and customize your course easily using this sample course outline.

• **PowerPoint Presentations**—Each unit has a corresponding PowerPoint presentation that you can use in lecture, distribute to your students, or customize to suit your course.

• **Figure Files**—The figures in the text are provided on the Instructor Resources CD to help you illustrate key topics or concepts. You can create traditional overhead transparencies by printing the figure files. Or you can create electronic slide shows by using the figures in a presentation program such as PowerPoint.

• **Solutions to Exercises**—Solutions to Exercises contains files students are asked to create or modify in the lessons and end-of-unit material. Also provided in this section is a document outlining the solutions for the end-of-unit Concepts Review, Skills Review, and Independent Challenges.

• **Data Files for Students**—To complete the units in this book, your students will need Data Files. You can post the Data Files on a file server for students to copy. The Data Files are available on the Instructor Resources CD-ROM, the Review Pack, and can also be downloaded from cengagebrain.com. For more information on how to download the Data Files, see the inside front cover.

• **ExamView**—ExamView is a powerful testing software package that allows you to create and administer printed, computer (LAN-based), and Internet exams. ExamView includes hundreds of questions that correspond to the topics covered in this text, enabling students to generate detailed study guides that include page references for further review. The computer-based and Internet testing components allow students to take exams at their computers, and also saves you time by grading each exam automatically.

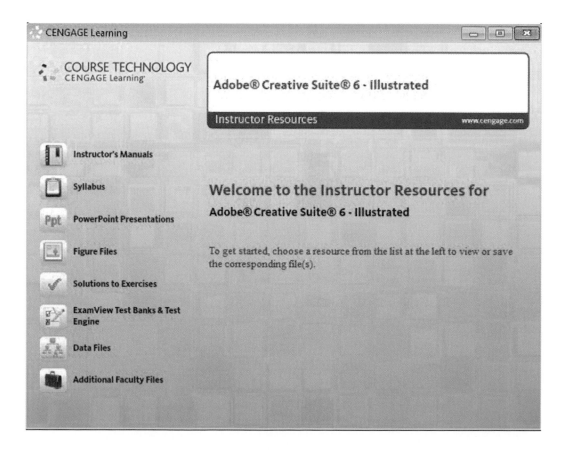

Other Adobe® CS6 Titles

Adobe® Dreamweaver® CS6—Illustrated
Sherry Bishop (9781133526025)

Eleven units provide essential training on using Adobe Dreamweaver CS6 to create websites. Coverage includes creating a web site, developing web pages, formatting text, using and managing images, creating links and navigation bars using CSS to layout pages, and collecting data with forms.

Adobe® Flash® Professional CS6—Illustrated
Barbara M. Waxer (9781133526001)

Eight units provide essential training on using Adobe Flash Professional CS6, including creating graphics, text, and symbols, using the Timeline, creating animation, creating buttons and using media, adding interactivity, and integrating Flash projects with other CS6 programs.

Adobe® Illustrator® CS6—Illustrated
Chris Botello (9781133526407)

Eight units cover essential skills for working with Adobe Illustrator CS6 including drawing basic and complex shapes, using the Pen tool, working with blends, compound paths and clipping masks, creating pattern fills and gradient fills for objects, and designing stunning 3D effects.

Adobe® InDesign® CS6—Illustrated
Ann Fisher (9781133187585)

Eight units provide essential training on using Adobe InDesign CS6 for designing simple layouts, combining text, graphics, and color, as well as multi-page documents, layered documents, tables, and InDesign libraries.

Adobe® Photoshop® CS6—Illustrated
Chris Botello (9781133190394)

Eight units offer thorough coverage of essential skills for working with Adobe Photoshop CS6 from both the design and production perspective, including creating and managing layer masks, creating color effects and improving images with adjustment layers, working with text and combining text and imagery, and using filters and layer styles to create eye-popping special effects.

Adobe® Creative Suite 6 Web Tools: Dreamweaver, Photoshop, Flash Illustrated (9781133629740)

Covers essential skills for working with Adobe Dreamweaver® CS6, Adobe Photoshop® CS6, and Adobe Flash® CS6 with ten Dreamweaver units, one Bridge unit, four Photoshop units, five Flash units, and one unit on integration.

Adobe® Creative Suite 6 Design Tools: Photoshop, Illustrator, InDesign Illustrated (9781133562580)

Covers essential skills for working with Adobe Photoshop® CS6, Adobe Illustrator® CS6, and Adobe InDesign® CS6 with seven Photoshop units, seven Illustrator units, six InDesign units, and one unit on integration.

For more information on the Illustrated Series, please visit:
www.cengage.com/ct/illustrated

Getting Started with Photoshop CS6

Photoshop CS6 is the latest version of the revolutionary, best-selling photo editing software from Adobe. Photoshop offers a set of powerful tools and easy-to-use panels that let you perform all kinds of image editing, from simple to complex. In this unit, you will learn essential skills for viewing and navigating a document and investigate the basic building blocks of a Photoshop image. The information you learn in this unit will form an important foundation for everything else covered in the book. MegaPixel is a graphic arts service bureau and design agency. Laura Jacobs, the owner of MegaPixel, has hired you as a production artist. Your job will involve using Photoshop CS6 to address a variety of image-processing issues to produce high-quality Photoshop files.

OBJECTIVES

Define photo editing software

Start Photoshop and view the workspace

Use the Zoom tool and the Hand tool

Save a document and understand file formats

Understand and change resolution

Change image size

Create a new document

Transform the canvas

Crop an image

Crop an image to a specific size

Defining Photo Editing Software

Photoshop CS6 is photo editing software. In a nutshell, Photoshop offers you a variety of tools, menu commands, and panels that allow you to edit and manipulate **digital images**—images that you get from a digital camera, scan from a photograph or a slide, or create from scratch. Photoshop CS6 allows you to edit images in a variety of ways in order to enhance or process them for different types of uses, such as for print or for the web. Laura Jacobs invites you to her office for an orientation meeting on your first day at MegaPixel. The conversation turns to Photoshop, and you share with her some of your experiences with the many uses of the application.

The following are just some of the tasks you can use Photoshop CS6 to accomplish:

- **Acquire images from a variety of devices**

  Transfer images from CDs, DVDs, digital cameras, and scanners into Photoshop. Download images from the web and open them in Photoshop. With some digital cameras, you can use Photoshop to preview images from your camera before you open them in Photoshop.

- **Apply basic processing procedures**

  Crop an image to get rid of unwanted elements or to focus more dramatically on your subject. Rotate an image if it is upside down, on its side, or crooked. Resize an image so that it prints to fit the frame you just bought. All of these are essential and practical procedures that Photoshop can do quickly and efficiently.

- **Improve the color and quality of images**

  Photoshop has many sophisticated color tools that allow you to enhance the appearance of photographs. You can brighten images that are too dark, or darken images that are overexposed. Turn an otherwise plain image into something striking with a quick increase in contrast. Make the color more vivid or remove it entirely to create a dramatic black-and-white image.

- **Fix image flaws**

  Photoshop's retouching tools and production filters offer you many options for fixing flaws in an image, such as dust and scratches, graininess, and red eye. You can also retouch photos of your family and friends—best of all, retouch and restore old family photos and give them as gifts to be treasured. Figure A-1 shows an image with various effects applied.

- **Add special effects**

  If you can think of it, you can probably do it in Photoshop. Turn a brand-new photo into an old-looking photo, or take a typical black-and-white photo and make it look hand-tinted. Add grain effects or blur effects to give an ordinary photo a custom look. Distort photos by giving your friends big heads on little bodies or making your sister appear to be a giant 40-foot woman crashing her way down Fifth Avenue. Photoshop makes your imagination a reality.

- **Batch-process image files**

  Photoshop is also a production workhorse. For example, Photoshop can automatically process a batch of files for one type of output, such as professional printing, and then reprocess the same batch of files by reducing their physical size and file size, and changing their format for use on the web. And that's literally with the click of one button.

- **Output to various devices**

  You can use Photoshop to create graphics for slide shows, video presentations, and electronic billboards. Photoshop is used every day to create elements for on-screen animation projects. Photoshop comes complete with software you can use to save images for your cell phone or your iPod. Photoshop can even process a bunch of different-sized images into one contact sheet.

FIGURE A-1: Various effects with an old photo

Understanding graphics programs

The term **graphics program** can refer to a wide range of software applications. Generally speaking, though, graphics programs fall into three basic categories: bitmap, vector, and animation. You can think of **bitmap graphics** (also called **raster graphics**) as very sophisticated mosaics. Instead of using colored tiles, bitmap graphics use **pixels**—colored squares that are so small that your eye perceives only the whole image, not the pixels themselves. All digital photographs are bitmap graphics, and all Photoshop images are bitmap graphics. **Vector graphics** are often created on a computer, not through scanning or downloading. Many times, vector-based programs are called **draw programs**, because vector graphics are created by drawing lines, creating objects, and filling them with color. Adobe Illustrator is a vector-based program. Finally, **animation programs**, such as Adobe Flash, use timeline structures to create sequences of graphics—both bitmap and vector—then create the illusion of motion and animation by presenting that sequence of images so quickly that your eye perceives movement.

Starting Photoshop and Viewing the Workspace

You start Photoshop by launching the program or by opening a Photoshop file that is already created. Once in Photoshop, before you open or create a new document, the **workspace** becomes available. The workspace consists of the Menu bar at the top of the screen, the Options bar below the Menu bar, the Tools panel on the left of the screen, and the dock of panels on the right of the screen. Most of the panels are expanded while a few others are closed and represented by thumbnail images. Clicking a panel thumbnail opens the panel. The Menu bar contains the Photoshop menus and the Minimize, Restore, and Close buttons. You can rearrange the elements of the workspace to your liking to create and save your own customized workspace. Laura has shown you your office and new computer. You start Photoshop and familiarize yourself with the workspace.

STEPS

1. Click the Start button ⊕ on the taskbar, point to All Programs, click Adobe Design Standard CS6 (or the name of your specific Adobe Creative Suite package) if necessary, then click Adobe Photoshop CS6 (Win); or Open the Finder, double-click Applications, double-click Adobe Photoshop CS6, then double-click Adobe Photoshop CS6 (Mac)

2. **Verify that Essentials is the chosen workspace on the Options bar, as shown in Figure A-2.**
   The Essentials workspace is one of many preset workspaces in Photoshop. Different workspaces are designed for different tasks. For example, the Painting workspace opens a number of panels that are very useful when painting.

> **QUICK TIP**
> If your workspace is different from the figure, click the workspace list arrow on the Options bar, and then click Reset Essentials.

3. **Note the Tools panel on the left, then click the double arrows at the top of the Tools panel repeatedly to toggle between a single and double row of tools**

4. **In the panels dock on the right, click the tabs of each panel to show each panel**
   These are the panels that are displayed when the Essentials workspace is chosen.

> **QUICK TIP**
> You can click the Collapse to Icons button to view panels as icons.

5. **Click Window on the Menu bar, then click Character**
   The Character panel opens. Note that by default it is grouped with the Paragraph panel. Use the Window menu to access all of the panels in Photoshop.

6. **Drag the Character panel name tab to the center of the workspace**
   The Character panel is separated from the Paragraph panel.

7. **Drag the Paragraph panel name tab over the Character panel until you see a light blue frame around the Character panel, then release the mouse button**
   The panels are grouped once again.

8. **Double-click the name tab of any visible panels in the panels dock**
   Double-clicking the name tab of an open panel minimizes the panel.

9. **Click the workspace list arrow on the Options bar, then click Reset Essentials**
   The panels are restored to their original locations.

FIGURE A-2: The Essentials workspace

Menu bar

Options bar

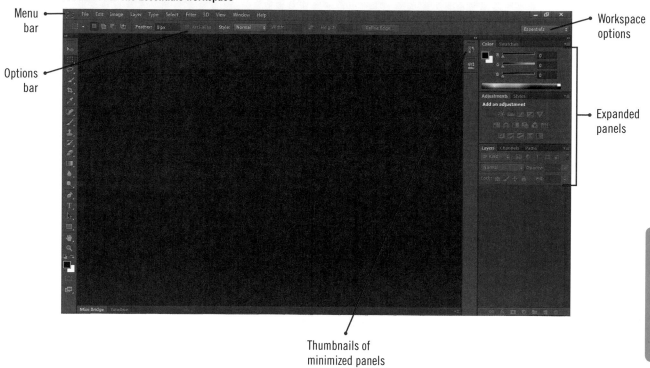

Workspace options

Expanded panels

Thumbnails of minimized panels

Getting help in Photoshop CS6

Whenever you have a question about what you're doing in Photoshop or want to learn more about a tool or a feature, remember that you always have the Help menu close at hand. Installing Photoshop on your computer automatically gives you access to Adobe's online help site.

To access Photoshop Help, click Help on the Menu bar, and then click Photoshop Online Help. The Photoshop Help page of the Adobe.com website opens in your browser. At the top of the page are help categories, such as What's new, Image adjustments, and Repair and restoration. Clicking a category brings you to that section of help and offers more specific topics within the chosen category. Clicking a topic opens a new web page with information about the chosen topic.

Managing the workspace

Think of the Photoshop workspace just as you would your own home or apartment; you want to have things how you like them and where you like them. For example, click the double arrows above the Tools panel to display the tools in one or two rows. Your biggest consideration with the workspace is always maximizing the room available to view the image you are working on. For this reason, managing the panels on the right of the window is important, because open panels can take up a lot of space in the Document window. Condensing panels by grouping them with other panels is a smart choice for maximizing working space. Minimizing panels is the best choice for keeping essential panels open but out of the way.

Using the Zoom Tool and the Hand Tool

When you work with Photoshop files, you will often be viewing them from different perspectives. You use the Zoom tool to enlarge and reduce the image on your screen. When the image is enlarged so much that you can't see the whole image, you can use the Hand tool to scroll around to see other areas of the image. Because the Zoom and Hand tools are used so often when working in Photoshop, it's important to learn keyboard commands to access the tools. See Table A-1 for a list of useful quick keys. Laura asks that you open a file and demonstrate your abilities with using the Zoom and Hand tools and viewing the workspace.

STEPS

1. **Click File on the Menu bar, click Open, navigate to the location where you store your Data Files, click PS A-1.psd, then click Open**

   Figure A-3 shows the opened file in the default workspace. The name of the file appears in the document tab, which is located in the upper-left corner of the file.

   > **QUICK TIP**
   > Double-clicking the Hand tool on the Tools panel also fits the image on the screen.

2. **Click View on the Menu bar, then click Fit on Screen**

   This command resizes the view to fit the entire canvas on your screen. The current magnification is listed in the document tab and also in the lower-left corner of the document window.

   > **QUICK TIP**
   > The pixels are outlined in white. To hide the white outline, press [Ctrl][H] (Win) or ⌘[H] (Mac).

3. **Click the Zoom tool 🔍 on the Tools panel, position it over the bird's eye, then click the eye eight times to zoom in on the image**

   Each time you click, the image is enlarged. Note that the magnification level on the document tab changes to show the percentage at which you are viewing the image each time you click.

4. **Click the Hand tool ✋ on the Tools panel, then click and drag the Hand tool pointer over the image to see other areas of the bird**

5. **Double-click ✋, click 🔍, position it directly above the eye, drag the Zoom tool pointer to create a marquee as shown in Figure A-4, then release the mouse button**

   As you drag, a dotted rectangle, called a **marquee**, appears around the area that you drag over. When you release the Zoom tool pointer, the area inside the marquee is enlarged in the window. Dragging the Zoom tool on the image is called a **marquee zoom**. Make sure the Scrubby Zoom check box is not checked on the Options bar. If the Scrubby Zoom check box is checked, you will not be able to create a marquee zoom using the Zoom tool.

   > **QUICK TIP**
   > Press and hold [Ctrl] (Win) or ⌘ (Mac) then press [-] repeatedly to reduce the view. See Table A-1 for other useful quick keys.

6. **Press and hold [Alt] (Win) or [option] (Mac), then click ten times anywhere on the image**

   The image's magnification level is reduced. When you press and hold [Alt] (Win) or [option] (Mac), the Zoom tool shows a minus sign, indicating that it will reduce the view, rather than magnify it.

7. **Press and hold [Ctrl] (Win) or ⌘ (Mac) then press [+] repeatedly to enlarge the view**

8. **Click View on the Menu bar, then click Fit on Screen**

Accessing the Zoom and Hand tools

When you're working with various tools, you will find yourself having to continuously switch to the Zoom tool to enlarge your view or to the Hand tool to change your view. This will slow you down. Take time to practice and master the quick keys that allow you to temporarily switch to the Zoom or Hand tool while remaining in the current tool. Press and hold [Spacebar] to access the Hand tool. Press and hold [Spacebar] [Ctrl] (Win) or [Spacebar] ⌘ (Mac) to access the Zoom Plus tool. Press and hold [Spacebar] [Alt] (Win) or [Spacebar] [option] (Mac) to access the Zoom Minus tool. When you release the quick keys, the current tool is active again. These three keyboard commands will help you enormously in speeding up your workflow.

FIGURE A-3: Viewing the document in the Essentials workspace

FIGURE A-4: Creating a marquee with the Zoom tool

This area will be magnified

TABLE A-1: Useful quick keys

command	Windows	Macintosh
Open	[Ctrl][O]	⌘[O]
Fit on Screen	[Ctrl][0] (zero)	⌘[0] (zero)
Fit on Screen	Double-click Hand tool	Double-click Hand tool
Zoom In	[Ctrl][+]	⌘[+]
Zoom Out	[Ctrl][-]	⌘[-]
Access Zoom Plus tool	[Spacebar][Ctrl]	[Spacebar]⌘
Access Zoom Minus tool	[Spacebar][Alt]	[Spacebar][option]
Access Hand tool	[Spacebar]	[Spacebar]

Photoshop CS6

Saving a Document and Understanding File Formats

File formats are specific types of computer code that you use to save an image for various types of output or use with other applications. Table A-2 shows a list of common file formats you can use with Photoshop. PSD stands for Photoshop Document and is the basic format for saving a Photoshop file. All other Adobe programs can open and/or place a file saved as a PSD. You refresh your knowledge of file formats by saving the bird image as a PSD, a TIFF, and a JPEG.

STEPS

1. **Click File on the Menu bar, click Save As, then navigate to the location where you store your Data Files**

QUICK TIP

If you are using a Macintosh, you will not see the file format suffixes in the file format name.

2. **Type birdie_PS-A in the File name text box (Win) or the Save As text box (Mac), click the Format list arrow, click Photoshop (*.PSD, *.PDD), if necessary, then click Save**
   The filename in the document tab changes to birdie_PS-A.psd.

3. **If the Photoshop Format Options dialog box opens, click OK to close it**
   This dialog box is for maximizing the compatibility of the file with other programs. To prevent the dialog box from opening each time you save a document, click the Don't show again check box in the dialog box before clicking OK.

QUICK TIP

The items in parentheses next to the format name refer to the various suffixes used for the format. Using TIFF as an example, .tiff is sometimes used for Macintosh files, while .tif is the standard for Windows files.

4. **Click File on the Menu bar, click Save As, click the Format list arrow, click TIFF (*.TIF, *.TIFF), then compare your dialog box to Figure A-5**

5. **Click Save, then click OK in the TIFF Options dialog box**
   TIFF is an acronym for Tagged Image File Format. TIFF is a standard file format for placing digital images for print in page layout programs.

6. **Click File on the Menu bar, click Save As, click the Format list arrow, click JPEG (*.JPG, *.JPEG, *.JPE), then click Save**
   The JPEG Options dialog box opens, as shown in Figure A-6. The JPEG file format is a lossy compression format often used for images on the web and for images that will be emailed. Because it compresses a file by removing data, the JPEG format always reduces an image's file size.

7. **Drag the Quality slider to 6**
   The file size is reduced to approximately 176 KB.

8. **Click OK, click File on the Menu bar, then click Close**

TABLE A-2: Standard file formats for Photoshop files

file format	extension	use
Bitmap	.bmp	Bitmap images, popular with Windows operating systems
CompuServe GIF	.gif	Web graphics
Photoshop EPS	.eps	Photoshop graphics with live type or shape layers
Photoshop PSD	.psd	Basic format for all Photoshop documents
JPEG	.jpg, .jpeg	Web graphics, images to be emailed
PICT	.pct, .pict	Graphics to be used in presentation programs, such as PowerPoint
PNG	.png	High-quality web graphics
TIFF	.tif, .tiff	Graphics to be used for print in page layout programs

FIGURE A-5: Save As dialog box

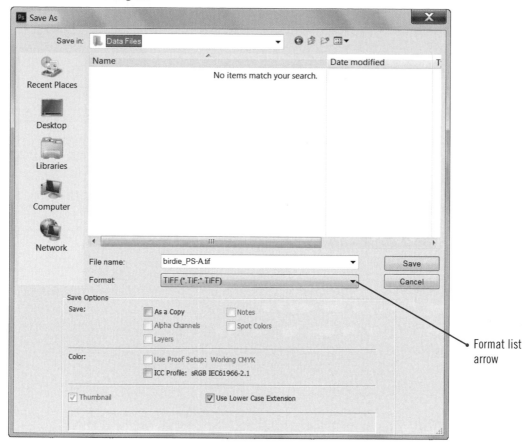

Format list
arrow

FIGURE A-6: JPEG Options dialog box

Choosing the right file format

In the real world, working with file formats is seldom challenging. You'll save the vast majority of your files as basic PSD documents, and if you're saving a file at work or for a client, usually you'll be told which format to choose. The key to choosing a file format is understanding what the file will be used for. For web graphics, you'll usually choose JPEG. For PowerPoint graphics, you'll usually choose PICT. With a little bit of experience, you will soon be comfortable knowing which file format to choose for a given output or to interface with another software package.

Understanding and Changing Resolution

A bitmap graphic is a graphic composed of pixels. The word *pixel* is derived from the words picture and element. You can think of a bitmap image as being a grid of pixels (abbreviated *px*)—thousands or millions of them. All Photoshop images are bitmap graphics. **Resolution** is a measurement: the number of pixels per inch (ppi). For example, if you had a 1" × 1" Photoshop file with a resolution of 100 ppi, that file would contain a total of 10,000 pixels (100 px wide × 100 px high = 10,000 pixels). In this lesson, you'll investigate how to change resolution in the Image Size dialog box. Jon Schenk, a senior art director at MegaPixel, asks that you to use the Image Size dialog box to change the resolution of an image. He asks that you change the resolution twice, first with no loss of image data, and then with a loss of data so that you can show him the difference.

STEPS

1. **Open PS A-2.psd, then save it as** birdie resize_PS-A

2. **Click** Image **on the Menu bar, then click** Image Size

   The Image Size dialog box opens. The Document Size section specifies that this is a 2" × 2" file with a resolution of 300 ppi—a high-resolution file. The Pixel Dimensions section specifies that the full width of the file is 600 pixels (300 ppi × 2"), and the height is 600 pixels. Therefore, this image is composed of exactly 360,000 pixels.

3. **Click the** Resample Image check box **to remove the check mark**

   Resampling means changing the total pixel count of an image. The Resample Image check box is perhaps the most important option in this dialog box. When the Resample Image check box is not checked, the total number of pixels in the image must remain the same. In other words, no matter how you resize the image or change the resolution, no pixels can be added or discarded.

4. **Double-click** 300 **in the Resolution text box, type** 100**, press [Tab], then note the changes in the Width and Height values**

   As shown in Figure A-7, the width and height of the file change to 6 inches. Because the pixel dimension of 600 pixels cannot change, when the number of pixels per inch is reduced to 100, the file must enlarge to 6" wide × 6" inches tall to accommodate all the pixels. In other words, no pixels were added or discarded with the change in resolution—they were simply redistributed.

5. **Press and hold [Alt] (Win) or [option] (Mac) so that the Cancel button changes to the Reset button, then click** Reset

   The Image Size dialog box returns to its original values and the Resample Image check box is checked.

6. **Change the resolution from 300 to** 150**, press [Tab], then note the changes to the Width and Height values and to the Pixel Dimension values**

   As shown in Figure A-8, the resolution is reduced to 150 ppi, but the width and height remain at 2 inches. The Pixel Dimensions show that the full width of the file is 300 pixels (150 ppi × 2") and the full height is 300 pixels. This means that, if you click OK, the total number of pixels will be 90,000. 75% of the original 360,000 pixels will be discarded because of the reduction in resolution from 300 to 150 ppi.

7. **Click** OK

   Though the image doesn't look much different on your screen, 75% of its original data has been discarded.

8. **Save your work, then close** birdie resize_PS-A.psd

FIGURE A-7: Decreasing resolution without resampling

FIGURE A-8: Decreasing resolution with resampling

Understanding the difference between image size and file size

Try not to confuse the terms image size and file size. Image size refers to the physical dimensions of the image—its width and height. So if you say an image is 8" × 10", you are referring to its image size. File size refers to how big the file is in computer memory—how much storage space it takes up on your computer. If an image is 42 MB (megabytes), that is its file size. Remember that every pixel in an image increases the file size of the image. Therefore, resolution and image size both affect file size. The greater the resolution—the more pixels per inch—the greater the file size. The greater the image size—the more inches of pixels—the greater the file size. If you were printing an 8" × 10" color poster at 300 ppi, your file size would be somewhere close to 27 MB, and the image would be composed of more than 7 million pixels!

Changing Image Size

Image size refers to the dimensions of the Photoshop file. Image size is not dependent on resolution; in other words, you could create two 3" × 5" inch files, one with a resolution of 72 ppi and the other with a resolution of 300 ppi. The two files would have the same image size but different resolutions. Image size is, however, related to resolution: all bitmap images, regardless of their physical dimensions, have a resolution. Changing the width and/or height of an image will affect its resolution. Also, because resolution is so closely associated with image quality, resizing an image may have a negative effect on its appearance. Jon Schenk gives you a 2" × 2" file from his client. The file needs to be printed at 4"× 4" for a glossy magazine then saved at the same size for the client's website. You create two files at two different resolutions for the two different types of use.

STEPS

1. **Open PS A-3.psd, click** Image **on the Menu bar, then click** Image Size

   The Document Size section specifies that this is a 2" × 2" file with a resolution of 300 ppi. The Pixel Dimensions section specifies that the full width of the file is 600 pixels (300 ppi × 2") and the height is 600 pixels. Thus, this image is composed of exactly 360,000 pixels.

2. **Verify that the** Resample Image check box **is checked**

   This file is 2"× 2" and you need it to be 4" × 4".

3. **Change the Width value to** 4, **then compare your dialog box to Figure A-9**

   In order to be used in a color magazine at the specified size of 4" × 4", the file must be 300 ppi at that size. Photoshop is able to scale the image to that size and resolution. However, note the pixel dimensions. Because we've doubled the size of the original, the new size now must contain 1,440,000 pixels to maintain a resolution of 300 pixels per inch. The supplied image was scanned at 360,000 total pixels. Where did all the new pixels come from? If you click OK, Photoshop will create them based on information from existing pixels in a process called **interpolation**.

4. **Click** OK, **then evaluate the enlargement in terms of image quality**

5. **Double-click the** Zoom tool 🔍 **to view the image at 100%**

   The image still looks good overall. However, for quality print reproduction, this image is unacceptable because it is composed of 75% interpolated data.

6. **Save the file with the name** birdie magazine_PS-A **as a Photoshop document, close it, then open PS A-3.psd again**

7. **Open the Image Size dialog box, and note that the Resample Image check box is checked**

   Now you will resize the file to be used on the client's website.

8. **Change the Width and Height values to** 4, **change the Resolution to** 72, **then compare your dialog box to Figure A-10**

   As shown in the Pixel Dimensions section, the file size will be reduced from 1.03 MB to 243KB. Even though the image was doubled in size, the reduction in resolution from 300 ppi to 72 ppi resulted in the need for fewer than 25% of the number of original pixels.

9. **Click** OK, **then evaluate the enlargement in terms of image quality**

   Viewed at 100%, the image looks great on screen, which is our goal, given that it will be used on a website. Even though Photoshop has discarded more than 75% of the original number of pixels, the reduced image contains only original data and no interpolated data.

10. **Save the file as a .jpg file with a Quality setting of** 10 **named** birdie web graphic_PS-A, **then close it**

FIGURE A-9: Increasing image size and resampling pixels

FIGURE A-10: Decreasing image size and resampling pixels

What is "hi-res" exactly?

Pixels must be small to create the representation of a photographic image—you want to see the image, not the pixels. 300 ppi is considered a high resolution for any file that will be professionally printed. For a home desktop printer, 150 ppi is generally enough resolution for a good-looking print. For the web and other "on-screen" graphics, the standard resolution is low—just 72 ppi. "Hi-res" is an abbreviation for "high-resolution", and generally speaking, a hi-res file pertains only to the world of printing. So when you think of hi-res, think of images—color or black-and-white—printing at a high quality, like in a magazine or a poster. This type of reproduction requires the industry standard of 300 pixels per inch.

Creating a New Document

Usually when you work in Photoshop, the image you're working on was either scanned or captured by a digital camera. You can also create pixels from scratch, simply by creating a new document in Photoshop. You create a new document in the New dialog box, where you specify its width, height, and its resolution. The information you enter will be reflected in the Image Size dialog box. Jon asks you to create a new document for a magazine cover. He tells you the document should be 8.125" × 11.25".

STEPS

1. Click **Edit (Win)** or **Photoshop (Mac)** on the Menu bar, point to **Preferences**, click **Units & Rulers**, then verify that Rulers is set to Inches and Type is set to Points

2. In the New Document Preset Resolutions section, verify that Print Resolution is set to 300 pixels/inch and Screen Resolution is set to 72 pixels/inch, then click **OK**

3. Click **File** on the Menu bar, then click **New**

   The New dialog box opens.

4. Click the **list arrow** next to Width, then click **Inches**

5. Change the Width value to **8.125**, change the Height value to **11.25**, then change the Resolution value to **300**

   You set the resolution to 300 ppi because you know in advance that the file will be used on a magazine cover.

6. Click the **Color Mode list arrow**, then click **CMYK Color**

   CMYK Color is the mode commonly used for images that will be printed using traditional printing methods.

7. Click the **button to the left of Advanced** to expand the New dialog box, click the **Color Profile list arrow**, then click **Don't Color Manage this Document**

   A **color profile** is a group of preset settings for controlling how color will appear on your monitor and in a printed document. Color profiles are used almost exclusively in professional settings such as ad agencies, service bureaus, and photography houses. For your own personal work, or if you're working for a business that hasn't incorporated color management, you can work without incorporating default color profiles.

8. Compare your dialog box to **Figure A-11**, then click **OK**

   A new document opens.

9. Click **File** on the Menu bar, click **Save As**, type **new document_PS-A** in the File name text box, choose **Photoshop** as the format, then click **Save**

   The filename new document_PS-A.psd appears in the document tab in the upper-left corner of the document. When you open one or more documents in Photoshop, the documents are docked together as tabbed documents. Click a document tab to activate that document in the window or rearrange the order of documents by dragging a document tab to a new location in the dock. You can undock a document from a group by pulling the document tab out of the group. The document will be in a free-floating window.

10. Close the document

Using the Revert command

The Revert command on the File menu is one of your best methods for undoing lots of moves. When you choose the Revert command, the file is reverted to the same status it was at when you last saved. This can be an enormous help if you've made more changes than you can undo with the Undo command. Simply click File on the Menu bar, click Revert, and you're back to where you were when you last saved. This is another reason to remember to save often when you work, preferably every 10 minutes.

FIGURE A-11: New dialog box

Introducing color models and color modes

A **color model** defines the colors we see and work with in digital images. RGB (red, green, blue), CMYK (cyan, magenta, yellow, black), and HSB (hue, saturation, brightness) are all color models, and each uses a different method for describing color.

In Photoshop, a document's **color mode** is listed on the Image menu. The color mode determines which color model is being used to display and print the image on which you are working. In most cases, you will be working in RGB Color for color images and Grayscale for black-and-white images. RGB Color is the standard color mode for working with color images. Choosing a color mode has an impact on which tools and file formats are available. All of Photoshop's tools and features are available to files in the RGB

Color mode. Many of them are not available to files in the CMYK Color mode. That's one of many reasons why it's best to do all of your color work in RGB, not CMYK.

All files that are printed professionally must at some point be CMYK files, so therefore it is likely that you will eventually switch to CMYK Color mode. However, most designers do all their color work in RGB Color then save a CMYK Color copy for printing. In other words, they use CMYK Color as part of the saving and output procedure, not part of the Photoshop design work itself. To change the color mode, click Image on the Menu bar, point to Mode, then click one of the color modes on the menu.

Transforming the Canvas

The bed of pixels that make up an image is referred to as the **canvas**. When you open an image, usually the image uses all of the pixels available on the canvas. However, the canvas can be enlarged to add more pixels to the file—perhaps to make room for another image to overlap or sit beside the original. In Photoshop, the term **transform** refers to specific operations that you make to change the location of pixels. Transformations include scaling, rotating, skewing, and distorting pixels. Jon asks you to increase the canvas size in an existing document to make room to place a second image over the first. You open the file and see that the image will also need to be rotated.

STEPS

1. **Open PS A-4.psd then save it as** parrots_PS-A

2. **Click** Image **on the Menu bar, point to** Image Rotation, **then click** 90° CW

3. **Click** Image **on the Menu bar, then click** Canvas Size

4. **Type** 6 **in the Width text box, type** 8 **in the Height text box, click the** Canvas extension color list arrow, **click** White, **then note the Anchor icon in the dialog box**

   The Anchor is used to determine where new pixels will be placed relative to the location of the existing canvas. By default, when you open the dialog box, the existing canvas is represented by the circle in the middle of eight directional arrows. If you were to add pixels, they would be evenly distributed on all sides of the existing canvas.

5. **Click the** lower-left arrow **in the grid**

   Clicking the lower-left arrow of the Anchor indicates that the new pixels will be positioned above and to the right of the existing canvas, as shown in Figure A-12.

6. **Click** OK, **then compare your canvas to Figure A-13**

   The canvas is enlarged to the new dimensions. White pixels are added above and to the right of the original canvas.

7. **Open PS A-5.psd, click** Image **on the Menu bar, point to** Image Rotation, **then click** Flip Canvas Horizontal

8. **Click** Select **on the Menu bar, click** All, **click** Edit **on the Menu bar, click** Copy, **then close the file without saving changes**

9. **Click** Edit **on the Menu bar, then click** Paste

   The image you copied is pasted into the parrots_PS-A.psd document.

QUICK TIP
For precise moves, use the arrow keys to move the image one pixel at a time. Press and hold [Shift] while pressing the arrow keys to move the image in 10-pixel increments.

10. **Click the** Move tool ▸⊕, **drag the** little parrot image **to the position shown in Figure A-14, save your work, click** OK **in the Photoshop Format Options dialog box, then close parrots_PS-A.psd**

"Res-ing up" when you have no choice

Inevitably, there will come a time when you have no other choice but to increase the resolution or the image size of a file and live with the results. In the working world, this often happens when a client delivers an original file at one size and wants you to use it at a much larger size. In that case, you'll want to be smart about how you increase the size or resolution of the image. Remember that Photoshop is running complex algorithms to create that new data. Don't make it more complicated by enlarging by odd numbers. For example, if you have a 3-inch square image that needs to print as a 5.75-inch square, double the image size to a 6-inch square. It's much easier for Photoshop to interpolate data with a simple doubling of the existing image size; this will result in a higher quality interpolation and a better result for your enlarged image. You can then import the image into your layout at 5.75".

FIGURE A-12: Canvas Size dialog box

FIGURE A-13: Viewing new pixels added to the canvas

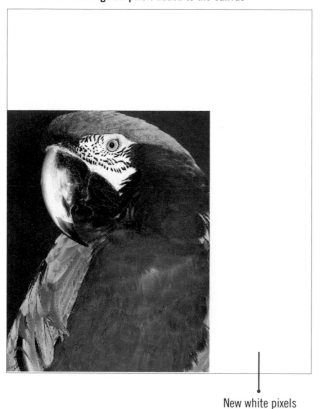

New white pixels added to canvas

FIGURE A-14: Positioning a second image over the new pixels

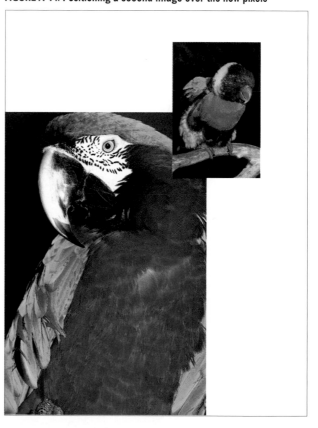

Cropping an Image

Cropping an image is a basic task in which you define an area of an image that you want to keep and then discard the remainder of the image. Photoshop's Crop tool makes it easy to execute a simple crop and also provides you with options for previewing the crop before you execute it. Cropping an image can often be an artistic choice: an interesting crop can turn a boring image into something eye-catching and intriguing. You are asked to crop an image for one of MegaPixel's clients, the United States office of the Estonia Travel and Tourism Board. They will use the cropped image as an email postcard.

STEPS

1. **Open PS A-6.psd, then save it as estonia house_PS-A**

2. **Click Window on the Menu bar, then click Info**

   The Info panel opens. The Info panel provides lots of information about a Photoshop document, everything from image size and file size to color information for every pixel on the canvas. The Info panel can help you determine the size of an image as you apply the Crop tool.

3. **Click the Info panel menu button ▦, then click Panel Options**

   The Info Panel Options dialog box is where you choose what type of information you want to view about your document. By default, the Info panel does not display the document size or document dimensions.

   QUICK TIP
   Viewing document dimensions in the Info panel is faster than relying on the Image Size dialog box.

4. **Click the Document Sizes and the Document Dimensions check boxes to select them, if they are not already checked, then click OK**

   The document size (Doc) refers to the size of the file in megabytes. The document dimensions refer to the physical dimensions of the file. They are listed below "Doc" at the bottom of the Info panel.

   QUICK TIP
   Click the list arrow next to Unconstrained to choose from preset crop ratios.

5. **Click the Crop tool ▦ on the Tools panel**

   A dotted line, called a **crop marquee**, appears around the image with crop handles at each corner and at the horizontal and vertical centers. You can drag the crop handles to crop the image or use the Crop tool inside the marquee by dragging it over the image. The Options bar displays settings for the Crop tool, such as width, height, and ratio settings. The default ratio setting is Unconstrained which means that you can crop the image without being constrained by a specific width to height ratio.

6. **Verify that Unconstrained appears as the crop ratio setting on the Options bar.**

   Choosing Unconstrained removes the previously used settings for the Crop tool.

7. **Using Figure A-15 as a guide, drag the Crop tool pointer around the house so that only the house remains and the two other buildings are discarded, then release the Crop tool pointer**

   As you drag, the crop marquee is created. When you release the Crop tool, the dotted line changes to solid. The area inside the crop marquee is what will remain after the crop is executed. You can continue to adjust the marquee by dragging the crop handles to resize it.

   QUICK TIP
   You can also press [Enter] (Win) or [return] (Mac) to execute a crop. To remove a crop marquee from the canvas, click the Crop tool, then click Don't Crop or press [Esc].

8. **Double-click inside the crop area, then click outside the image to deselect**

   The image is cropped. The pixels outside the crop still remain even though you do not see them. If you crop the image again, the original image appears in its full size. If you would like to permanently discard the pixels outside of the crop area, click the Delete Cropped Pixels check box on the Options bar before you commit to the crop. The crop marquee remains active on the image unless you select another tool when you are done with the Crop tool.

9. **Compare your result to Figure A-16, save your work, then close estonia house_PS-A.psd**

Getting Started with Photoshop CS6

FIGURE A-15: Creating a crop marquee

Click to change ratio

Width setting

Height setting

Crop border

Crop handles

Info panel

FIGURE A-16: The cropped image

Setting opacity for the Crop tool

Opacity refers to how opaque something is. It is a term you will see used for a number of different Photoshop elements. When using the Crop tool, you can change the shield color and opacity of the area outside the crop using the Color and Opacity settings on the Options bar. Click the Set additional Crop options button 🔧 on the Options bar, then verify that the Enable Crop Shield check box is checked. To choose a new shield color, click the Color list arrow, then click Custom. The Color Picker dialog box opens. Choose a color, then click OK. You can also change the opacity by dragging the Opacity slider. This is a great option for previewing the image as it would look if cropped, especially if you hide the crop marquee. The more you reduce the opacity, the more the pixels outside of the marquee will be visible, which is useful for seeing where your crop lines fall in the image and what would be discarded if you execute the crop. As a preview before cropping, many designers set the opacity to 50% while they're experimenting and then, when they think they've found a crop that they like, they increase the opacity to 100%. If you prefer to crop without using color or opacity, click the Enable Crop Shield check box to remove the check mark.

Cropping an Image to a Specific Size

The Crop tool has a number of options attached to it that enable the tool to execute more than just a simple crop. After you create a crop marquee, the Crop tool pointer becomes an arrow pointer when inside the marquee. Using the arrow, you can move the image to crop a different area. When the Crop tool pointer is outside of the crop marquee, it becomes a rotate pointer that allows you to rotate the image. You can also input specific width and height dimensions to create a crop marquee at a specific size. ▓▓▒▒▒ A client of MegaPixel has provided you with an image they would like cropped vertically to 2.25" × 4". You crop the image and then rotate it in order to improve the appearance of the image.

STEPS

1. Open PS A-7.psd, then save it as hotel postcard_PS-A

2. Click the Crop tool 🔲, type 2.25 in the Width text box on the Options bar, then type 4 in the Height text box

3. Drag any corner of the crop marquee to create a new crop marquee of any size

   As you drag, the crop marquee is constrained proportionally to the values you input.

4. Position the Crop tool pointer outside of the marquee

   The pointer changes to a rotate pointer.

5. Using Figure A-17 as a guide, drag the image to rotate it, then size and position it as shown, being sure that the crop marquee remains within the borders of the canvas

   Note that the bottom of the marquee is parallel to the step that the girl is standing on.

6. Execute the crop, then compare your result to Figure A-18

7. Save the document, then close hotel postcard_PS-A

8. Click File on the Menu bar, then click Exit (Win) or click Photoshop on the Menu bar, then click Quit Photoshop (Mac).

> **QUICK TIP**
> Once you enter values in the Width and Height text boxes, you cannot drag the Crop tool pointer inside the crop marquee.

> **QUICK TIP**
> You can hide the marquee if you find it distracting by clicking [Ctrl][H] (Win) or ⌘[H] (Mac).

Cropping, resolution, and image size

When you select the Crop tool, you can enter a specific width, height, and resolution to crop an image to. You can also enter a specific resolution in the Crop Image Size & Resolution dialog box. To access this dialog box, click the list arrow next to Unconstrained on the Options bar. It may occur to you that the options for the Crop tool make it function much like the Image Size dialog box. Think about it: in the Image Size dialog box, you modify width, height, resolution, or all three. The same is true in the Crop Image Size & Resolution dialog box. That being said, it's important that you don't mistakenly resample an image by using the Crop tool. The key to making sure this doesn't happen is to understand that if you input a new height or width value but leave the Resolution text box empty, the resolution cannot change. It's

like turning off the Resample Image option in the Image Size dialog box. No matter where you crop or what size crop marquee you create, new pixels cannot be added or deleted, only redistributed. Make no mistake, the Crop tool is not intended to be used as a practical alternative to the Image Size dialog box. However, the Crop tool options are most practical when you have a target size and resolution that you want as a result. For example, it's often the case that you will be given high-res files and asked to crop them to a specific size for use on a website. In that case, you could simply enter the specific width and height, enter a resolution of 72 ppi, and crop the image. Your result would be cropped to that size and resolution in one step.

FIGURE A-17: Rotating the image

FIGURE A-18: The cropped, rotated, and resized image

Practice

Concepts Review

Label the elements of the Photoshop screen shown in Figure A-19.

FIGURE A-19

Match each term with the statement that best describes it.

6. Pixel	**a.**	The bed of pixels in a Photoshop file
7. Resolution	**b.**	The physical dimensions of an image
8. Image Size	**c.**	Removing unwanted areas of an image
9. File Size	**d.**	File format often used for web graphics
10. Canvas	**e.**	Picture element
11. Menu bar	**f.**	The amount of memory a file takes up
12. JPEG	**g.**	Part of the workspace that contains menu items
13. Cropping	**h.**	The number of pixels per inch

Select the best answer from the list of choices.

14. What is the name of the tool that you use to enlarge and reduce the view of a document?

- **a.** Hand
- **b.** Window
- **c.** Zoom
- **d.** Control

15. Which dialog box do you use to change the resolution of a file?

- **a.** Image Size dialog box
- **b.** Canvas Size dialog box
- **c.** New dialog box
- **d.** Both a and b but not c

16. Which of the following can you not specify in the New dialog box?

- **a.** Resolution
- **b.** Units and Rulers
- **c.** Width and Height
- **d.** Color Mode

17. Which of the following can you use to change the size of an image after it has been created?

- **a.** Canvas Size dialog box
- **b.** Crop tool
- **c.** New dialog box
- **d.** Both a and b but not c

18. Which of the following occurs every time you enlarge an image?

- **a.** New pixels are added based on existing pixels
- **b.** Increase in file size
- **c.** Reduction in quality
- **d.** All of the above

19. When you enlarge an image and Photoshop creates pixels from existing pixels, what is that process called?

- **a.** Interpretation
- **b.** Intertranslation
- **c.** Interrelation
- **d.** Interpolation

Skills Review

1. Define photo editing software.

- **a.** List four tasks that you can accomplish with Photoshop CS6.
- **b.** If you were publishing a monthly magazine, what role would Photoshop play in the production of that magazine?
- **c.** If you have a box full of family photos, what could you use Photoshop to do with them?
- **d.** If you have an old photo that is torn and faded, what help would Photoshop be for that situation?

2. Start Photoshop and view the workspace.

- **a.** Click the Start button on the taskbar, point to All Programs, click Adobe Design Standard CS6 (or the name of your specific Adobe Creative Suite package) if necessary, then click Adobe Photoshop CS6 (Win) or open the Finder, then double-click Adobe Photoshop CS6, then double-click **Adobe Photoshop CS6**.
- **b.** Identify the Menu bar.
- **c.** Toggle the Tools panel between being a single and double row of tools.
- **d.** On the panels dock on the right, click the tabs of each panel to show each panel.
- **e.** Click the workspace list arrow on the Options bar, then click Painting.
- **f.** Click the workspace list arrow on the Options bar, then click Essentials.
- **g.** Click Window on the Menu bar, then click Character.
- **h.** Drag the Character panel to the center of the workspace, separating it from the Paragraph panel.
- **i.** Drag the Paragraph panel back over the Character panel name tab to group the two panels together.
- **j.** Double-click the name tab of any visible panels in the panels dock to minimize them.
- **k.** Click the workspace list arrow on the Options bar, then click Reset Essentials.

3. Use the Zoom tool and the Hand tool.

- **a.** Click File on the Menu bar, click Open, navigate to the location where you store your Data Files, click PS A-8.psd, then click Open.
- **b.** Click View on the Menu bar, then click Fit on Screen.
- **c.** Click the Zoom tool on the Tools panel, position it over the black steeple in the middle ground, then click five times to zoom in on the image.

Skills Review (continued)

    d. Click the Hand tool on the Tools panel, then drag the Hand tool pointer over the image to see other areas of the image.

    e. Double-click the Hand tool.

    f. Click the Zoom tool, then click and drag a marquee around the same steeple.

    g. Press and hold [Alt] (Win) or [option] (Mac), then click four times anywhere on the image.

    h. Press and hold [Ctrl] (Win) or ⌘ (Mac), then press [+] repeatedly to enlarge the view.

    i. Click View on the Menu bar, then click Fit on Screen.

4. Save a document and understand file formats.

    a. Click File on the Menu bar, click Save As, then navigate to the location where you store your Data Files.

    b. Type **tallinn_PS-A** in the File name text box, click the Format list arrow to see all the file formats available, click Photoshop (*.PSD, *.PDD) then click Save.

    c. Click File on the Menu bar, click Save As, click the Format list arrow, then click TIFF (*.TIF, *.TIFF).

    d. Click Save, accept the defaults in the TIFF Options dialog box, then click OK.

    e. Click File on the Menu bar, click Save As, click the Format list arrow, click JPEG (*.JPG, *.JPEG, *.JPE), then click Save.

    f. Drag the Quality slider so that the file size is less than 200 KB but greater than 100 KB.

    g. Click OK, then close tallinn_PS-A.jpg.

5. Understand and change resolution.

    a. Open PS A-9.psd, then save it as **eagle resize_PS-A**.

    b. Click Image on the Menu bar, then click Image Size.

    c. Click the Resample Image check box to remove the check mark.

    d. Change the value in the Resolution text box to 100, press [Tab], then note the changes in the Width and Height values.

    e. Press and hold [Alt] (Win) or [option] (Mac) so that the Cancel button changes to the Reset button, then click the Reset button.

    f. Change the resolution from 300 to 150, press [Tab], then note the changes to the Width and Height values and to the Pixel Dimensions.

    g. Click OK.

    h. Click File on the Menu bar, then click Revert.

6. Change image size.

    a. Click Image on the Menu bar, then click Image Size.

    b. Note that the Resample Image check box is checked by default.

    c. Change the Width value to 9.

    d. Click OK, then evaluate the enlargement in terms of image quality.

    e. Revert the file, open the Image Size dialog box, and note that the Resample Image check box is checked.

    f. Change the Width value to 9, then change the resolution to 72.

    g. Click OK, then evaluate the enlargement in terms of image quality.

    h. Save changes, then close the file.

7. Create a new document.

    a. Click Edit (Win) or Photoshop (Mac) on the Menu bar, point to Preferences, then click Units & Rulers.

    b. Verify that Rulers is set to Inches and Type is set to Points.

    c. In the New Document Preset Resolutions section, verify that Print Resolution is set to 300 ppi and Screen Resolution is set to 72 ppi.

    d. Click OK, click File on the Menu bar, then click New.

    e. Click the list arrow next to Width, then click Inches.

    f. Change the Width value to 5, change the Height value to 7, then change the resolution to 300.

    g. Click the Color Mode list arrow, then click CMYK Color.

Skills Review (continued)

h. Click the Advanced button to expand the New dialog box, if necessary, click the Color Profile list arrow, then choose Don't Color Manage this Document.

i. Click OK.

j. Save the file as **skills new_PS-A**, then close the file.

8. Transform the canvas.

a. Open PS A-10.psd, then save it as **title_PS-A**.

b. Click Image on the Menu bar, point to Image Rotation, then click Flip Canvas Horizontal.

c. Click Image on the Menu bar, then click Canvas Size.

d. Type **4** in the Height text box.

e. Click the lower-center arrow in the Anchor section, then click OK.

f. Save your work, then close title_PS-A.psd.

9. Crop an image.

a. Open PS A-11.psd, then save it as **email postcard_PS-A**.

b. Click Window on the Menu bar, then click Info to show the Info panel, if necessary.

c. Click the Info panel menu button, then click Panel Options.

d. In the Status Information section, verify that both the Document Sizes and Document Dimensions check boxes are checked, then click OK.

e. Click the Crop tool on the Tools panel.

f. Verify that the ratio setting on the Options bar is set to Unconstrained.

g. Drag the Crop tool anywhere on the canvas to create a crop marquee and note the width and height values on the Info panel as you drag.

h. Drag the crop handles to define an area similar to that shown in Figure A-20.

i. Click the Crop tool, verify that the Delete Cropped Pixels check box on the Options bar is checked, then click Crop.

j. Save your work, then close email postcard_PS-A.psd.

10. Crop an image to a specific size.

a. Open PS A-12.psd, then save it as **san francisco_PS-A**.

b. Click the Crop tool on the Tools panel.

c. Verify that the ratio setting on the Options bar is set to Unconstrained.

d. On the Options bar, type **6** in the Width field.

e. Float your cursor outside of the marquee to see the rotate pointer, then rotate the image so that the skyline is parallel to the bottom of the marquee.

f. Drag the crop handles of the marquee so that all four are on the canvas.

g. Execute the crop, then compare your result to Figure A-21.

h. Save changes, then close san francisco_PS-A.psd.

i. Click File on the Menu bar, then click Exit (Win) or click Photoshop on the Menu bar, then click Quit Photoshop (Mac).

FIGURE A-20

Crop marquee

FIGURE A-21

Independent Challenge 1

Your first client, the Estonia Travel and Tourism Board, has sent you three files that they want to put on their website to promote all the construction, development, and restoration going on in the city. Each image needs to be a 3" square with a file size less than 100 KB each.

a. Open PS A-13.psd.

b. Check the Image Size dialog box to verify that the image is larger than 3" × 3" and has a resolution higher than 72 ppi.

c. Click Image on the Menu bar, point to Mode, then click RGB Color.

d. Click the Crop tool, click the list arrow next to Unconstrained on the Options bar, then click Size & Resolution.

e. In the Crop Image Size & Resolution dialog box, type **3** in the Width and Height text boxes, type **72** in the Resolution text box, then click OK.

f. Crop the image in a way that you think is aesthetically pleasing.

g. Open the Image Size dialog box to verify the settings.

h. Open PS A-14.psd.

i. Using the same settings, crop PS A-14.psd in a way that the size and position within the frame of the subject's head and body are consistent with the cropped PS A-13.psd.

j. Open PS A-15.psd, then crop it in a way that is consistent with the two previous crops you executed.

k. Position the three documents side by side, then compare your screen to Figure A-22. (*Hint*: The sample in the figure shows the three heads on the same horizontal line and the subject's boot in the left photo is on the same baseline as his knee in the right photo.)

FIGURE A-22

PS A-13.psd

PS A-14.psd

PS A-15.psd

l. If you don't like the relationships between any of the three photos, revert the files and then recrop.

m. Save PS A-13.psd as a JPEG named **web graphic 1_PS-A**, then choose a compression setting that will compress the file to under 100 KB.

n. Save PS A-14.psd as a JPEG named **web graphic 2_PS-A**.

o. Save PS A-15.psd as a JPEG named **web graphic 3_PS-A**.

Advanced Challenge Exercise

- Verify that the web graphic 3_PS-A.psd file is active in the document window.
- Click Image on the Menu bar, point to Mode, then click CMYK Color. Click OK in the warning dialog box that follows, if necessary.
- Click Image on the Menu bar, point to Mode, then click Grayscale.
- Click OK in the dialog box that follows.

p. Close the three files without saving changes, then exit Photoshop.

Independent Challenge 2

The Estonia Travel and Tourism Board provides you with three images. They ask you to create one file with all three images displayed vertically. They ask that you leave 1/8-inch space between each image, and the space between should be black. You open the three Photoshop files. Each one is in RGB Color mode and has been cropped to 3" × 3" at 72 pixels per inch.

a. Open PS A-16.psd, PS A-17.psd, and PS A-18.psd.

b. Save PS A-16.psd as **triptych_PS-A**.

c. Open the Canvas Size dialog box.

d. Change the dimension of the canvas to accommodate the client's specifications.

e. triptych_PS-A.psd will be the topmost of the three images, so click the appropriate box in the Anchor section to accommodate the other two images.

f. Specify that the new pixels will be Black, then click OK.

g. In PS A-18.psd, select all, copy, then close the file.

h. Paste into the triptych_PS-A.psd file.

i. Click the Move tool, then use the arrow keys to move the image down to the bottom of the file.

j. Zoom in to be sure that the pasted image is at the very bottom of the file and no black pixels are showing beneath it.

k. Fit on screen.

l. Copy and paste PS A-17.psd into the file, then position it so that it is centered vertically between the other two images.

m. Close PS A-17.

n. Save triptych_PS-A.psd as a JPEG and choose a compression setting that will output the file at less than 200 KB.

o. Compare your result to Figure A-23, save and close triptych_PS-A.psd, then exit Photoshop.

FIGURE A-23

Independent Challenge 3

The city zoo is planning on creating a series of animal bookmarks that they will sell in their gift shop. They want you to create a preliminary design for the first bookmark. The width must be between 1 and 2.5 inches and the height must be between 6 and 7.5 inches. They want the bookmark to be "interesting and unexpected." Since there's a range of acceptable sizes, you decide to first experiment with the Crop tool to find an interesting crop, then change the physical size after you crop. Because this is just a preliminary design, you're not worried about resolution or quality issues that might occur with resizing the file after you crop.

a. Open PS A-19.psd then save it as **bookmark_PS-A**.

b. Click the Crop tool, then verify that the ratio setting on the Options bar is set to Unconstrained.

c. Create a crop marquee of any size anywhere on the canvas.

d. Click the Set additional Crop options list arrow on the Options bar, then click the Enable Crop Shield check box to select it, if necessary.

e. Drag the Opacity slider to 100%.

f. Experiment with different crops of different sizes, being sure to stay within the parameters of between 1 and 2.5 inches in width and between 6 and 7.5 inches in height.

Independent Challenge 3 (continued)

Advanced Challenge Exercise

- Verify that you have an active crop marquee. Click the Set additional Crop options list arrow on the Options bar, then click the Enable Crop Shield check box, if necessary.
- Click the Color list arrow, then click Custom.
- Click in the red area of the Color Picker, then click OK.
- Drag the Opacity slider to 50%.

f. Decide on a crop that you feel is "interesting and unexpected", then execute the crop. (*Hint*: Remember that you can rotate the image, which could produce interesting results.)

g. Open the Image Size dialog box, then verify that the Resample Image check box is checked.

h. Change the Height value to 6 inches, note the new Width value, then click OK.

i. Compare your result to the sample shown in Figure A-24, save your work, then exit Photoshop.

FIGURE A-24

Real Life Independent Challenge

You have a digital camera, and you've just captured a great picture of your sister and her young daughter. You want to email it to your aunt and uncle who live on the opposite coast—just so they can see it. You know they don't have a high-speed Internet line, but you want it large enough for them to enjoy, and you want the image quality to be there, too. You decide to make the image 5 inches wide on its longest side and the resolution 150 ppi. Your goal is to get the image at that resolution and the size to be under 750 KB when saved.

a. Open PS A-20.psd, then save it as **mother's love_PS-A**.

b. Look at the image size and resolution of the file.

c. Click the Crop tool, then verify that the ratio setting on the Options bar is set to Unconstrained.

d. Crop the image (without changing the resolution) in a way that you think is aesthetically pleasing.

e. Open the Image Size dialog box to see the physical size you cropped the image to.

f. Change the width or the height—whichever is largest—to 5 inches.

g. Reduce the resolution to 150 ppi.

Real Life Independent Challenge (continued)

h. Check the before-and-after file size at the top of the dialog box to verify that the file size is being reduced, not enlarged.

i. Click OK, then compare your screen to Figure A-25 and Figure A-26. (*Hint*: The figures show two sample crops—the first is more of a standard crop. In the second, the very tight crop conveys a sense of the closeness of the mother and daughter.)

j. Save your file as a JPEG and choose a quality setting that produces a file size that's less than 750 KB.

k. Close mother's love_PS-A.psd, then exit Photoshop.

FIGURE A-25

FIGURE A-26

Visual Workshop

Open PS A-21.psd, then save it as **visual solution_PS-A**. Crop the image so that it resembles the one shown in Figure A-27.

FIGURE A-27

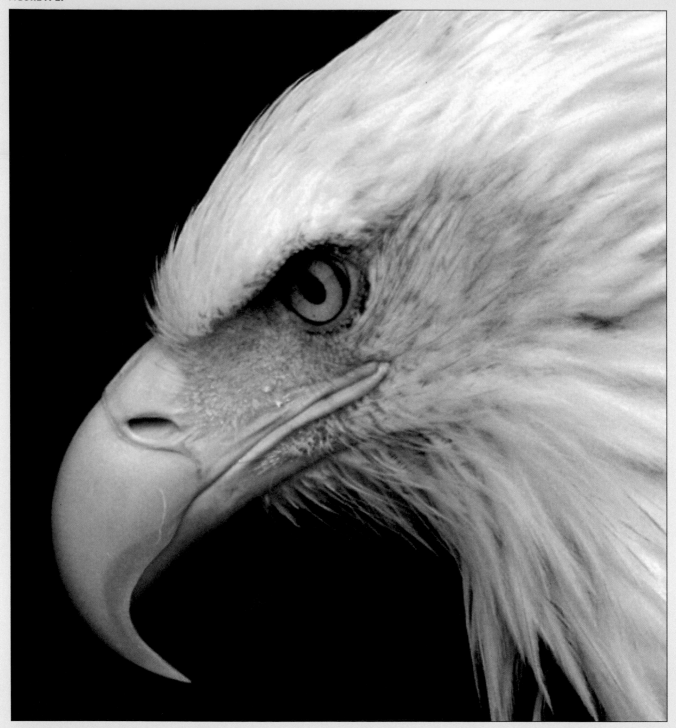

Selecting Pixels

In order to modify specific pixels, you first need to select them. Making selections is one of the most fundamental procedures you'll do in Photoshop. The Tools panel houses three types of selection tools: the Marquee tools, the Lasso tools, and the Tolerance tools—the Magic Wand and Quick Selection tools. Making selections is just one component of working with selections. In this unit, you'll learn how to define a selection edge—with a feather, for example—how to save a selection, how to preview a selection in Quick Mask, and how to refine a selection's edge. You'll also gain an understanding of issues involved with moving pixels to a new location on the canvas. At MegaPixel, Laura has prepared a number of projects for you that will test your abilities with making selections, previewing them, saving them, and refining selection edges.

OBJECTIVES

Use the marquee tools

Use the lasso tools

Use the Magic Wand tool

Save and load selections

Work with and save alpha channels

Understand anti-aliased edges

Work with a feathered edge

Refine selection edges

Using the Marquee Tools

The Marquee tools are the most basic tools available for making selections in Photoshop. The Rectangular Marquee tool is used for making rectangular or square selections and the Elliptical Marquee tool is used for making oval or circular selections. You can add to an existing selection and remove pixels from a selection using simple quick keys. If you are not happy with a selection, you can deselect and start over. ▒▒▒▒▒ Laura has given you a Photoshop file which is a puzzle that the company uses to test new employees' understanding of basic selections. You use the Rectangular Marquee tool and the Elliptical Marquee tool to select the first four pieces of the puzzle.

STEPS

QUICK TIP
The white triangle on some tool icons indicates that there are more tools hidden beneath the current tool.

QUICK TIP
If you need to start over, deselect by pressing [Ctrl][D] (Win) or ⌘[D] (Mac) or click Select on the Menu bar, then click Deselect.

Before starting these steps, verify that only the Tools panel is open. Press [D] so that the foreground and background colors on the Tools panel are black over white. Use all the zooming and scrolling techniques you learned in Unit A.

1. Open PS B-1.psd, save it as selections puzzle_PS-B, zoom in on the #1 piece, then click the Rectangular Marquee tool ▣

2. Position the center of the crosshair on the upper-left corner of the puzzle piece, drag downward until the center of the crosshair is on the lower-right corner, then release the mouse pointer

3. Click View on the Menu bar, then click Fit on Screen, click the Move tool ⊹, drag the piece to the correct position on the hot air balloon image, as shown in Figure B-1, then deselect

   You will be positioning puzzle pieces 2, 3, and 4 for the remainder of this lesson. Each time you select a puzzle piece, zoom in on the piece, select it, zoom out, move it to the correct position on the hot air balloon using the Move tool, then deselect. The point of this exercise is to practice making selections, adding to, and removing from selections. Do not worry if your selections include extra white pixels.

4. Click ▣, select the top square in the #2 piece, press and hold [Shift], position the crosshair over the lower-right corner, drag a second marquee that overlaps the first, then release the mouse pointer

   The entire piece is selected. Pressing and holding [Shift] when making a selection adds pixels to the existing selection.

QUICK TIP
To switch quickly between the marquee tools and the Move tool, press [M] to select the current marquee tool and [V] to select the Move tool.

5. Select the outer square in the #3 piece, press and hold [Alt] (Win) or [option] (Mac), then select the white inner rectangle

   The white inner rectangle is removed from the selection. Pressing and holding [Alt] (Win) or [option] (Mac) when making a selection removes pixels from the existing selection.

6. Press and hold ▣, click the Elliptical Marquee tool ◯, then position the crosshair icon over the white pixel at the center of the #4 piece

7. Press and hold [Alt][Shift] (Win) or [option][Shift] (Mac), then drag to the edge of the circle to complete the selection

   Pressing and holding [Alt] (Win) or [option] (Mac) when no pixels are selected creates a marquee selection that starts in the center and grows outward. Pressing and holding [Shift] while dragging a marquee tool constrains the marquee selection to a perfect circle or square. Don't worry if you have a slight white halo at the edge of your selection.

TROUBLE
If you're using a Macintosh computer and you see a dialog box asking what you want to use ⌘[H] for, click Hide Extras.

8. Press [Ctrl][H] (Win) or ⌘[H] (Mac) to hide the marquee, then move the piece into position so that your canvas resembles Figure B-2

9. Deselect, then save your work

Selecting Pixels

FIGURE B-1: Positioning the first piece

FIGURE B-2: Positioning the circle piece

Circle piece in place

The Shift key: doing double duty

As you've seen in this lesson, the Shift key does two important things: it adds to an existing selection, and it constrains a selection to a perfect shape. What if you wanted to do both—to select two perfect squares? You would press and hold [Shift] while selecting the first square to make a square marquee. To select the second square, you would need to press [Shift] to add to the first selection. So how would you use the Shift key to add to the first square *and* constrain the shape of the second selection as a square? Release the Shift key while dragging, then press it again and it will constrain the selection.

Using the Lasso Tools

There are three types of Lasso tools in Photoshop: Lasso, Polygonal Lasso, and Magnetic Lasso. Lasso tools are also used for making free-form selections: simply click and drag anywhere on the canvas to create a section of pixels. When selecting a complex shape with the Lasso tool, you will usually find it easier to make small selections then add to them with the Shift key. The Polygonal Lasso tool functions like the Lasso tool, but it does so with straight lines. This makes the tool very effective for making quick selections or selecting areas of the canvas that are geometric in shape, as the tool's name implies. Laura instructs you to move on to select the free-form pieces of the puzzle. You use the Lasso tool to select an organically shaped object and the Polygonal Lasso tool to select a multi-lateral object.

STEPS

QUICK TIP

If you do not see the Lasso tool, press and hold the Polygonal Lasso tool or the Magnetic Lasso tool to expose the Lasso tool.

1. Zoom in on the #5 piece, then click the Lasso tool

2. Click and drag to select just an interior section of the piece, as shown in Figure B-3
   Your selection may differ from the figure.

3. Press [Shift] while using the Lasso tool to keep adding to the selection until the entire shape is selected

4. If necessary, press [Alt] (Win) or [option] (Mac) while using the Lasso tool to remove unwanted selected areas you might create outside of the shape

5. Move the piece into place in the puzzle, as shown in Figure B-4
   Don't worry if the selection isn't perfect. This is just for practice with the Lasso tool; you will learn more precise methods for selecting these types of shapes.

6. Zoom in on the #6 piece, click the Polygonal Lasso tool , then press [Caps Lock] so that the Lasso tool icon is a precise crosshair

7. Position the crosshair at the tip of the upper-right point of the shape, click, release the mouse button, then move the mouse pointer to the next corner on the shape and click

8. Using the same method, move the mouse pointer around the shape, clicking on the next 12 corners of the shape

9. Float over the original point you clicked so that the Polygonal Lasso tool icon appears with a small "o" beside it, then click to close the selection

10. Move the piece into place in the puzzle, deselect, then compare your result to Figure B-5

Working with the foreground and background colors

As shown in Figure B-15, the Foreground and Background colors are the colors that you paint with and fill selections with. You can click the Switch Foreground and Background Colors button or press [X] to switch the foreground and background colors. Click the Default Foreground and Background Colors button or press [D] to revert the foreground and background colors to black and white.

FIGURE B-15: Foreground and Background colors

Press [X] to access this function

Press [D] to access this function

FIGURE B-3: Selecting the interior of the object

Selection marquee

FIGURE B-4: Positioning piece #5

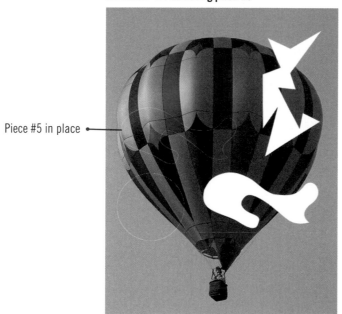

Piece #5 in place

FIGURE B-5: Positioning piece #6

Piece #6 in place

Selecting Pixels

Using the Magic Wand Tool

The Magic Wand tool is a very powerful selection tool. Click any pixel on the canvas, and the Magic Wand tool selects other pixels based on tolerance—the similarity of their color. The greater the tolerance value you set for the tool, the more pixels the Magic Wand tool will select. By clicking the Contiguous check box on the Options bar, you can specify that the Magic Wand tool selects only pixels that are contiguous to (touching) the area where you click the image. Otherwise, it will select similar pixels throughout the image. For more information about the Magic Wand tool, see the Clues to Use, called *Understanding tolerance*, on the next page. As with any selection, once you select all of the pixels that you want, you can modify them in many ways, such as by changing their color in the Hue/Saturation dialog box. ▚▚▚ Laura tells you to complete the test using the Magic Wand tool, and then to show her a method for changing selected pixels' color using the Hue/Saturation dialog box.

STEPS

QUICK TIP

The Magic Wand tool may be hidden behind the Quick Selection tool ▨.

1. Release [Caps Lock] if it is activated, click the Magic Wand tool ▨, then, on the Options bar, change the Tolerance setting to **8** and verify that the Anti-alias and Contiguous check boxes are both checked

2. Click anywhere in the white area that represents the missing piece in the puzzle, then compare your selection to Figure B-6

   The Magic Wand tool selected other white and almost-white pixels, but did not select pixels of the balloon image because they are outside of tolerance. Because the Contiguous option was checked, the white pixels on the left of the canvas are not selected because they are not contiguous—they don't touch the area that you clicked.

QUICK TIP

Once the marquee is close to the #7 piece, zoom in and use the arrow keys to align it precisely.

3. Float over the selected area so that the Magic Wand pointer changes to a white arrow, then drag to move the marquee and align it with the #7 piece on the left of the canvas

4. Click the Move tool ▸⊕, position the #7 piece in the puzzle, deselect, then save your work

5. Open PS B-2.psd, save it as air balloon_PS-B, click the Magic Wand tool ▨, then click in the center red rectangle of the hot air balloon

   Only a small selection is created because the tolerance setting is low, and there are a variety of red pixels in this area.

6. Deselect, increase the Tolerance value on the Options bar to **48**, then click the same place in the red rectangle

   The increased tolerance value allows for a broader range of reds to be selected. The entire red rectangle is selected, but the selection does not extend into the yellow areas because they are out of tolerance.

7. Deselect, click the Contiguous check box on the Options bar to remove the check mark, click the same place in the red rectangle, then compare your selection to Figure B-7

   With the Contiguous option deactivated, the red pixels within tolerance throughout the image are selected.

QUICK TIP

Zooming in on areas of the image that you want to select always helps when making selections

8. Press and hold [Shift], then click unselected red areas in the balloon to add them to the selection

9. Hide the marquee, click Image on the Menu bar, point to Adjustments, click Hue/Saturation, then drag the Hue slider to **126**

   All of the selected pixels—and only the selected pixels—are changed to a green hue, as shown in Figure B-8.

10. Click OK, save your work, then close air balloon_PS-B.psd and selections puzzle_PS-B.psd

FIGURE B-6: Selecting the white pixels

Selected pixels

FIGURE B-7: Selecting pixels without the Contiguous option

FIGURE B-8: Results of changing the hue of selected pixels

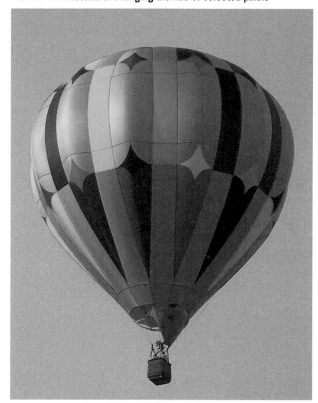

Understanding tolerance

The Magic Wand tool and many other tools in Photoshop do their work based on the function of tolerance. The key to understanding tolerance is to understand that in every Photoshop file, every pixel has a number. The clearest example of that concept can be found in a grayscale image. In a grayscale image, each pixel can be one—and only one—of 256 shades of gray. Tolerance settings work and interact directly with those pixel numbers. For example, let's say you set the tolerance option for the Magic Wand tool to 10. Next, you click the Magic Wand tool on a pixel whose grayscale value is 75. The Magic Wand tool would select all contiguous pixels whose grayscale value falls within the range of 65–85; ten grayscale values higher and lower than the pixel that you clicked. If the Contiguous option is not activated, the Magic Wand tool would select all the pixels throughout the image whose grayscale values were 65–85. Of course, you don't need to know the number of the pixel you are clicking. Your goal is simply to select pixels of similar color. All you need to do is experiment with different tolerance settings until you get the selection you want.

Saving and Loading Selections

Making selections can be some of the most complex and time-consuming work you'll do in Photoshop, so it makes sense that you can save selections with the Photoshop file. Saving a selection is always a smart idea because you never know when you might want to access the selection again in the future. ⬛⬛⬛ You've been assigned to work on a design project for a client. Jon explains that the client wants to see color applied to a posterized image. You posterize the file, then create and save four selections in order to load them and fill them with four different colors.

STEPS

Before starting these steps, open the Swatches and Color panels.

1. **Open PS B-3.psd, click** Image **on the Menu bar, point to** Adjustments, **then click** Posterize

   Posterize is a special effect that is created by reducing the number of colors available for the image.

2. **Drag the** Levels slider **to 4, then click** OK

   With the Posterize effect set to four, each pixel in the image can be one—and only one—of four available shades of gray: black, dark gray, light gray, or white.

3. **Click** Image **on the Menu bar, point to** Mode, **then click** RGB Color

   Changing the color mode to RGB Color will allow you to add color to the selections.

4. **Click the** Magic Wand tool ✦, **set the Tolerance to 1 on the Options bar, verify that the Anti-alias and the Contiguous check boxes are not checked, then click a white area of the image**

5. **Click** Select **on the Menu bar, click** Save Selection, **then type** White **in the Name text box**

   The Save Selection dialog box, shown in Figure B-9, shows that the new selection will be saved with the file PS B-3.psd when you save the file.

6. **Click** OK **to close the dialog box, then repeat Steps 4 and 5 to make three more selections, named** Light Gray, Dark Gray, **and** Black, **by clicking a light gray area, a dark gray area, and a black area with the Magic Wand tool, then saving each selection**

7. **Deselect the last selection by pressing [Ctrl][D] (Win) or ⌘[D] (Mac), click** Select **on the Menu bar, click** Load Selection, **click the** Channel list arrow, **click** Light Gray, **then click** OK

   The saved selection is loaded.

8. **Float the pointer over the Swatches panel, then click the swatch named** Pure Yellow Orange, **as shown in Figure B-10**

   Pure Yellow Orange becomes the foreground color on the Tools panel.

9. **Click** Edit **on the Menu bar, click** Fill, **click the** Use list arrow, **click** Foreground Color, **verify that the Opacity setting is 100%, click** OK, **then deselect**

   The Light Gray selection is filled with Pure Yellow Orange.

10. **Repeat Steps 7–9 to load the** White, Dark Gray, **and** Black **selections, filling each with a color of your choice on the Swatches panel**

    Figure B-11 shows one possible result.

QUICK TIP
Press [Alt] [Delete] (Win) or [option] [delete] (Mac) to fill a selection with the foreground color and [Ctrl][Delete] (Win) or ⌘ [delete] (Mac) to fill a selection with the background color. Press [Delete] (Win) or [delete] (Mac) to open the Fill dialog box.

Selecting Pixels

FIGURE B-9: Save Selection dialog box

FIGURE B-10: Pure Yellow Orange swatch on the Swatches panel

FIGURE B-11: The image with different fill colors for each selection

Saving color swatches

There are many ways to change the foreground and background colors. On the Swatches panel, for example, if you click a swatch, the foreground changes to that color. Press [Ctrl] (Win) or ⌘ (Mac) when you click a swatch to change the background color. You can also click the Eyedropper tool and sample any pixel from the image. Doing so changes the foreground color to the color of the pixel. You can also drag the sliders on the Color panel to modify the current foreground color. To save colors that you create, simply float the pointer over a dark gray area of the Swatches panel. The pointer changes to a paint bucket icon. Click and the color will be added as a new swatch. You're even given the option to name it. The new swatch will remain on the Swatches panel for every new file that you create from that point forward. To delete a swatch from the Swatches panel, press and hold [Alt] (Win) or [option] (Mac), then click to delete the swatch.

Selecting Pixels
Photoshop 39

Photoshop CS6

Working with and Saving Alpha Channels

Alpha channels are saved selections. To put it another way, when you save a selection, the selection is saved as an alpha channel. Alpha channels are listed on the Channels panel in Photoshop. They are displayed as black and white thumbnail images. The selected areas are represented by white, and the areas not selected are represented by black. You can save selections as you are working, but alpha channels are not automatically saved when you save the file. You must specify that they be saved when you save the file. ▰▰▰ Now that you have four new alpha channels, you view them on the Channels panel. You load the Dark Gray alpha channel, change its color, then save all of the alpha channels with the file.

STEPS

1. **Click Window on the Menu bar, then click Channels**

   The Channels panel holds four default channels: the "composite" RGB channel, and one channel each for Red, Blue, and Green. In addition are the four alpha channels representing the selections you saved: White, Light Gray, Dark Gray, and Black.

QUICK TIP
Many users like to think of alpha channels as stencils and the white areas as that which has been "cut out" of the stencil.

2. **Click the Channel thumbnail on the Dark Gray channel, then compare your canvas to Figure B-12**

   The alpha channel is the selection that you saved. The dark gray pixels that you selected are represented by white pixels. Everything that wasn't selected is represented by black pixels.

3. **Click the Channel thumbnails for the other three alpha channels that you saved, then click the RGB channel thumbnail to see the composite image with all of its colors**

4. **Press and hold [Ctrl] (Win) or ⌘ (Mac), then click the Channel thumbnail of the Dark Gray alpha channel**

   The Dark Gray alpha channel is loaded as a selection. Pressing and holding [Ctrl] (Win) or ⌘ (Mac) while clicking a channel thumbnail is a quicker way to load a selection.

5. **On the Swatches panel, click Pure Yellow Green**

   Pure Yellow Green becomes the foreground color.

6. **Fill the selection with the foreground color, deselect, then compare your result to Figure B-13**

7. **Click File on the Menu bar, click Save As, type save selections_PS-B in the File name text box (Win) or the Save As text box (Mac), verify that the Alpha Channels check box is checked, as shown in Figure B-14, then click Save**

   All of the saved selections—the alpha channels—are saved with the file. Every time you save a selection and add a channel to a file, you are increasing the file size substantially. Delete alpha channels when you no longer need them.

8. **Close save selections_PS-B.psd**

FIGURE B-12: The Dark Gray alpha channel

FIGURE B-13: Filling the loaded selection with a new color

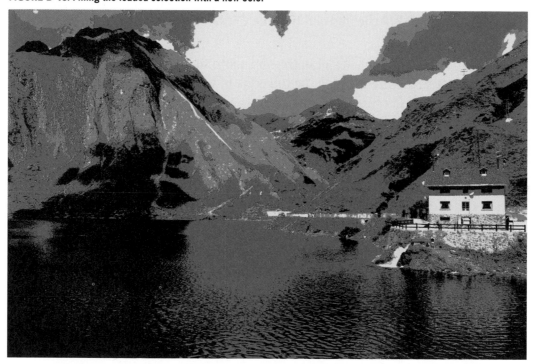

FIGURE B-14: Save Alpha Channels option in the Save As dialog box

Alpha Channels
check box

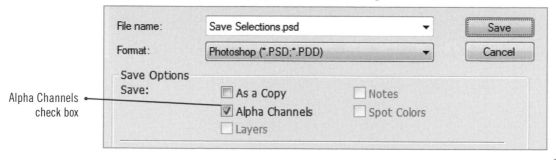

Understanding Anti-Aliased Edges

The outline of a selection is called the **edge** of a selection; the type of edge that you choose will have a big impact on how your work appears. The edge of a selection is always either aliased or anti-aliased. An **aliased** edge is a hard edge—the hard "stair-stepped" pixels are very obvious. The edge is noticeably blunt. This is why aliased edges are seldom used. An **anti-aliased** edge is a crisp but smoother edge. With an anti-aliased edge, Photoshop creates a smooth transition between the edge and its background using many shades of the edge pixel color. Jon provides you with an image he needs for an educational poster. He asks you to try to improve the appearance of an apple against a blue background. You apply an aliased edge and an anti-aliased edge to compare the difference between the two.

STEPS

1. Open PS B-4.psd, then save it as apple edges_PS-B

2. Press and hold [Ctrl] (Win) or ⌘ (Mac), then click the yellow swatch (RGB Yellow) in the top row on the Swatches panel

   The background color changes to RGB Yellow.

QUICK TIP
You will need to make more than one selection to select the entire apple.

3. Click the Magic Wand tool 🪄, set the Tolerance value to 72, verify that the Anti-alias check box is *not* checked and that the Contiguous check box *is* checked, then select the entire apple

4. Click the Move tool ⊕, drag the apple into the black area on the right, hide the marquee, then zoom in on the top edge of the apple

   Figure B-16 is an enlarged view of the top edge of the apple and shows the hard aliased edge; the square shapes of the pixels are clearly visible.

5. Double-click the Hand tool 🖐 to fit the page in the window, then note on the left of the canvas that the yellow background color fills the remaining area after the move and has the same aliased edge

6. Click Edit on the Menu bar, click Undo Move, then deselect

QUICK TIP
You will need to make more than one selection to select the entire apple.

7. Click the Magic Wand tool 🪄, click the Anti-alias check box on the Options bar, then select the apple

8. Click ⊕, drag the apple into the black area, hide the marquee, then zoom in on the top edge

   As shown in Figure B-17, the apple has an anti-aliased edge. Edge pixels of various shades of green create the illusion of a smooth edge where the apple meets the black background.

9. Click 🖐, then move the canvas to the right so that you can examine the edge where the yellow fill meets the blue background

   The anti-aliased edge creates a crisp and smooth transition between the solid yellow and the almost-solid blue background.

10. Save your work, then close apple edges_PS-B.psd

FIGURE B-16: Viewing the aliased edge

FIGURE B-17: Viewing the anti-aliased edge

How anti-aliasing works

As has been said before, a Photoshop image is made up of pixels, and pixels are square. By definition, a square does not have a soft edge. So think about this: How do you create a soft edge for a curved object using only squares? The answer is that you can't create a soft edge with squares; squares have right-angle corners. All you can do is create the *illusion* of a soft edge. That's what an anti-aliased edge is: an illusion. Anti-aliasing manipulates the color of edge pixels in a selection to create a visual transition between the selected object and the background. So the soft edge is an optical illusion made by manipulating color—the color of square pixels.

Computer monitors and viewing edges

Your computer monitor acts as the middleman between you and the Photoshop image. Everything you are seeing is through your monitor. Monitors also use red, green, and blue pixels of transmitted light. Using these three colors, your monitor is able to show you millions of colors—more than your eye can differentiate. Monitors have resolution as well; most have a resolution of 72 pixels per inch. This fact has a big impact on how you view your Photoshop image, because at all times the monitor's resolution is trying to match the image's resolution. When you're viewing your image at less than 100%, your monitor is not giving you an accurate visual representation of the pixels in your image. When you're analyzing subtle components of your image—like selection edges!—be sure that you're viewing your canvas at least at 100%.

Working with a Feathered Edge

A **feathered edge** is a blended edge. Photoshop creates a blend at the edge of a selection between the selected pixels and the background image. Photoshop offers settings for controlling the length of the blend at the edge. The feather value is equal to the length of the feathered edge. When you apply a feathered edge to a selection, the edge is equally distributed inside and outside the selection edge. In Photoshop, vignettes are created with feathered edges. A **vignette** is a visual effect in which the edge of an image—usually an oval—gradually fades away. A MegaPixel client has given you a picture and asked that you create a vignette effect. You create an oval with a feathered edge, preview it in Quick Mask Mode, then save the selection.

STEPS

1. Open PS B-5.psd, then click the Default Foreground and Background Colors button on the Tools panel

QUICK TIP

The Rectangular Marquee tool and the Lasso tool also offer feather options.

2. Click the Elliptical Marquee tool , type 32 in the Feather text box on the Options bar, then verify that the Anti-alias check box is checked

3. Position the mouse pointer on the jewelry at the woman's neck, press [Alt] (Win) or [option] (Mac), then draw an oval from the center that resembles the shape and size of the one shown in Figure B-18

TROUBLE

The Quick Mask in Figure B-19 uses the default red Quick Mask color. Your quick mask color and degree of transparency may differ.

4. Click the Edit in Quick Mask Mode button on the Tools panel to preview the selection

   Quick Mask Mode provides a preview of how the feathered edge will appear when you save the selection. The Quick Mask Mode feature shows the selected pixels and hides or "masks" unselected pixels. As shown in Figure B-19, the 32-pixel blend created a very soft and smooth edge that progressively fades out the edge of the selected image. The Quick Mask is very helpful because without it, you would not be able to see the result of the feathered edge until after you saved the selection. To learn more information about Quick Mask Mode, see the Clues to Use on the next page called *Understanding Quick Mask Mode*.

5. Click the Edit in Standard Mode button to return to the Standard view

6. Click the Select menu, click Save Selection, save the selection as Vignette, then deselect

   The selection is now an alpha channel saved on the Channels panel.

7. Open the Channels panel, then click the Vignette channel thumbnail to view the saved selection

   In this selection, which transitions gradually from selected pixels to unselected pixels, the alpha channel transitions gradually from white to black. See the Clues to Use called *Understanding gray pixels in alpha channels*.

QUICK TIP

Use the Select menu to load the selection.

8. Click the RGB channel thumbnail on the Channels panel, then load the Vignette selection

9. Click the Move tool , drag the selected pixels into the green area on the right, then deselect

   Figure B-20 shows the moved pixels with the feathered edge and also the feathered edge remaining after the move.

10. Save the file with its alpha channels as vignette_PS-B, then close vignette_PS-B.psd

FIGURE B-18: Drawing the feathered oval selection

FIGURE B-19: Previewing the selection in Quick Mask Mode

FIGURE B-20: The selected pixels relocated

Understanding Quick Mask Mode

Many graphic arts professionals refer to alpha channels as "masks" because the non-selected areas are "masked" by the black areas in the alpha channel. Quick Mask works with the same concept as alpha channels. Quick Mask is a visual aid that gives you a preview of your selection. It helps you to see your selection by "masking out" the areas that aren't selected and showing only the areas that are. You can increase or decrease the opacity of the Quick Mask by double-clicking the Edit in Quick Mask Mode button on the Tools panel. The Quick Mask Options dialog box opens. In this dialog box, you can change the color and the opacity as well as decide whether you want the color to indicate the masked area or the selected area. You can toggle between Quick Mask Mode and Standard Mode by pressing [Q].

Understanding gray pixels in alpha channels

How does Photoshop save a selection? By creating an alpha channel. Selected areas are white, and non-selected areas are black. But what if the selection has a feathered edge? The only way an alpha channel can render that is with gray pixels. This is the concept of opacity. Here's the easiest way to understand this concept in relation to alpha channels: The feathered edge makes the image fade away to nothing outside the selection. In the case of the previous lesson, the center of the oval is where the pixels have 100% opacity—they are fully visible, and they are represented by 100% white pixels in the alpha channel. The pixels completely outside the selection have 0% opacity—they are completely transparent, and thus represented by 100% black pixels in the alpha channel. In a feathered edge, the opacity fades from 100% to 0%, so in the alpha channel, that area fades from white to black. For example, the pixels smack in the middle of the feathered edge would be 50% black; in other words, gray. Pixels closer to the outer edge would be dark gray, almost black, and therefore fading out to nothing.

Refining Selection Edges

The Refine Edge dialog box offers you a number of useful options for viewing and refining the edge of a selection. The two key options in this dialog box are the Feather slider, which you can use to dynamically feather a selection while you preview the result, and the Shift Edge slider, which expands or contracts a selection marquee. The Contrast slider is especially useful for removing halos from the edge of a selection. Table B-1 on the next page offers useful keyboard commands for the Refine Edge dialog box. ▓▓▓▓ MegaPixel's city zoo client has asked that you create a preliminary design that involves a silhouette of a bird's head on a white background. You note immediately that this will be challenging because the background is so dark and the white head feathers are so numerous. You decide to make a quick selection and tweak it in the Refine Edge dialog box.

STEPS

1. **Open PS B-6.psd, then save it as** eagle silhouette_PS-B

2. **Press and hold the** Magic Wand tool ▨, **click the** Quick Selection tool ▨, **click the Brush Picker list arrow on the Options bar, then set the Size setting to** 10 px

   The Quick Selection tool is a selection tool that you use by dragging the tool pointer over the item you wish to select until you have all of it selected. The Quick Selection tool selects pixels based on their similarity, but there's no option to set a tolerance value. Instead, the Quick Selection tool offers you the Add to selection and Subtract from selection tools that you can use to either enlarge an existing selection or remove unwanted areas from a selection. In addition, you can reduce the brush size to select smaller or more specific areas.

3. **Position the Quick Selection tool pointer at the top of the eagle's head, then drag the brush slowly down over the eagle's white feathers and then down over the eagle's brown feathers**

   Compare your result to Figure B-21.

4. **Click** Select **on the Menu bar, then click** Refine Edge

   By default, the selection should appear against a white background.

5. **Click the** View list arrow, **sample all seven views, then choose** On White

6. **In the Edge Detection section, verify that the Smart Radius check box is not checked, drag the** Radius slider **to experiment with changing the size of the refinement area, then set the Radius value to** 30

   The Radius setting improves the selection of the long white feathers on the eagle's neck.

7. **Experiment with the** Smooth slider, **then set the Smooth value to** 3

   The Smooth option will reduce bumps and stair-stepping at the edges of the selection.

8. **Experiment with the** Contrast slider, **set the Contrast value to** 12, **then compare your Refine Edge dialog box to Figure B-22**

9. **Click** OK, **click** Select **on the Menu bar, then click** Inverse

   Everything outside of the eagle selection is selected.

10. **Click** Edit **on the Menu bar, click** Fill, **click the** Use list arrow, **click** White, **click** OK, **then deselect**

    The original background is now filled with white. The Refine Edge dialog box did a great job on the white feathers of the head, but the brown edges on the top and breast are unacceptable and would need to be corrected.

11. **Compare your canvas to Figure B-23, save your changes, then close eagle silhouette_PS-B.psd**

Selecting Pixels

FIGURE B-21: Quick selection made from the Quick Selection tool

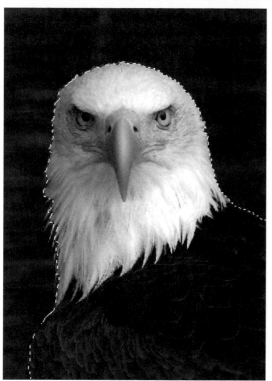

FIGURE B-22: Refine Edge dialog box

View list arrow

FIGURE B-23: The silhouette of the eagle against white

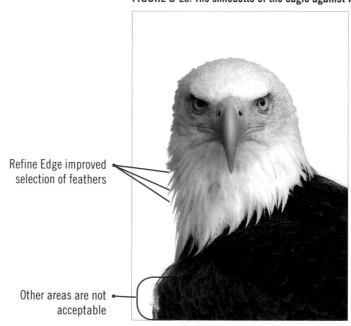

Refine Edge improved selection of feathers

Other areas are not acceptable

TABLE B-1: Useful keyboard commands for the Refine Edge dialog box (Win & Mac)

keyboard	action
[P]	Toggles the Preview option on and off
[F]	Cycles through the preview modes
[Shift][F]	Cycles backward through the preview modes
[X]	Temporarily displays the entire image

Practice

Concepts Review

Label the elements of the Photoshop screen shown in Figure B-24.

FIGURE B-24

Match each term with the statement that best describes it.

  8. **Alpha channel**

  9. **Quick Mask Mode**

10. **Aliased edge**

11. **Anti-aliased edge**

12. **Tolerance**

13. **Feather**

14. **Posterize**

15. **Vignette**

a. Hard edge showing pixels stair-stepping

b. Setting that controls the Magic Wand tool

c. Useful for previewing selections

d. Blended edge

e. To reduce the colors in an image

f. Created whenever a selection is saved

g. Effect made with a feathered edge

h. Smooth and crisp edge

Select the best answer from the list of choices.

16. Which of the following offers the hardest edge for a selection?
a. Alias
b. Anti-alias
c. Feather
d. Tolerance

17. Which of the following would be the best tool for selecting an image of a stop sign?
a. Rectangular Marquee tool
b. Elliptical Marquee tool
c. Lasso tool
d. Polygonal Lasso tool

18. Which of the following is not true about saved selections?
a. Saving a selection creates an alpha channel
b. An alpha channel is a selection
c. Alpha channels are saved automatically when you save a file
d. Saving alpha channels increases file size

19. Which of the following is true about alpha channels?
a. White pixels represent selected pixels
b. Saving a selection with a feathered edge results in an alpha channel with gray pixels
c. The Load Selection command is the only way to load a saved selection
d. Both a and b but not c

20. Which of the following quick keys is used to fill a selection with the foreground color?
a. [Alt][Enter] (Win) or [option][return] (Mac)
b. [Alt][Backspace] (Win) or [option][Delete] (Mac)
c. [Shift][Enter] (Win) or [Shift][return] (Mac)
d. [Backspace] (Win) or [Delete] (Mac)

21. What are the default foreground and background colors in Photoshop?
a. Black over White
b. White over Black
c. Black over Black
d. White over White

Skills Review

1. Use the marquee tools.
a. Open PS B-7.psd, save it as **shapes_PS-B**, zoom in on the #1 piece, then click the Rectangular Marquee tool.
b. Press [D] to access the default colors on the Tools panel.
c. Position the center of the crosshair on the upper-left corner of the #1 puzzle piece, drag downward until the center of the crosshair is on the lower-right corner, then release the mouse pointer.
d. Click View on the Menu bar, click Fit on Screen, click the Move tool, drag the piece to the corresponding position in the puzzle on the right, then deselect. You will be positioning puzzle pieces 2, 3, and 4 for the remainder of this exercise. Each time you select a puzzle piece, zoom in on the piece, select it, zoom out, move it to the correct position on the puzzle on the right, then deselect.
e. Click the Rectangular Marquee tool, select the top square in the #2 piece, press and hold [Shift], position the crosshair over the lower-right corner, drag a second marquee that overlaps the first, then release the mouse pointer.
f. Select the outer square in the #3 piece, press and hold [Alt] (Win) or [option] (Mac), then select the blue inner rectangle so that it is removed from the selection.
g. Using the same method, click the Elliptical Marquee tool, verify that the Feather value on the Options bar is 0, press and hold [Alt] (Win) or [option] (Mac), then remove the circle from the selection.
h. Press [Ctrl][H] (Win) or ⌘[H] (Mac) to hide the marquee, then move the piece into position.
i. Deselect, then save your work.

2. Use the lasso tools.
a. Zoom in on the #4 piece, then click the Lasso tool.
b. Click and drag to select just an interior section of the piece.
c. Use the [Shift] key in conjunction with the Lasso tool to keep adding to the selection until the entire shape is selected.
d. Press [Alt] (Win) or [option] (Mac) while using the Lasso tool to remove unwanted selected areas you might have created outside of the shape.

Skills Review (continued)

e. Move the piece into place in the puzzle on the right.

f. Zoom in on the #5 piece, click the Polygonal Lasso tool, then press [Caps Lock] so that the Lasso tool icon is a precise crosshair.

g. Position the crosshair at the tip of the upper-right point of the shape, click, release the mouse button, then move the mouse pointer to the next corner on the shape and click.

h. Using the same method, move the mouse pointer around the shape, clicking on the remaining corners of the shape.

i. Float over the original point you clicked so that the Polygonal Lasso tool icon appears with a small "o" beside it, then click to close the selection.

j. Move the piece into place in the puzzle on the right, then deselect.

3. Use the Magic Wand tool.

a. Verify that Caps Lock is not active, then click the Magic Wand tool.

b. Change the Tolerance setting to 4.

c. Verify that the Anti-alias check box is checked.

d. Verify that the Contiguous check box is checked.

e. Click anywhere in the #6 puzzle piece to select it.

f. Click the Move tool, move the piece into position, and keep the piece selected.

g. Hide the marquee, click Image on the Menu bar, point to Adjustments, click Hue/Saturation, then drag the Hue slider to -112.

h. Click OK, then compare your screen to Figure B-25.

i. Save your work, then close shapes_PS-B.psd.

FIGURE B-25

Skills Review (continued)

4. **Save and load selections.**
   a. Open PS B-8.psd.
   b. Click Image on the Menu bar, point to Adjustments, then click Posterize.
   c. Drag the Levels slider to 4, then click OK.
   d. Click Image on the Menu bar, point to Mode, then click RGB Color.
   e. Click the Magic Wand tool, set the Tolerance to 1, then verify that the Anti-alias check box is not checked and that the Contiguous check box is not checked.
   f. Click a white area of the image.
   g. Click Select on the Menu bar, click Save Selection, type **White** in the Name text box, then click OK.
   h. Repeat Steps f and g to save three new selections named **Light Gray**, **Dark Gray**, and **Black**.
   i. Click Select on the Menu bar, click Load Selection, click the Channel list arrow, click Light Gray, then click OK.
   j. Float your cursor over the Swatches panel so that it changes to the Eyedropper, then click Pure Yellow Orange to make it the foreground color.
   k. Click Edit on the Menu bar, click Fill, click the Use list arrow, click Foreground Color, then click OK.
   l. Repeat Steps i–k to load and fill the three other saved selections with different colors. Figure B-26 shows one possible result.

5. **Work with and save alpha channels.**
   a. On the Channels panel, click the Dark Gray channel thumbnail to view the channel itself.
   b. Click the thumbnails for the three other alpha channels that you saved, then click the RGB channel to return to the image on the canvas.
   c. On the Swatches panel, choose Pastel Violet Magenta as a new foreground color.
   d. Press and hold [Ctrl](Win) or ⌘ (Mac) then click the Dark Gray channel thumbnail.
   e. Fill the selection with the foreground color.
   f. Click File on the Menu bar, click Save As, type **clown posterize_PS-B** in the Name text box, then verify that the Alpha Channels check box is checked.
   g. Click Save, then close clown posterize_PS-B.psd.

FIGURE B-26

Skills Review (continued)

6. **Understand anti-aliased edges.**
   a. Open PS B-9.psd, then save it as **skills edges_PS-B**.
   b. On the Swatches panel, press and hold [Ctrl](Win) or ⌘ (Mac), then click the RGB Yellow swatch in the top row to make it the background color.
   c. Click the Magic Wand tool, set the Tolerance value to 4, verify that the Anti-alias check box is not checked and that the Contiguous check box is not checked, then click the center of any orange shape.
   d. Click the Move tool, then drag the selected pixels into the white area on the right.
   e. Hide the selection, then examine the edges of various shapes.
   f. Undo the move, deselect, click the Magic Wand tool, check the Anti-alias check box, then select all the shapes again.
   g. Move the selected pixels into the white area, then hide the selection marquee.
   h. Zoom in and examine the edges of various shapes.
   i. Examine the edges where the yellow fills meet the blue background on the left of the canvas.
   j. Undo the move, then save your work.

7. **Work with a feathered edge.**
   a. Verify that all pixels are deselected, then set the foreground and background colors on the Tools panel to the default colors.
   b. Click the Magic Wand tool, then click the center of any orange shape.
   c. Click Select on the Menu bar, point to Modify, then click Feather.
   d. Type **12** in the Feather Radius text box, then click OK.
   e. Click the Edit in Quick Mask Mode button on the Tools panel to preview the selection.
   f. Click the Edit in Standard Mode button to return to Standard view.
   g. Click the Move tool, then drag the selected pixels into the white area on the right.
   h. Hide the selection, then examine the edges of the shapes on the right and left.
   i. Compare your results with Figure B-27.
   j. Save your work, then close skills edges_PS-B.psd.

FIGURE B-27

Skills Review (continued)

8. **Refine selection edges.**

   a. Open PS B-10.psd, then save it as **apple silhouette_PS-B**.

   b. Click the Quick Selection tool, click the Brush Picker list arrow on the Options bar, then set the Size setting to 10 px.

   c. Click and drag the brush slowly over the apple until the entire apple is selected.

   d. Click Select on the Menu bar, then click Refine Edge.

   e. Verify that Smart Radius is not checked, then drag the Radius slider to 3.

   f. Drag the Smooth slider to 25, then click OK.

   g. Click the Move tool, then move the selected pixels into the black space on the right part of the canvas.

   h. Deselect, compare your canvas to Figure B-28, save your work, then close apple silhouette_PS-B.psd.

FIGURE B-28

Independent Challenge 1

The Estonia Travel and Tourism Board has sent you a great image of a hot air balloon to promote sightseeing around Tallinn. They tell you that they love the image, but they don't like the colors of the balloon—they think the primary palette of yellow, red, and blue is "not exciting or magical." They ask that you change the colors of the balloon to something more interesting. You realize that you'll need to make a really good selection of the balloon so that the color changes won't show.

a. Open PS B-11.psd, then save it as **magic wand mask_PS-B**.

b. Click the Magic Wand tool.

c. Set the Tolerance to 20, then verify that the Anti-alias and Contiguous check boxes are both checked.

d. Use the Magic Wand tool to select the sky. (*Hint*: You will need to click multiple times with the Magic Wand tool to select the entire sky.)

e. Click Select on the Menu bar, then click Inverse.

f. Use the Lasso tool to remove the basket from the selection so that only the balloon is selected.

g. Click Select on the Menu bar, then click Refine Edge.

h. Click the View list arrow, then click On Black. (*Hint*: The selection is clearly outside of the edge of the balloon and is a very hard edge.)

i. Verify that the Smart Radius check box is not checked, then drag the Radius slider to 3.0.

j. Drag the Smooth slider to 9.

k. Drag the Contrast slider to 13, and note how the edge is improved.

l. Click OK, then hide the selection marquee.

m. Click Image on the Menu bar, point to Adjustments, then click Hue/Saturation.

n. Drag the Hue slider to -84, then click OK.

o. View the image at 100%, then scroll around to examine the edges.

p. Save your work, compare your screen to Figure B-29, then close magic wand mask_PS-B.psd.

FIGURE B-29

Independent Challenge 2

Your client has called, asking that you modify a file that shows balloons against the sky. They tell you that they would like you to posterize the balloons and change their color so that the yellow balloons are orange. They have created and saved a selection of the balloons to make your work easier.

   a. Open PS B-12.psd, then save it as **orange balloons_PS-B**.

   b. Posterize the image to 4 levels.

   c. Open the Channels panel.

   d. Press and hold [Ctrl](Win) or ⌘ (Mac), then click the Balloons channel thumbnail to load the selection.

   e. Click Image on the Menu bar, point to Adjustments, then click Hue/Saturation.

   f. Drag the Hue slider to -45, then click OK.

   g. Deselect, then compare your result to Figure B-30.

   h. Save your work, then close orange balloons_PS-B.psd.

FIGURE B-30

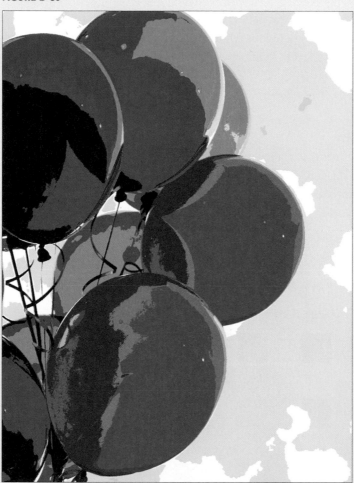

Independent Challenge 3

Your company has a client that specializes in online IQ tests. You've worked on producing more than 100 visual puzzles in the last month. Two of the puzzles have come back with requests for changes. The client has supplied two low-res examples of the changes for you to match.

a. Open PS B-13.psd, then save it as **iq test_PS-B**.

b. Open PS B-14.psd. (*Hint*: If you can, make room on your screen for both files. You need to make iq test_PS-B.psd match the small file.)

c. Use the Rectangular Marquee tool to draw one marquee around all four red boxes—be precise.

d. Draw one marquee around the four blue squares to deselect that entire area. (*Hint*: Use [Alt] (Win) or [option] (Mac) when drawing to deselect the area.)

e. Use the Magic Wand tool to remove the black squares from the selection with one click. (*Hint*: Deselect the Anti-alias and Contiguous check boxes on the Options bar and press [Alt] (Win) or [option] (Mac) when clicking a black square.)

f. Use the same method to remove the red squares from the selection.

g. Fill the remaining selection with the 50% gray swatch on the Swatches panel.

h. Deselect.

i. Click the first yellow swatch on the Swatches panel to make it the foreground color.

j. Use the Magic Wand tool to select only the white squares in the center, then fill them with yellow.

k. Use the Magic Wand tool to select the blue squares, then fill them with the first green swatch on the Swatches panel.

l. Select the four red squares, then fill them with the same yellow you used in Step j so that your screen resembles Figure B-31.

Advanced Challenge Exercise

- Expand the Swatches panel so that you can see all the swatches.
- Float your cursor in the gray area beneath the swatches so that your cursor turns into a paint bucket icon.
- Click the mouse pointer.
- Type **Yellow I Used** in the Name text box, then click OK.

m. Close PS B-14.psd.

n. Save your work, then close iq test_PS-B.psd.

FIGURE B-31

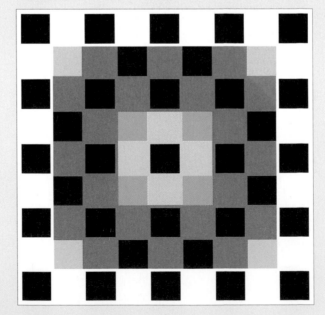

Real Life Independent Challenge

Your sister has just bought a new condo and has lots of wall space to fill. You have a great photo of her and decide to apply an "Andy Warhol" effect to the photo and give it to her to enlarge and frame.

   a. Open PS B-15.psd, then posterize the file to 6 levels.

   b. Click Image on the Menu bar, point to Mode, then click RGB Color.

   c. Open the Channels panel and keep it visible while you work.

   d. Click the Magic Wand tool, set the Tolerance to 8, then verify that the Anti-alias check box is not checked and that the Contiguous check box is not checked.

   e. Click the lightest gray area in the woman's cheek.

   f. Save the selection as **Lightest Gray**.

   g. Save three new selections named **Light Gray**, **Dark Gray**, and **Darkest Gray**. (*Hint*: Don't select any of the white areas or the black areas.)

   h. Use the Channels panel to load the Lightest Gray selection.

   i. Fill the selection with a color of your choice.

   j. Load and fill the three other saved selections with different colors. Figure B-32 shows one possible solution.

Advanced Challenge Exercise

   ■ Load the Lightest Gray selection.

   ■ Double-click the Edit in Quick Mask Mode button.

   ■ Click the Color box and set the color to R255/G0/B0.

   ■ Set the Opacity to 100%.

   ■ Click OK.

   ■ Click the Edit in Standard Mode button.

   k. Save the file with the alpha channels as **posterized woman_PS-B**.

   l. Close posterized woman_PS-B.psd.

FIGURE B-32

Visual Workshop

Open PS B-16.psd, then save it as **visual solution_PS-B**. Create a feathered selection so that the canvas resembles Figure B-33.

FIGURE B-33

Working with Layers

Files You Will Need:

To view a list of files needed for this unit, see the Data Files Grid in the back of the book.

The Layers panel is one of Photoshop's greatest features because it allows you to segregate various art components onto different layers within a single document. Working with layers allows you to apply various effects, like drop shadows or glows, to individual art components without affecting others. Layers give you options for positioning artwork in relation to other artwork and allow you to move that artwork without affecting the content on other layers. At MegaPixel, you're given artwork for a print ad for a local jewelry retailer. The artwork involves a **montage**: multiple art components overlapping to create a single composition. You prepare yourself to work extensively with layers and the Layers panel.

OBJECTIVES

Work with the Layers panel

Merge layers and manipulate opacity

Duplicate, delete, and paste new layers

Scale artwork

Flip and rotate artwork

Add an Outer Glow layer style

Add a Drop Shadow layer style

Work with a layer mask

Working with the Layers Panel

The Layers panel houses all the layers in a document and offers you many options for manipulating those layers. Some basic operations you can do with the Layers panel and layered artwork are to hide or show various art components and move them independently of one another. ▰▰▰ Jon asks that you spend a few minutes examining the supplied document. He asks that you examine the layer structure and move items around just to get a sense of how the montage has been built.

STEPS

1. **Open PS C-1.psd, then save it as** roman holiday 1_PS-C

2. **Click the** Layers panel menu button ▦, **click** Panel Options, **click the** medium Thumbnail Size option button, **then click OK**

   The thumbnails in the figures throughout this unit are the medium size.

3. **Press and hold [Alt] (Win) or [option] (Mac), then click the** Indicates layer visibility button ◉ **on the Passport layer**

   Only the artwork on the Passport layer is visible. Pressing and holding [Alt] (Win) or [option] (Mac) and clicking the Indicates layer visibility button shows only that layer and hides all other layers.

4. **Click the** Indicates layer visibility button ◉ **on the Coin and Colosseum layers, then compare your screen to Figure C-1**

   The artwork on the two layers becomes visible.

5. **Make all the remaining layers visible**

6. **Click the** Move tool ⯭, **click the** Pen layer name **on the Layers panel, then click and drag the** pen artwork **to move it to the left side of the canvas**

   Only the artwork on the selected layer moves. Note that when you are directed to click or target a layer, click the layer name once. Only click the layer thumbnail when you are told to specifically.

7. **Click the** Couple layer name **on the Layers panel to target it, press and hold [Ctrl] (Win) or ⌘ (Mac), then click the** Couple Shadow layer name **so that both are selected**

   Pressing and holding [Ctrl] (Win) or ⌘ (Mac) allows you to select multiple layers on the Layers panel.

8. **Drag the** Couple **and** Couple Shadow **artwork to the upper-right corner of the canvas**

   Because both layers are selected on the Layers panel, the artwork on both layers moves as you drag.

9. **Target the** Coin layer, **then drag the** Coin artwork **down so that its bottom edge is behind the title**

   Compare your screen to Figure C-2. Your results will vary from the figure.

10. **Click** File **on the Menu bar, then click** Revert

FIGURE C-1: Viewing the visible layers

Three
layers
showing

FIGURE C-2: Canvas with repositioned artwork

Life without layers

It seems quite hard to believe now, but in the early versions of Photoshop, there were no layers! It was possible to overlap various components of artwork, but once you deselected, those components would become embedded in the canvas. So, if the montage we worked on in this lesson was created in Photoshop

2.0, all of the elements would have existed on one canvas, one bed of pixels. If you think about that for a moment, you get a real sense of the true benefit of working with layers: the options to edit, rethink, and redesign.

Merging Layers and Manipulating Opacity

On the Layers panel, artwork on a top layer appears in *front* of artwork on layers beneath it. Thus, artwork on the bottom layer would be behind the artwork on layers above it. You can use the Layers panel to reorder layers and also to merge layers. When you merge multiple layers, separate artwork on those layers is merged onto one layer and can no longer be manipulated individually. In Photoshop, the term opacity refers to how opaque artwork is. For example, if artwork has 100% opacity, it is completely opaque—no part of it is transparent. Conversely, artwork with 0% opacity is completely transparent and thus invisible. In between the two extremes, artwork with 50% opacity would be visible, but any artwork on a layer or layers beneath it would be visible *through* it. You decide to experiment with reordering the layers in hopes of improving the impact of the montage. You also experiment with merging layers and reducing the opacity of various artwork components.

STEPS

1. **Verify that all layers are visible on the Layers panel, then target the Coin layer**

2. **Drag the Coin layer above the Colosseum layer on the Layers panel until you see a horizontal gray line, as shown in Figure C-3, then release the mouse**
   The coin artwork appears in front of the Colosseum artwork.

3. **Click the Pen layer on the Layers panel, then drag it down below the Euros layer so that your canvas resembles Figure C-4**

   > **QUICK TIP**
   > When you merge artwork, the resulting merged layer takes on the name of the top of the original layers.

4. **Target both the Coin and the Colosseum layers, click the Layers panel menu button ▼≡, then click Merge Layers**
   The artwork is merged onto one layer as one piece of art. See the Clues to Use titled *Merging layers and memory* on the next page.

5. **Click the Move tool ▶⊹, then click and drag to move the artwork in any direction**
   Both the Coin and Colosseum artwork move because they are now one piece of art on the same layer.

6. **Click Edit on the Menu bar, click Undo Move, then drag the Opacity slider on the Layers panel to 50%**
   The Coin and Colosseum artwork becomes 50% transparent. The Opacity slider can set a layer's opacity to any percentage between 0% and 100%.

7. **Target the Couple Shadow layer, then reduce its opacity to 75%**

   > **QUICK TIP**
   > With the Move tool or any selection tool selected, pressing [5] changes the opacity of a targeted layer to 50%, pressing [6] changes it to 60%, and so on. Pressing [0] results in 100% opacity.

8. **Verify that the Move tool is selected, target the Passport layer, then press [5]**
   The opacity of the Passport layer is reduced to 50%.

9. **Compare your canvas to Figure C-5, save your work, then close roman holiday 1_PS-C.psd**

FIGURE C-3: Moving the Coin layer above the Colosseum layer

Moving the layer

FIGURE C-4: Moving the Pen layer beneath the Euros layer

FIGURE C-5: Canvas with transparent artwork

Merging layers and memory

The more layers in a file, the larger the file size, and therefore merging layers reduces file size. Remember, though, that merging layers is a commitment: once artwork is merged onto a single layer, it can't be unmerged later on in the project (other than by undoing, reverting, or using the History panel). For example, if you merge two layers and then exit Photoshop, there will be no way to unmerge that artwork. Generally speaking, it's best to keep artwork segregated on different layers simply to keep your options open for any modifications you might need to make as your project evolves.

Duplicating, Deleting, and Pasting New Layers

Layers are created in Photoshop in a variety of ways. You can click the Create a new layer button on the Layers panel or use the New Layer command on the Layers panel menu. However, some of the most common ways that new layers are created are when you duplicate an existing layer or when you paste artwork copied from another file. ▰▰▰ Now that you've studied the layers in the document and made some changes to them, you decide to duplicate one layer to make a more interesting montage. Then Jon asks you to remove one piece of artwork and replace it with artwork from another file.

STEPS

1. **Open PS C-2.psd, save it as** roman holiday 2_PS-C, **target the** Coin layer, **click the** Layers panel menu button ▰, **then click** Duplicate Layer

2. **Type** Top Coin **in the As text box, then click** OK

   A duplicate of the original artwork is created in the same position on a layer immediately above the targeted layer.

3. **Use the Move tool** ▰ **or the arrow keys to reposition the Top Coin artwork as shown in Figure C-6**

   QUICK TIP

   Pressing [Ctrl][J] (Win) or ⌘[J] (Mac) is the fastest and easiest way to duplicate a layer.

4. **With the Top Coin layer still targeted, press [Ctrl][J] (Win) or ⌘[J] (Mac)**

   The layer is duplicated.

5. **Double-click the** Top Coin copy layer name **on the Layers panel, type** Bottom Coin **to rename the layer, press [Enter] (Win) or [return] (Mac), drag the** Bottom Coin layer **beneath the Couple Shadow layer, then reposition the Bottom Coin artwork, as shown in Figure C-7**

   QUICK TIP

   Click the Don't show again check box in the warning dialog box if you don't want to be asked to confirm that you want to delete future layers.

6. **Target the** Colosseum layer, **click the** Delete layer button ▰ **on the Layers panel, then click** Yes **to confirm that you want to delete the layer**

7. **Open Colosseum.psd, then view each layer separately to understand how the file was built**

8. **Show both layers, select all, click** Edit **on the Menu bar, then click** Copy Merged

   Clicking Copy Merged copies the visible image on the canvas as a single image. In other words, Copy Merged copies a combined, or "merged," result of all the visible layers.

9. **Close Colosseum.psd without saving changes, return to the roman holiday 2_PS-C.psd file, target the** Euros layer, **click** Edit **on the Menu bar, then click** Paste

   The artwork is pasted as a new layer, named Layer 1, directly above the targeted Euros layer.

10. **Name the new layer** Colosseum, **move it to the position shown in Figure C-8, then save your work**

FIGURE C-6: Repositioning the Top Coin artwork

FIGURE C-7: Repositioning the Bottom Coin artwork

FIGURE C-8: Positioning the Colosseum artwork

Pasting new layers

Whenever you copy artwork and then paste, the copied artwork is pasted onto a new layer, above the targeted layer on the Layers panel. This is a great feature in Photoshop, because you can always be confident that when you paste artwork, the new artwork will always be isolated on its own layer and will not directly affect any existing artwork in the file. If you use the Fit on Screen command on the View menu so that your entire canvas is visible before you paste, when you paste, the pasted artwork will be centered on the canvas. This knowledge can be very useful for alignment considerations.

Scaling Artwork

One of the preeminent features of Photoshop is the ability to **transform** artwork—moving, scaling, rotating, flipping, and distorting it. Transforming skills become important especially when creating a montage, because montages involve specific positioning relationships between elements. Resizing or **scaling** artwork is one of the most basic transformations, and one you'll use often. ▓▓▓▒▒ Now that the montage contains all of the elements that you want to work with, Jon asks you to reduce the size of the Colosseum and the Bottom Coin images.

STEPS

QUICK TIP

Throughout this lesson, keep an eye on the W and H text boxes on the Options bar to see the percentage of enlargement or reduction you are making to the width and height of the selected artwork.

1. **Verify that the Colosseum layer is targeted, click Edit on the Menu bar, point to Transform, then click Scale**

   The transform bounding box appears around the artwork. The bounding box has a square handle at each corner that you click and drag to transform artwork. The handles are sometimes referred to as resizing handles.

2. **Position the mouse pointer on the lower-right corner handle until a double-headed arrow appears, click and drag in many directions to modify the image, then release the mouse pointer**

   Clicking and dragging the corner handle allows you to enlarge, reduce, and/or distort the image.

3. **Undo your last step, position the mouse pointer on the lower-right corner handle, press and hold [Shift], click and drag in different directions, then release the mouse pointer**

   The [Shift] key constrains the scale proportionately. You can enlarge or reduce the artwork, but you can't modify the proportional relationship between the width and height.

4. **Undo the move, then note the crosshair icon in the middle of the bounding box**

   The crosshair icon is automatically positioned at the center of the bounding box and therefore at the center of the artwork.

QUICK TIP

If you activate the Maintain aspect ratio button (the link icon) between the W and H text boxes, any change you make to one will automatically be made to the other.

QUICK TIP

Press [Enter] (Win) or [return] (Mac) to apply a transformation quickly.

5. **On the Options bar, double-click the W text box, type 80, press [Tab], type 80 in the H text box, press [Tab], then compare your screen to Figure C-9**

   The artwork is scaled 80% at the crosshair, which is at the artwork's center point. By default, when you enter a scale value in the W and/or H text boxes on the Options bar, the artwork is scaled using the crosshair icon as the point of origin for the scale.

6. **Click the Move tool ▶✛, then click Apply to apply the scale**

   You can press [Esc] to cancel a transformation.

7. **Target the Bottom Coin layer, press [Ctrl][T] (Win) or ⌘[T] (Mac), then drag the crosshair icon to the position shown in Figure C-10**

QUICK TIP

[Ctrl][T] (Win) or ⌘[T] (Mac) are the quick keys for accessing the Transform command.

8. **Press and hold [Shift][Alt] (Win) or [Shift][option] (Mac), position the mouse pointer over the lower-left handle, drag to experiment with resizing the coin artwork, then release the mouse pointer**

   Pressing and holding the [Alt] (Win) or [option] (Mac) key ensures that any transformation will be executed using the location of the crosshair as the point of origin. The [Shift] key is used in this step to constrain the width/height proportion of the artwork while scaling.

9. **Undo the move, double-click the W text box on the Options bar, type 67, press [Tab], type 67 in the H text box, press [Tab], then compare your screen to Figure C-11**

10. **Click ▶✛, click Apply, then save your work**

FIGURE C-9: Using the Options bar to scale the artwork

Width and Height text boxes on Options bar

FIGURE C-10: Moving the crosshair icon

Crosshair icon determines the point of origin for a transformation

FIGURE C-11: Scaling the artwork from the relocated crosshair icon

Flipping and Rotating Artwork

Flipping and rotating are two transformations that can be very useful when creating a montage of various images. **Flipping** artwork creates a mirror image of the artwork. You can flip images horizontally or vertically. **Rotating** moves an object clockwise or counterclockwise around its center point, much like a windmill spins. You can rotate an image by hand or by entering a specific rotation value on the Options bar. Jon directs you to flip the main image in the montage and asks that you rotate the coins in the image so that it is not so obvious that they are duplicate images.

STEPS

1. Target the Colosseum layer, click Edit on the Menu bar, point to Transform, then click Rotate

   The transform bounding box appears around the artwork.

2. Position the mouse pointer outside of the bounding box so that a curved double-arrow icon appears, click and drag to rotate the artwork to various rotations, then release the mouse pointer

QUICK TIP

Entering a positive value in the Set rotation text box rotates artwork in a clockwise direction. Entering a negative value in the Set rotation text box rotates artwork in a counterclockwise direction.

3. Undo the move, type 17 in the Set rotation text box on the Options bar, apply the transformation, then compare your result to Figure C-12

   The image is rotated 17 degrees (clockwise) around its center point.

4. Drag the Colosseum layer down on the Layers panel so that it is immediately above the Passport layer

5. Target both the Couple and the Couple Shadow layers, click Edit on the Menu bar, point to Transform, then click Flip Horizontal

   The artwork on both layers is flipped horizontally.

6. Verify that the Couple and Couple Shadow layers are still selected, add the Bottom Coin layer to the selection, then move the artwork down slightly to the position shown in Figure C-13

QUICK TIP

Pressing and holding [Shift] when rotating rotates the artwork in 15 degree increments.

7. Click the Bottom Coin layer so that it is the only targeted layer, press [Ctrl][T] (Win) or ⌘[T] (Mac), press and hold [Shift], then click and drag to rotate the bottom coin –45 degrees

   The bottom coin is rotated and no longer appears as an obvious duplicate of the larger coin.

8. Apply the rotation, then compare your artwork to Figure C-14

9. Save your work

Rotating vs. flipping

Rotating and flipping are two very different transformations that produce different results. You can compare rotating artwork with the tire on your car turning on a specific point. By default, artwork in Photoshop is rotated around its center point unless you move the crosshair icon to a new location. When you flip artwork, you create a mirror image of the artwork. Photoshop offers you the ability to flip artwork horizontally (across an imaginary vertical axis) or vertically (across an imaginary horizontal axis). Flipping an image can produce odd results, especially when the image shows peoples' faces. Nobody's face is perfectly symmetrical, and flipping a face can yield unflattering results. Also remember, if there's text anywhere in an image when flipped, that text is going to read backwards, which is a dead giveaway that the image has been flipped! If you want to flip an image, target the layer that the image is on, click Edit on the Menu bar, point to Transform, then click Flip Horizontal or Flip Vertical.

FIGURE C-12: Rotating the Colosseum artwork

FIGURE C-13: Moving the artwork on three layers

FIGURE C-14: Rotating the bottom coin artwork

Rotated coin

Working with Layers

Adding an Outer Glow Layer Style

Layer styles are built-in effects that you can apply to layers; they include glows, shadows, bevels, embosses, and chiseled edges, among many others. When you apply a layer style to a layer, all the artwork on that layer inherits the layer style. Layer styles are listed on the Layers panel beneath the layer they've been applied to. Click the small black triangle to the right of the layer to expand or collapse the list of layer effects for that layer. ▰▰▰▰▰ Jon asks you to apply a gold outer glow to the pen artwork, similar to the glow around the bouquet of roses.

STEPS

QUICK TIP
Move the Layer Style dialog box to the side, if necessary, so that you can see the pen artwork on the canvas.

1. **Target the Pen layer, click Layer on the Menu bar, point to Layer Style, then click Outer Glow**

   The Layer Style dialog box opens. Note that on the left side is a list of all the available layer styles and that Outer Glow is checked and highlighted. The settings you see in the dialog box are settings for an outer glow.

2. **Enter the values shown in Figure C-15 and verify that the Preview check box is checked**

   As you change settings in the Layer Style dialog box, you will see changes made to the selected artwork in real time.

QUICK TIP
You can also choose a glow color by placing the mouse pointer over the canvas and then clicking a color with the eyedropper pointer when the Color Picker dialog box is open.

3. **Click the Set color of glow square, type 253 in the R text box, 226 in the G text box, and 162 in the B text box, click OK to close the Color Picker, then click OK to close the Layer Style dialog box**

4. **Compare your canvas and Layers panel to Figure C-16**

   The Outer Glow layer style is listed on the Layers panel as a component of the Pen layer; the Indicates layer effects icon appears on the layer, indicating a layer style has been applied to it.

5. **Click the Eye button 👁 on the Outer Glow layer style to hide and show the style**

6. **Double-click the Outer Glow layer style on the Layers panel to open the Layer Style dialog box**

   The Layer Style dialog box opens with the Outer Glow layer style settings.

7. **Drag the Opacity, Spread, and Size sliders to see the effect that each has on the outer glow effect, then click Cancel to close the Layer Style dialog box without saving the changes, then save your work**

Understanding the point of origin in a transformation

The point of origin defines the point from which a transformation occurs. For example, if you create a 2" × 2" square and then reduce it by 50% using its center point as the point of origin, all four sides of the square would move equally towards the center until the new size of the square was 1" × 1". Before you transform, move the crosshair icon to the point that you want to remain fixed, then transform the artwork using that point as the point of origin for the transformation.

Remember that the crosshair icon determines the point of origin automatically when you enter values on the Options bar. If you transform by hand by clicking and dragging the bounding box, you must press and hold [Alt] (Win) or [option] (Mac) to transform using the location of the crosshair as the point of origin.

FIGURE C-15: Settings for an Outer Glow layer style

Set color of glow square

FIGURE C-16: Viewing the layer style on the canvas and on the Layers panel

Indicates layer effects icon

Outer Glow layer style listed on Layers panel

Working with Layers

Adding a Drop Shadow Layer Style

A **drop shadow**, an effect where artwork appears to cast a shadow, is one of the most commonly used Photoshop effects. There are many methods for creating a drop shadow, and one method is to use Photoshop's Drop Shadow layer style. One of the many great features about all layer styles is that you can copy them from one layer to another, which saves lots of time and speeds up your work. See Table C-1 for an explanation of Drop Shadow layer style settings. Jon asks that you use a Drop Shadow layer style as an alternate to the drop shadow that is already being used for the main artwork in the montage. He also asks that you apply a Drop Shadow layer style to the Colosseum artwork.

STEPS

1. **Hide the Couple Shadow layer, then target the Couple layer**
   The Couple Shadow layer is not a drop shadow layer style. It was created using the Brush tool.

2. **Click Layer on the Menu bar, point to Layer Style, then click Drop Shadow**
   The Layer Style dialog box opens, showing settings for the Drop Shadow layer style.

3. **Verify that the Preview check box is checked, then enter the values shown in Figure C-17**

4. **Click OK, then compare your canvas to Figure C-18**

5. **Click the Eye button 👁 on the Drop Shadow layer style to hide and show the style**

6. **Press and hold [Alt] (Win) or [option] (Mac), drag the Indicates layer effects icon 𝑓𝑥 to the Colosseum layer, then release the mouse pointer when a white frame surrounds the Colosseum layer**
   As shown in Figure C-19, the drop shadow appears behind the Colosseum artwork, and the Drop Shadow layer style is added to the Colosseum layer.

7. **Double-click the Drop Shadow layer style on the Colosseum layer to open the Layer Style dialog box, change the Spread value to 12 and the Size value to 40, then click OK**
   The drop shadow on the Colosseum artwork is updated.

8. **Save your work**

TABLE C-1: Drop Shadow layer style options

setting	purpose
Angle	Determines the lighting angle at which the effect is applied to the layer
Distance	Specifies the offset distance for the shadow—how far it is away from the artwork
Spread	Determines the size of the shadow effect before the edge blurs
Size	Controls the size of the blur at the edge of the effect

FIGURE C-17: Settings for a Drop Shadow layer style

FIGURE C-18: Viewing the Drop Shadow layer style on the canvas and on the Layers panel

FIGURE C-19: Viewing the Drop Shadow layer style behind the Colosseum artwork and on the Layers panel

Working with Layers

Working with a Layer Mask

A **layer mask** allows you to define which areas of artwork on a single layer are visible, not visible, or partly visible. The basic concept of a layer mask is very simple: white areas of the layer mask represent art on the layer that is 100% visible. Black areas of the layer mask represent art on the layer that is 100% masked (and therefore invisible). Gray areas of the layer mask represent art on the layer that is semitransparent. You can use many methods to apply black, white, or gray to a layer mask. One common method is to use the Brush tool to paint in the layer mask, thus adjusting the opacity of the artwork by hand. You can set size and hardness options for the Brush tool on the Options bar. ▓▓▓▓ Jon feels that the green leaves on the bouquet of roses might be distracting to the overall color palette of the montage. He asks that you use a layer mask to provide the client with two alternative montages: one with the leaves and one without the leaves.

STEPS

QUICK TIP

When you create a new layer mask, the foreground color changes to white and the background color changes to black.

1. **Target the Roses layer, click Layer on the Menu bar, point to Layer Mask, then click Reveal All**

   As shown in Figure C-20, a layer mask is added to the layer. By default the new layer mask is targeted, which is indicated by the heavy white border around the mask. When you click Reveal All, an all-white layer mask is added to the layer; therefore, all of the artwork on the layer remains visible, or revealed. The Hide All type of layer mask creates an all-black layer mask in which all of the artwork is hidden.

2. **Click the small gray triangle on the Roses layer to reveal the layer effects, then hide the Outer Glow layer style on the Roses layer**

QUICK TIP

The Brush tool *always* paints using the foreground color.

3. **Click the Default Foreground and Background Colors button 🔲 on the Tools panel, click the Switch Foreground and Background Colors button ↺ so that the foreground color is white, then click the Brush tool 🖌**

4. **On the Options bar, verify that the Opacity setting is 100%, click the Brush Preset picker list arrow, set the Size to 15 px, then set the Hardness to 30%**

5. **Zoom in so that the top green leaf in the bouquet is large on your screen, then paint over the leaf until the entire leaf is no longer visible**

   The areas you paint become invisible because you are painting black in the layer mask, not on the canvas.

6. **Scroll, then paint to mask out the bottom leaf, as shown in Figure C-21**

7. **Press and hold [Alt] (Win) or [option] (Mac), click the layer mask thumbnail on the Layers panel, then compare your canvas and Layers panel to Figure C-22**

   Pressing and holding [Alt] (Win) or [option] (Mac) and clicking the layer mask thumbnail displays the layer mask on the canvas.

QUICK TIP

Pressing and holding [Shift] when clicking a layer mask toggles a layer mask between being active and inactive.

8. **Click the Roses Layer thumbnail to the left of the layer mask thumbnail**

   The canvas displays the artwork on the layer. The layer mask is no longer targeted, but it is still active.

9. **Press and hold [Shift], then click the layer mask thumbnail on the Roses layer**

   As shown in Figure C-23, the layer mask is inactive, and the green leaves are visible once again.

10. **Save your work, close roman holiday 2_PS-C.psd, then exit Photoshop**

Three Brush tool techniques

Practice these three techniques that will make you much more effective with the Brush tool:

1. Press the right bracket key repeatedly to increase the brush size.
2. Press the left bracket key repeatedly to decrease the brush size.
3. [Shift]-click the brush to cover large areas. Click the brush once anywhere on the canvas. Move the brush pointer to a different location. Press and hold [Shift], then click the brush at the new location. The Brush tool will paint from the first click and connect to the second click.

FIGURE C-20: Layer mask added to the Roses layer

— Layer mask

FIGURE C-21: Artwork with both leaves masked out

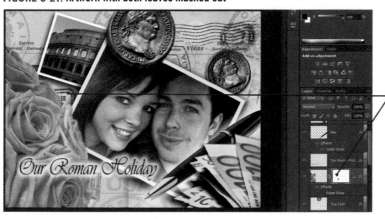

Masked pixels in the layer mask and on the artwork

FIGURE C-22: Viewing the layer mask

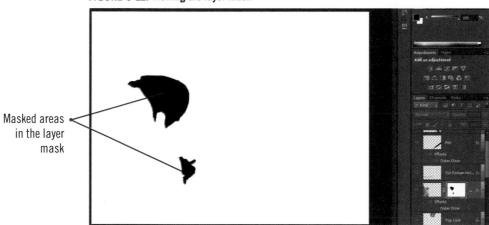

Masked areas in the layer mask

FIGURE C-23: Deactivating the layer mask

Leaf is visible because layer mask is inactive

Red X indicates layer mask is inactive

Practice

Concepts Review

Label the elements of the Photoshop screen shown in Figure C-24.

Match each term with the statement that best describes it.

6. **Transform**
7. **Layer style**
8. **Layer mask**
9. **Opacity**
10. **Flipping**
11. **Merging**
12. **Indicates layer effects icon**

a. Used to affect image opacity in specific areas
b. Appears when layer styles are applied
c. Transformation that creates a mirror image
d. The measure of how opaque artwork is
e. Effects such as a drop shadow or an outer glow
f. Condensing layered artwork onto one layer
g. To move, scale, or rotate an image

Select the best answer from the list of choices.

13. **Which of the following is not a benefit of using layers?**
   a. Organization
   b. Segregation
   c. Editing ability
   d. Saving file space

14. **Which of the following is not a layer style?**
   a. Outer Glow
   b. Blur
   c. Drop Shadow
   d. Inner Shadow

15. **Which of the following is not a transformation option?**
   a. Rotate
   b. Blend
   c. Scale
   d. Move

16. **Which of the following is not true about the Opacity slider?**
   a. It can be applied to specific areas of a layer.
   b. It can be applied at 52%.
   c. It can be used to make pixels semitransparent.
   d. It is manipulated only on the Layers panel.

17. **Which of the following is not true about a layer mask?**
   a. It can be used to manipulate opacity in specific areas of a layer.
   b. One layer mask affects all areas of the layer.
   c. It is created by default when you create a new layer.
   d. It can be shown and hidden.

18. **Which of the following is true about a layer mask?**
   a. An all-black layer mask means all the artwork on the layer is visible.
   b. An all-white layer mask means all the artwork on the layer has 0% opacity.
   c. Pixels in a layer mask are either black or white.
   d. A light gray layer mask means all the artwork on the layer is semitransparent.

Skills Review

1. **Work with the Layers panel.**
   a. Open PS C-3.psd, then save it as **shining future 1_PS-C**.
   b. Click the Layers panel menu button, click Panel Options, choose the medium Thumbnail Size option button, then click OK.
   c. Press and hold [Alt] (Win) or [option] (Mac), then click the Indicates layer visibility button on the Flower layer.
   d. Click the Indicates layer visibility button on the Background and Flower Shadow layers.
   e. Make all the remaining layers visible.
   f. Click the Move tool, click the Moon layer on the Layers panel, then drag the moon artwork to move it to the right side of the canvas behind the flower.
   g. Click the Child layer to select it, press and hold [Ctrl] (Win) or ⌘ (Mac), then click the Child Shadow layer so that both are selected.
   h. Drag to move the Child and Child Shadow artwork up so that the child is "standing" in the water.
   i. Target the Type artwork, then move it to the left so it is outside of the flower's shadow.
   j. Save your work, then close shining future 1_PS-C.psd.

2. **Merge layers and manipulate opacity.**
   a. Open PS C-4.psd, then save it as **shining future 2_PS-C**.
   b. Verify that all layers are visible, then target the Moon layer on the Layers panel.
   c. Drag the Moon layer down below the Flower Shadow layer on the Layers panel.
   d. Click the Type layer, then drag it to the top of the Layers panel so that it is the top layer.
   e. Target both the Flower and the Purple Center layers, click the Layers panel menu button, then click Merge Layers.
   f. Click the Move tool, then drag the merged artwork to the right of the canvas.

Skills Review (continued)

    g. Undo the move, target the Moon layer, then drag the Opacity slider on the Layers panel to 55%.

    h. Target the Dolphin layer, then reduce the Opacity to 75%.

    i. Verify that the Move tool is selected, then press [5].

    j. Save your work, then close shining future 2_PS-C.psd.

3. Duplicate, delete, and paste new layers.

    a. Open PS C-5.psd, save it as **bright shining future_PS-C**, target the Moon layer, click Layer on the Menu bar, then click Duplicate Layer.

    b. Type **Middle Moon** in the As text box, then click OK.

    c. With the Middle Moon layer still targeted, press [Ctrl][J] (Win) or ⌘[J] (Mac).

    d. Double-click the Middle Moon Copy name, then rename the layer as **Little Moon**.

    e. Target the Purple Center layer, click the Delete layer button on the Layers panel, then click Yes to confirm that you want to delete the layer.

    f. Open Globe.psd, then note that the file has three layers.

    g. Click Select on the Menu bar, click Load Selection, click the Channel list arrow, click Globe Only, then click OK.

    h. Click Edit on the Menu bar, then click Copy Merged.

    i. Close Globe.psd without saving changes, return to the bright shining future_PS-C.psd file, target the Flower layer, then paste.

    j. Name the new layer **Globe**, move it to the position shown in Figure C-25, then save your work.

4. Scale artwork.

    a. Target the Little Moon layer, click Edit on the Menu bar, point to Transform, then click Scale.

FIGURE C-25

    b. Position the mouse pointer over the lower-right corner handle until a double-headed arrow appears, click and drag in many directions to modify the image, then release the mouse pointer.

    c. Undo the move, position the mouse pointer over the lower-right corner handle, press and hold [Shift], click and drag in different directions, then release the mouse pointer.

    d. Undo the move, then note the crosshair icon in the middle of the bounding box.

    e. On the Options bar, double-click the W text box, type **10**, press [Tab], type **10** in the H text box, then press [Tab].

    f. Click the Move tool, then click Apply to apply the scale.

    g. Target the Middle Moon layer, then press [Ctrl][T] (Win) or ⌘[T] (Mac).

    h. Press and hold [Shift][Alt] (Win) or [Shift][option] (Mac), position the mouse pointer over the lower-right selection handle, click and drag to experiment with different sizes, then release the mouse pointer.

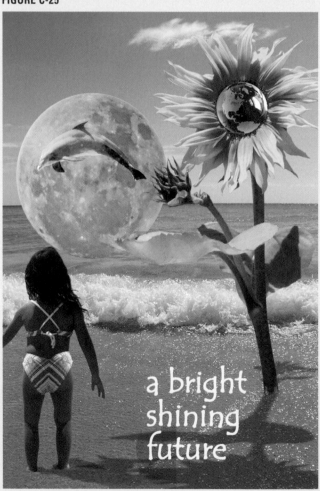

a bright shining future

Skills Review (continued)

    i. Undo the move, double-click the W text box, type **28**, press [Tab], type **28** in the H text box, press [Tab], then click the Move tool to apply the scale.

    j. With the Move tool, move the Little Moon and Middle Moon artwork to the positions shown in Figure C-26, then save your work.

5. Flip and rotate artwork.

    a. Target the Middle Moon layer, click Edit on the Menu bar, point to Transform, then click Rotate.

    b. Position the mouse pointer outside of the bounding box so that a curved double-arrow icon appears, click and drag to rotate the artwork to various rotations, then release the mouse pointer.

    c. Undo the move, type **27** in the Set rotation text box on the Options bar, then apply the transformation.

    d. Target both the Child and the Child Shadow layers, click Edit on the Menu bar, point to Transform, then click Flip Horizontal.

    e. Target the Little Moon layer, press [Ctrl][T] (Win) or ⌘ [T] (Mac), press and hold [Shift], then drag the rotate pointer to rotate the artwork –45 degrees.

    f. Apply the rotation, then save your work.

6. Add an Outer Glow layer style.

    a. Target the Dolphin layer, click Layer on the Menu bar, point to Layer Style, then click Outer Glow.

    b. Verify that the Preview check box is checked, set the Blend mode to screen, set the Opacity to 75%, set the Noise to 0, set the Spread to 27%, then set the Size to 40.

    c. Click the Set color of glow square, type **255** in the R text box, **190** in the G text box, and **255** in the B text box, click OK to close the Color Picker, then click OK to close the Layer Style dialog box.

    d. Hide and show the Outer Glow layer style on the Layers panel to hide and show the effect on the artwork.

    e. Double-click the Outer Glow layer style on the Layers panel to open the Layer Style dialog box.

    f. Drag the Opacity, Spread, and Size sliders to see the effect that each has on the outer glow effect, then click Cancel to close the Layer Style dialog box without applying the changes.

    g. Save your work, then compare your screen to Figure C-27.

7. Add a Drop Shadow layer style.

    a. Target the Type layer.

    b. Click Layer on the Menu bar, point to Layer Style, then click Drop Shadow.

    c. Verify that the Preview check box is checked, set the Blend Mode to Multiply, set the Opacity to 100%, set the Distance to 9, set both the Spread and Size to 0, then click OK.

    d. On the Layers panel toggle the Drop Shadow layer style off and on to hide and show the effect.

    e. Target the Dolphin layer, press and hold [Alt] (Win) or [option] (Mac), click and drag the Indicates layer effects icon to the Globe layer, then release the mouse pointer when a white frame appears around the Globe layer.

    f. Save your work.

FIGURE C-26

FIGURE C-27

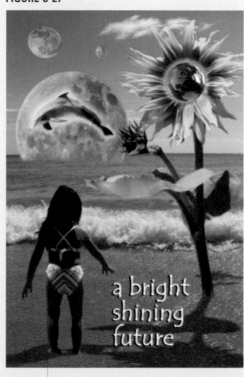

Working with Layers

Skills Review (continued)

8. Work with a layer mask.

   a. Target the Moon layer, click Layer on the Menu bar, point to Layer Mask, then click Reveal All.

   b. Click the Default Foreground and Background Colors button on the Tools panel, click the Switch Foreground and Background Colors button, then click the Brush tool.

   c. On the Options bar, verify that the Opacity setting is 100%, click the Brush Preset picker list arrow, set the Size to 125 pixels, then set the Hardness to 40%.

   d. Paint over the bottom third of the moon so that it is no longer visible.

   e. Press and hold [Alt] (Win) or [option] (Mac), then click the layer mask thumbnail on the Layers panel to view the mask.

   f. Click the Moon layer thumbnail to the left of the layer mask thumbnail to view the artwork again.

   g. Press and hold [Shift], then click the layer mask thumbnail on the Moon layer to make it inactive.

   h. Press and hold [Shift], then click the layer mask thumbnail on the Moon layer to make it active.

   i. Compare your results to Figure C-27.

   j. Save your work, close bright shining future_PS-C.psd, then exit Photoshop.

Independent Challenge 1

The Web Design department at your advertising agency has asked you to create a drop shadow to create a "white on white" effect that they will be using for graphics on a website they are building.

   a. Open PS C-6.psd, then save it as **roman numerals_PS-C**.

   b. Hide the Background layer to see the contents of the XVII layer, show the Background layer again, then target the XVII layer.

   c. Click Layer on the Menu bar, point to Layer Style, then click Drop Shadow.

   d. Verify that the Preview check box is checked, set the Opacity to 80%, set the Distance to 34, set the Spread to 0, set the Size to 40, then click OK.

   e. Click Layer on the Menu bar, point to Layer Style, then click Stroke.

   f. Experiment with the Size slider to see the effect on the XVII artwork.

   g. Enter the values shown in Figure C-28 then click OK.

   h. Save your work, compare your result to Figure C-29, then close roman numerals_PS-C.psd.

FIGURE C-28

FIGURE C-29

Independent Challenge 2

The web design department at your advertising agency is designing a splash page for a website that shows an image of a dolphin in front of a large moon. You are asked to copy the dolphin image into the moon file, then use a layer mask to remove the background from the dolphin image.

a. Open PS C-7.psd, then save it as **dolphin moon_PS-C**.

b. Open Dolphin Sky.psd, select all, copy, then close Dolphin Sky.psd.

c. Return to dolphin moon_PS-C.psd, paste, then name the new layer **Dolphin**.

d. Click Layer on the Menu bar, point to Layer Mask, then click Reveal All.

e. Set the foreground color on the Tools panel to black.

f. Click the Brush tool, verify that the Opacity is set to 100%, change the Size to 40 pixels, then set the Hardness to 80% on the Options bar.

g. Paint over the big areas of blue sky to mask them out.

h. Zoom in on the dolphin's head, reduce the Master Diameter of the Brush to 7 px, then paint along the edges of the dolphin to remove the sky completely. (*Hint*: Use the Hand tool to scroll around the magnified image.)

i. Compare your result to Figure C-30, save your work, the close dolphin moon_PS-C.psd.

FIGURE C-30

Independent Challenge 3

You have been asked to take over the design of a splash page for an important client. You are given the artwork that the Web Design department has created so far, along with notes on how to finish the job.

a. Open PS C-8.psd, then save it as **double dolphins_PS-C**.

b. Drag the Green Moon layer beneath the Purple Moon layer.

c. Target the Dolphin layer, then duplicate the layer.

d. Rename the new layer **Small Dolphin**.

e. Click the Move tool, press and hold [Shift], then click and drag the Small Dolphin artwork straight down and center it over the Green Moon artwork.

f. Select both the Green Moon layer and the Small Dolphin layer.

g. Scale the artwork 50%.

h. Save your work, then compare your canvas to Figure C-31.

FIGURE C-31

Independent Challenge 3 (continued)

Advanced Challenge Exercise

- Target just the Small Dolphin layer.
- Rotate the small dolphin 180 degrees.
- Target the Dolphin layer.
- Flip it horizontally.

i. Close double dolphins_PS-C.psd, then exit Photoshop.

Real Life Independent Challenge

It's the end of the summer and you have some great photos to share with family and friends. Rather than just send out an individual photo, you decide to make a montage of three photos, two of them inset into a larger photo.

a. Open PS C-9.psd, then save it as **sisters postcard_PS-C**.

b. Open Jenny.tif, select all, copy, then close Jenny.tif.

c. Paste the artwork into sisters postcard_PS-C.psd, then rename the layer **Jenny**.

d. Open Annie.tif, select all, copy, then close Annie.tif.

e. Paste the artwork into sisters postcard_PS-C.psd, then rename the layer **Annie**.

f. Move the Jenny artwork to the upper-right corner.

g. Scale the Jenny artwork so that it fits into the upper-right corner without overlapping the girls in the main image.

h. Move the Annie artwork to the lower-left corner.

i. Scale the Annie artwork so that it fits into the lower-left corner over the girl's legs.

j. Add a light yellow outer glow layer style to the Jenny artwork.

k. Copy the layer style from the Jenny artwork to the Annie artwork.

l. Compare your result to Figure C-32, then save your work.

Real Life Independent Challenge (continued)

Advanced Challenge Exercise

- Double-click the Outer Glow layer on the Annie layer, then drag the Layer Style dialog box to the right so that you can see the canvas.
- Click the Set color of glow box in the Layer Style dialog box.
- Position the eyedropper pointer over the pink stripe in the little girl's dress, then click.
- Close the Color Picker dialog box, then close the Layer Style dialog box.

m. Close sisters postcard_PS-C.psd, then exit Photoshop.

FIGURE C-32

Visual Workshop

Open PS C-10.psd, then save it as **three glowing globes_PS-C**. Reorder the layers and move the globes to the position shown in Figure C-33. Add a gold Outer Glow layer style to the large gold globe. Copy the Outer Glow layer style from the Gold Globe layer to the Pink Globe and the Blue Globe layers. Change the color of the glow on the two smaller globes to match the figure. Close three glowing globes_PS-C.psd, then exit Photoshop.

FIGURE C-33

Improving Images with Adjustment Layers

In our digital world, images can come from just about anywhere. Photoshop offers many practical **adjustment** operations to improve characteristics of images: their color, their contrast, their overall effect. An adjustment layer is called "non-destructive" because it exists as a layer on the Layers panel and allows you to apply adjustments to images without directly affecting the artwork. Brightness/Contrast, Levels, and Color Balance are three common, powerful, and highly useful adjustments for improving the overall appearance of an image. When you understand the basics of Grayscale and RGB color modes, then you're ready and able to dramatically improve your images with adjustments. Jon asks you to improve the appearance of a number of grayscale and RGB images using adjustments.

OBJECTIVES

Understand grayscale

Investigate a grayscale image

Use the Brightness/Contrast adjustment

Adjust black and white points with levels

Adjust the midpoint with levels

Investigate an RGB image

Use the Color Balance adjustment

Use the Vibrance adjustment

Understanding Grayscale

A **grayscale** image is a digital image in which each pixel can be one—and only one—of 256 shades of gray. With 256 shades of gray available per pixel, the illusion of a continuous tone image can be created. The grayscale range is 0–255. Pixels with a grayscale value of 0 are black. Pixels with a grayscale value of 255 are white. Any number in between 0 and 255 is gray—light gray or dark gray—with 128 being the middle point in the grayscale range. ⬛⬛ Jon tells you about a new client who will be supplying imagery that will require lots of analysis and correction for quality and color. He gives you a grayscale image and asks that you analyze it.

STEPS

1. **Open PS D-1.psd, then save it as** grayscale_PS-D

2. **Click** Image **on the Menu bar, point to** Mode, **then note that** Grayscale **is checked**

   This image has been saved in Grayscale mode, meaning that one of 256 shades of gray is available per pixel.

3. **Click the** Window menu, **then click** Info **to open the Info panel, click the** Info panel menu **button** ▤, **click** Panel Options, **enter the settings shown in Figure D-1, then click** OK

   When you set the readouts on the Info panel to RGB, they indicate the grayscale value of each pixel, from 0–255. The three readouts—R, G, and B—will always be the same for a grayscale image; you can think of them as a single number.

QUICK TIP
Identifying pixel information on the Info panel is referred to as **sampling** pixels.

4. **Click the** Eyedropper tool ✎, **then position it over different areas of the image, noting the readouts on the Info panel**

5. **Position the Eyedropper tool at the very bottom of the gradient on the right, then move slowly to the top of the gradient**

   The pixels in the gradient range from 0 at the bottom to 255 at the top.

6. **Sample areas in the man's shoulder to see the grayscale information for the darker areas of the image, then see if you can find pixels with a value of 0, the darkest pixels in the grayscale range**

7. **Sample areas in the white stripe in the hat and parts of the hood to find mid-range areas of the image, then see if you can find pixels with a value near 128, which is the exact middle of the grayscale range**

8. **Position the Eyedropper tool over the man's cheek and the light area at the lower right to find light areas of the image**

   Figure D-2 identifies some of the lightest pixels in the image.

Improving Images with Adjustment Layers

FIGURE D-1: Info Panel Options dialog box

FIGURE D-2: Sampling the lightest pixels in the image

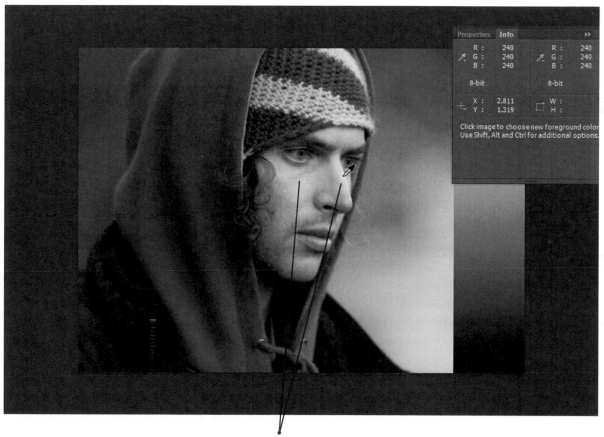

Very light pixels

Choosing settings on the Info panel

Why do you set the readouts on the Info panel to RGB if you are sampling a pixel in a grayscale image? Because the RGB readouts identify pixel values in grayscale, from 0–255. If you sampled pixels using the Grayscale setting on the Info panel, the readouts would identify pixels in ink percentages. In other words, the readouts would provide information for what would be a printed reproduction of the image. In a printed piece, a pixel with the value of 100% is a black printed dot. Zero percent means no ink, and on white paper, where there's 0% ink, that area remains white. So generally speaking, when adjusting an image, you'll want to use the RGB settings on the Info panel, because that setting presents pixels' grayscale values.

Investigating a Grayscale Image

The first step in analyzing the appearance of any image is to identify the highlights, midtones, and shadows. **Highlights** are the lightest areas of the image and are represented by pixels whose value falls in the upper third of the grayscale range. **Shadows** are the darkest areas represented by pixels in the low third of the grayscale range. **Midtones**, as the name suggests, fall into the middle range of the grayscale. When you look at a digital image, you don't see individual pixels, you see the illusion of **continuous tone**: a smooth transition from shadows to midtones to highlights. In order to create this illusion, a sufficient number of grays must be available per pixel so that the eye perceives smooth transitions between tones. ▚▚▞▞ Jon asks you to continue working with the image to identify the basic overall shadow, midtone, and highlight areas.

STEPS

1. Move the Info panel to the upper-left corner of the canvas, then close the Properties panel, if necessary

2. On the Layers panel, make the Chart layer visible, then compare your canvas to Figure D-3
   The chart uses a gradient to identify the shadow, midtone, and highlight areas of the grayscale image.

3. Look at the image of the man and try to see it not as a picture but as a range of tones from shadows to midtones to highlights

4. Using the chart as a guide, sample different areas of the image to identify shadows, midtones, and highlights

5. Target the Background layer on the Layers panel

6. Click the Image menu, point to Adjustments, click Posterize, drag the Levels slider to 3, and keep the Posterize dialog box open

7. Drag the Posterize dialog box out of the way, if necessary, then compare your image and the gradient on the right to Figure D-4
   At this posterize setting, only three shades of gray are available per pixel: 0, 148, and 255. Each pixel can be one and only one of these grayscale values. This image now has one color for highlights, one for midtones, and one for shadows. In the same way that those three shades are unable to render a smooth gradient on the right, they are unable to render the image as a smooth continuous-tone image.

8. Position the pointer over the image and note the readouts on the Info panel

9. In the Posterize dialog box, change the Levels value to 16, then compare your result to Figure D-5
   At this setting, 16 shades of gray are available per pixel. The image has clearly improved, but not nearly enough to create the illusion of continuous tone. The effect on the gradient at the right of the window mirrors the effect of the image. Just as the gradient shows distinct steps between grays, the image shows the same effect, especially in the hood and in the image background areas on the right side. However, note that at a very quick glance, your eye might accept the appearance of the knitted hat and—to some degree—the man's face as continuous tone.

10. Change the Levels value to 200
    At this level—still inferior to the standard 256 levels available in a grayscale image—the eye cannot identify any stair-stepping effect in the image; it appears to be continuous tone. The gradient on the right, however, still shows some signs of stair-stepping.

11. Click Cancel, hide the Chart layer on the Layers panel, save your work, then close grayscale_PS-D.psd

FIGURE D-3: Shadows, midtones, and highlights identified on the gradient

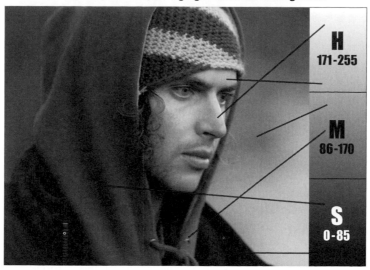

FIGURE D-4: Image with three shades of gray available per pixel

Every pixel can be one of three shades of gray

FIGURE D-5: Image with 16 shades of gray available per pixel

Background and gradient show stair-stepping

Using the Brightness/ Contrast Adjustment

Adjustments are operations you do that affect the appearance of an image, such as manipulating brightness and contrast. You can make adjustments directly to pixels on a layer, but you can't go back and re-adjust at a later time. **Adjustment layers** are adjustments you make that exist as layers on the Layers panel. Once created, they affect the image, but they can be manipulated at a later time. You can hide an adjustment layer or show it, and you can delete it at any time.

The Brightness/Contrast adjustment, as the name suggests, affects the brightness and contrast in an image. **Brightness** is defined by a pixel's grayscale value: the higher the number, the brighter the pixel. **Contrast** is represented by the relationship between the highlights and shadows. When the highlights aren't bright enough and the shadows aren't dark enough, the image will lack contrast and appear "flat" in its tonal range. Good contrast is created when highlights and shadows are distinctly different in tonal range: bright vs. dark. ▰▰▰ Jon gives you an image that overall is too dark and has poor contrast. He asks that you use the Brightness/Contrast adjustment to improve the tonal range of the image.

STEPS

QUICK TIP
Press [Ctrl][J] (Win) or ⌘[J] (Mac) to duplicate a layer quickly.

1. **Open PS D-2.psd, then save it as** adjust brightness contrast_PS-D

2. **Sample the highlight areas of the face, including the whites of the eyes, to get a general range of the values of the highlights in the image**

   The values are generally 140–170, far too low for highlights, which should be over 200. This image is not bright enough.

3. **Sample the hair and the image background area to the left of the face to get an idea of the general range of the shadows in the image**

   The values are generally 40–70, which puts them at the high end of the shadow range. The image lacks contrast because the highlight values are too close to the shadow values.

QUICK TIP
You can also create an adjustment layer by selecting a layer on the Layers panel, then clicking an adjustment icon on the Properties panel.

4. **Press and hold [Alt] (Win) or [option] (Mac), click the Create new fill or adjustment layer button ◙. on the Layers panel, drag the mouse pointer while holding down the mouse button, then click Brightness/Contrast**

   The New Layer dialog box and the Properties panel open. The Properties panel displays the settings for the current adjustment.

5. **Click OK to close the New Layer dialog box**

   As shown in Figure D-6, the Properties panel shows Brightness and Contrast sliders, and a Brightness/Contrast layer appears on the Layers panel.

6. **Drag the Brightness slider on the Properties panel to 75**

   With a Brightness value of 75, the pixels in the face fall into the 200–225 range. As shown in Figure D-7, with increased brightness, the appearance of the image improves dramatically.

7. **Drag the Contrast slider on the Properties panel to 80**

   The shadows darken and the highlights brighten. The shadows are improved dramatically, especially in the hair and the dark details of the face, like the pupils and the eyelashes.

8. **Reduce the Brightness to 65, then compare your result to Figure D-8**

   The reduced brightness deepens the shadows and increases the visible details of the face. Note the freckles. The face pixels still fall into the highlight range and are bright enough to give the image stunning contrast.

9. **Hide and show the Brightness/Contrast adjustment layer, save your work, then close adjust brightness contrast_PS-D.psd.**

FIGURE D-6: Brightness/Contrast adjustment layer on the Layers panel

Use Legacy check box is not checked

New adjustment layer

FIGURE D-7: Increasing the brightness

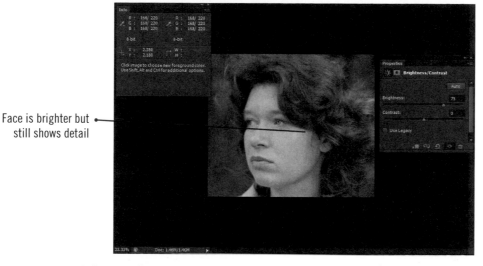

Face is brighter but still shows detail

FIGURE D-8: Before and after the adjustment

Extreme working behavior

A key to making adjustments is to sometimes walk the fine line between going far enough to make the adjustment the best it can be and going too far. When making adjustments, the first thing many designers do is push the adjustment to the extreme to see what the adjustment looks like when it's too much. When you work this way, seeing what you don't want can make it easier to find what you do want. Experiment with adjustments to see them at their extreme first. You're training your eye to recognize when an image looks its best, and recognizing when an image looks *bad* is a big part of that training.

Adjusting Black and White Points with Levels

In addition to shadows, midtones, and highlights, every image has a **black point**, representing the darkest pixel in the image, and a **white point**, representing the brightest pixel in the image. The black and white points represent the start and the end of the tonal range of the image.

Black and white points have a substantial effect on contrast. Often, photographers will capture an image with settings defined that the darkest pixel be no darker than, say, 15, and the brightest no lighter than 240. This forces the camera not to make shadows too dark or highlights too white. It results in an image that has a smooth tonal range from shadow to highlight but still lacks contrast because the darkest shadows aren't dark enough and the whitest highlights aren't white enough. This can be fixed using a Levels adjustment. For more information about levels, read the Clues to Use on the next page titled *How the Levels adjustment works.* Jon gives you an image with poor contrast and says he suspects the problem is with the black and white points.

STEPS

1. **Open PS D-3.psd, then save it as** adjust white and black points_PS-D

2. **Take a moment to make a visual analysis of the image and its tonal range**
   The image looks good, with a smooth range from shadow to highlight. However, it has low contrast-it lacks "snap," and it's "flat."

3. **Sample the image to find the darkest and lightest pixels in the image**
   The darkest pixels are in the low 20s and the lightest pixels are around 230. No pixels have a grayscale value of 0–19 or 234–255.

4. **Click the** Create new fill or adjustment layer button 🔘 **on the Layers panel, then click** Levels
   The Properties panel displays settings for the Levels adjustment layer.

5. **Resize the Properties panel so that you can see all of it, as shown in Figure D-9**
   The histogram, shown on the panel, reflects exactly what you learned when sampling the image. The **histogram** is a visual reference of every pixel in the image, or in a selection if only part of the image is selected. The black point on the histogram is represented by the black triangle, and the white point is represented by the white triangle. The tonal range of the image does not use the entire grayscale, represented by the gradient ramp below the histogram. Note how far to the right of the black triangle the histogram begins, and how far it ends from the white triangle.

QUICK TIP
The repositioned black and white triangles determine the new range of the histogram. The pixels at the far left of the histogram now have a grayscale value of 0, and those at the far right now have a grayscale value of 255.

6. **Drag the** black triangle **immediately beneath the histogram towards the right to the beginning of the histogram, drag the** white triangle **towards the left to the end of the histogram, then compare your result to Figure D-10**

7. **Hide and show the Levels 1 adjustment layer on the Layers panel to see the before and after view of the image**
   The *lengthened* tonal range is a stunning improvement in overall contrast for the image.

8. **Save your work**

FIGURE D-9: Properties panel with Levels adjustment layer settings

No pixels in this range

No pixels in this range

Histogram

Black point

White point

FIGURE D-10: Adjusting the black and white points

Repositioned

How the Levels adjustment works

The Levels type of adjustment, shown in Figure D-11, is a powerful adjustment option for affecting the tonal range of images. The most striking component of the Levels adjustment is the histogram.

Imagine that the histogram has 256 slots, one for each of the 256 available colors in the grayscale image. The slot for the 0-value pixels is on the left, and the slot for the 255-value pixels is on the right. Now imagine that there are a total of 1000 pixels in the image with a grayscale value of 64. Using a black marble to represent each pixel, imagine that you drop 1000 marbles into the 64 slot on the slider. Next, imagine that the image contains 1500 pixels with a grayscale value of 72, and you drop 1500 black marbles into the 72 slot. Imagine that you do this for each of the 256 slots on the slider. Your result would be the histogram—exactly what you see on the Properties panel. The height of the histogram, from left to right, shows the relative number of pixels that the whole file—or a selection of pixels—has for each of the 256 grayscale values.

You adjust the image by manipulating the sliders at the bottom of the histogram. The black triangle represents the 0 on the grayscale. The white triangle represents 255 on the grayscale.

The gray triangle represents the 128 midpoint. When you move any of the triangles, you readjust how the histogram relates to the full grayscale range, from shadow to highlight.

FIGURE D-11: Levels adjustment options on the Properties panel

Improving Images with Adjustment Layers

Adjusting the Midpoint with Levels

Adjusting the tonal range of an image is a lot like knowing which fork to use in fine dining. You start at the outside and work your way in. First, you set your black and white points—the extremes. Then, you verify that there's satisfactory contrast between the highlight and shadow range. Once those are established, you are ready to—if you want—adjust the midpoint. The **midpoint** defines which areas of the image fall into the middle range of the available grayscale. In other words, it separates the bright half from the dark half. Moving the midpoint darkens or lightens the image. Interestingly, a midpoint adjustment is often only subjective—do you like the image better if it's brighter or darker? Jon thinks you've been very successful adjusting the black and white points. He tells you to "play" with the midpoint and "see what you come up with."

STEPS

1. **Take a moment to note the overall "feel" of the image, then relate that impression to the histogram on the Properties panel**

   Overall, the image has more dark areas than light areas. The hood is such a big part of the image and mostly falls into the mid-upper shadow range. This is represented in the histogram, which shows significantly more pixels to the left of the midpoint than to the right.

   > **QUICK TIP**
   > If you have trouble dragging to the exact value, you can double-click the text box, then type 1.20.

2. **Drag the gray midpoint triangle left until the text box reads 1.20**

   Moving the midpoint triangle left by definition places more of the histogram to the right of the midpoint. Now, pixels that were in the lower half of the histogram are being defined as the midpoint of the grayscale.

3. **Evaluate the feel of the adjusted image, then compare your image to Figure D-12**

   Brightened, the image feels less heavy, but it also has less tension overall. The midpoint adjustment also makes the face too bright.

4. **Drag the gray midpoint triangle right until the text box reads .70**

   Artistically, this was a much better move than brightening the midpoint. The darkening has given great intensity to the face and the eyes. But it has also made the shadow areas so dark that they no longer show any detail, and this is not acceptable.

5. **Set the foreground color to black, click the Brush tool , then on the Options bar set the Size to 300 px and the Hardness to 0%**

6. **Click the Opacity list arrow on the Options bar, then change the Opacity to 10%**

7. **Target the layer mask on the Levels adjustment layer, then paint to lighten the shoulders and darkest areas of the jacket**

   Because the opacity of the brush is set to only 10%, you are essentially painting with a light gray. You are masking the adjustment very gradually.

8. **When you are done masking, press and hold [Shift] then click the layer mask thumbnail on the Layers panel to hide it, then click again to show it**

9. **Compare your result to Figure D-13, save your work, then close adjust white and black points_PS-D.psd**

FIGURE D-12: Brightening the midtones

FIGURE D-13: Masking areas of the image from the adjustment

Adjustment is reduced in these areas

Using layer masks with adjustments

When you create an adjustment layer—a Levels adjustment layer, for example—it is created automatically with a layer mask. It's a smart idea to think of the layer mask as less of an option and more of an essential component of working with adjustment layers. Sometimes, you will make an adjustment that you can apply completely to the artwork beneath, but more often, you will want to use the layer mask to apply the adjustment selectively in different strengths to different areas of the artwork.

When you set a low percentage of opacity on the Brush tool and then paint in the layer mask, the brush has reduced impact. In other words, if you set the brush to 10% opacity and paint in the layer mask with a black foreground color, each stroke of the brush will mask the artwork very gradually. This allows you to show or mask the adjustment very subtly and to be very specific as to how you want to affect the artwork beneath. Some designers automatically mask the adjustment completely then use a low-opacity brush to paint white in the mask, thus "brushing in" the adjustment gradually in specific areas. The layer mask allows you to apply it in a way that is unique and expresses your artistic vision.

Using the Color Balance Adjustment

Color Balance is an adjustment that allows you to control the balance of red, green, and blue in an image. It's a great tool for adjusting any color problems with an image. For example, many images from a digital camera are often too red. You can use the Color Balance adjustment to fix that. This lesson is closely related to what you learned in the previous lesson: when you work with the Color Balance adjustment, you'll see that you are manipulating the relationships between RGB and CMY. Jon asks you to open an image in Photoshop and improve the color by removing blue and green, using the Color Balance adjustment.

STEPS

1. **Open PS D-5.psd, then save it as** color balance_PS-D

2. **Take a moment to look at the image and get a feel for what it looks like, and how you think it could be made better**

   The image has good contrast but is "cold" overall. The colors are muted, and the flesh tone has underlying hints of blue and purple.

3. **Click the Eyedropper tool ![icon], position the tool over the background, note the RGB readouts on the Info panel, then sample the shadows in the hair**

   The background is a natural setting, probably green leaves, so you would expect to see larger concentrations of green in these pixels. However, the shadows in the hair also reflect this green: where the shadows in the hair should be neutral gray, they show dominance in green.

4. **Sample the whites in the eyes**

   Whites in eyes are great places to sample for midtones and highlights. The RGB values should all be relatively close; in this image, the whites show dominance in blue.

5. **Click the Create new fill or adjustment layer button ![icon] on the Layers panel, then click Color Balance**

   The Properties panel opens displaying the Color Balance options, shown in Figure D-17. The sliders represent what you learned in Lesson 6. Cyan is opposite Red, Magenta is opposite Green, and Yellow is opposite Blue.

6. **Experiment with the sliders by dragging them in each direction, noting the effect on the image, then click the Reset to adjustment defaults button ![icon] on the Properties panel**

7. **Verify that Midtones appears as the Tone setting on the Properties panel, drag the Yellow/Blue slider to –26, then sample the white of the eye on the left side of the screen**

   With the adjustment, the values are all much closer: 187R/197G/197B. Thus, the blue dominance is reduced.

8. **Click the Tone list arrow on the Properties panel, click Shadows, then drag the Magenta/Green slider left to –16**

   The move has a dramatic improvement on the image. Colors become more vibrant, and the face becomes a warmer pink because reducing green increases the magenta balance. Green is much less dominant in the shadows in the hair.

9. **Close the Properties panel, hide and show the Color Balance 1 adjustment layer to see the before and after view of the image as shown in Figure D-18, then save your work**

FIGURE D-17: Color Balance adjustment

Cyan = Minus Red

Magenta = Minus Green

Yellow = Minus Blue

FIGURE D-18: Before and after the adjustment

Looking for neutral grays

In an RGB file, color is created by an imbalance in the three channels. For example, when a pixel's red component is substantially greater than the green and blue components, the pixel's color will tend to fall into the red hue. However, when the three numbers are close in value, the pixel becomes neutral in color. Whenever the three components are the same, the pixel will have no color and can be only a neutral gray. For example, 20R/20G/20B would produce a dark gray, and 210R/210G/210B would produce a light gray.

Sampling an image for neutral grays can lead to many insights for improving color. If you sample areas that should be neutral—like shadows in hair—and they show a substantial dominance in one color, that's a good hint that you should reduce that color in the shadows.

On the other hand, if an area that should have vibrant color is grayish and neutral, that tells you that the color balance in that area is too close between the three and one or two need to be more dominant.

Using the Vibrance Adjustment

The Vibrance adjustment is a very useful method for quickly making colors in an image more vibrant. **Vibrance** refers to the intensity of a color. The measure of a pixel's vibrance is called its **saturation**. High saturation produces a vibrant color, like the red of a tomato. Reduced saturation produces a dull, more neutral color, like the dull red of a radish. A pixel with no saturation is a neutral gray. The Vibrance adjustment provides two settings: Vibrancy and Saturation. The Saturation setting is more of a blunt instrument; it simply increases or decreases the saturation value of all the pixels selected. The Vibrancy setting uses a more complex method for improving the image. It increases the saturation of pixels that need it without affecting pixels that are already saturated. Jon is pleased with the adjustments you made to the image with the Color Balance adjustment but asks that you improve the overall vibrancy of the color in the image.

STEPS

1. **Verify that the Color Balance 1 adjustment layer is targeted on the Layers panel, click the Create new fill or adjustment layer button [icon], then click Vibrance**

    The Properties panel opens with settings for the Vibrance adjustment.

2. **Drag the Saturation slider all the way to the left**

    The image is completely desaturated and resembles a black-and-white image. Even though the image appears black-and-white, the file is still an RGB file and all pixels still have an RGB component. In this case, all RGB values are all equal for all pixels.

3. **Drag the Saturation slider all the way to the right, then compare your result to Figure D-19**

    The image is oversaturated.

4. **Click the Reset to adjustment defaults button [icon], then drag the Vibrance slider all the way to the right**

5. **Hide and show the Vibrance 1 adjustment layer on the Layers panel to see a before and after view of the image**

    Even though the move is extreme, the result is very acceptable. The color is vibrant but not oversaturated.

6. **Click the Reset to adjustment defaults button [icon], then drag the Saturation slider to +37**

7. **Hide and show the Vibrance 1 adjustment layer on the Layers panel to see a before and after view of the image**

8. **Compare your result to Figure D-20**

9. **Save your work, then close color balance_PS-D.psd**

Using a group layer for adjustment layers

When you use multiple adjustment layers on the Layers panel, you will often want to see a before/after view of the image, with and without the adjustments. When you have many adjustment layers, it can be a little tricky to turn them all on and off simultaneously. For this reason, many designers place their adjustment layers in a group. A group is a new layer on the Layers panel with a folder icon. When you hide and show a group layer, you hide and show all the adjustment layers in the group. To create a group layer, click the Create a new group button [icon] on the Layers panel. Drag adjustment layers into the group layer, as necessary.

FIGURE D-19: Oversaturating the image

Note oversaturated "hot spots"

FIGURE D-20: Before and after the adjustment

Doing a "super-undo" with the History panel

The History panel, shown in Figure D-21, offers lots of great features; one of them is the ability to quickly revert a file to its state when you first opened it, then to undo the revert to bring it back to its current state. As you work, the History panel records your steps and lists the last 20 of them, called **states**, in the panel. You can increase or decrease the default number of states in the Preferences dialog box. The last state in the list represents the last change you made to the file. You can click a state in the list to go back to that point of your work, and then continue working from that state. At the top of the panel is a thumbnail that represents the file the way that it looked when it was first opened. If you click the thumbnail you will undo all states in the panel. All of the states in the History panel are grayed out. Click any state to continue working from that particular state. For example, if you want to continue working with the file the way it was before you clicked the thumbnail image, click the last state before you continue working. If you undo all states and continue working by

accident, you can click File on the Menu bar, then click Revert. This will take you back to the status of the file when you last saved it. You may lose some of your work, but at least not *all* of your work.

FIGURE D-21 The History panel

Improving Images with Adjustment Layers

Practice

Concepts Review

Label the elements of the Photoshop screen shown in Figure D-22.

FIGURE D-22

Match each term with the statement that best describes it.

6. **Grayscale mode**
7. **RGB mode**
8. **Shadow point**
9. **Cyan**
10. **Magenta**
11. **Yellow**
12. **Continuous tone**
13. **Vibrance**

a. Darkest pixels in an image
b. "Minus blue"
c. Intensity of a pixel's color
d. "Minus green"
e. 256 shades of gray available per pixel
f. "Minus red"
g. 256 shades available per pixel per channel
h. Smooth transition from shadows to highlights

Select the best answer from the list of choices.

14. Which of the following is not an adjustment you can make in Photoshop?
    a. Levels   **c.** Color Balance
    b. Bevel and Emboss   **d.** Vibrance

15. Which of the following is not true of an RGB file?
    a. It has three color channels.
    b. It is larger in file size than a grayscale version of the same file.
    c. Each pixel can be one of 256 shades of gray.
    d. The image can appear to be black-and-white.

16. Which of the following is not true about a Levels adjustment?
    a. A histogram is involved.
    b. You can use levels to adjust a color or a black-and-white image.
    c. You can choose a Tone setting so that the Levels adjustment will affect only shadows, midtones, or highlights.
    d. You can brighten the midpoint.

17. Which of the following is not true about the Color Balance adjustment?
    a. You can move a slider between Magenta and Cyan.
    b. You can move a slider between Blue and Yellow.
    c. You can move a slider between Cyan and Red.
    d. You can move a slider between Green and Magenta.

18. Which of the following is not involved in assessing the appearance of an image?
    a. Contrast   **c.** Shadows
    b. Color balance   **d.** Grayscale

Skills Review

1. Understand grayscale.
    a. Open PS D-6.psd, verify the Background layer is targeted, then save the file as **grayscale skills_PS-D**.
    b. Click the Background layer, click Image on the Menu bar, point to Mode, then note that Grayscale is checked.
    c. Open the Info panel, click the Info panel menu button, click Panel Options, then verify that First Color Readout and Second Color Readout are both set to RGB Color.
    d. Click the Eyedropper tool and position it over different areas of the image, noting the readouts on the Info panel.
    e. Position the Eyedropper tool at the very bottom of the gradient on the right, then move slowly to the top of the gradient, sampling as you go.
    f. Sample areas in the background to see grayscale information for the darker areas of the image.
    g. Sample areas in the flower at the center to find mid-range areas of the image.
    h. Sample the petals and try to find the lightest pixels in the image.

Skills Review (continued)

2. **Investigate a grayscale image.**

   a. On the Layers panel, make the Chart layer visible.

   b. Look at the flower image and the background and try to see it not as a picture but as a range of tones from shadows to midtones to highlights.

   c. Using the chart as a guide, sample different areas of the image to identify shadows, highlights, and midtones.

   d. Move the Info panel to the upper-left corner, click Image on the Menu bar, point to Adjustments, click Posterize, then drag the Levels slider to 3.

   e. Position the cursor over the image and note the before/after readouts on the Info panel.

   f. In the Posterize dialog box, change the Levels value to 16.

   g. Change the Levels value to 200.

   h. Click Cancel, then hide the Chart layer.

   i. Save your work, then close grayscale skills_PS-D.psd.

FIGURE D-23

3. **Use the Brightness/Contrast adjustment.**

   a. Open PS D-7.psd, then save it as **brightness contrast skills_PS-D**.

   b. Sample the highlight areas in the river and where sunshine strikes the rocks to get a general range of the values of the highlights in the image.

   c. Sample the dark areas of the rocks to get a general range of the shadows in the image.

   d. Click the Create new fill or adjustment layer button on the Layers panel, then click Brightness/Contrast.

   e. On the Properties panel, drag the Brightness slider and sample the image until the lightest pixels in the water fall into the 220–235 range.

   f. Drag the Contrast slider to 90.

   g. Reduce the Brightness to 58.

   h. Close the Properties panel.

   i. Hide and show the Brightness/Contrast 1 adjustment layer and compare your before and after appearance to Figure D-23.

   j. Save your work, then close brightness contrast skills_PS-D.psd.

Skills Review (continued)

4. Adjust black and white points with levels.

   a. Open PS D-8.psd, then save it as **levels skills_PS-D**.

   b. Take a moment to make a visual analysis of the image and its tonal range.

   c. Sample the image to find the darkest and lightest pixels in the image.

   d. Click the Create new fill or adjustment layer button on the Layers panel, then click Levels.

   e. Drag the black triangle toward the right to the beginning of the histogram, and drag the white triangle toward the left to the end of the histogram.

   f. Sample the image, trying to find shadow pixels that have a value of 10 or lower and highlight pixels that have a value of 240 or higher.

   g. Adjust the black and white triangles as necessary to produce the best shadow and highlight points.

   h. Hide and show the Levels 1 adjustment layer on the Layers panel to see the before and after view of the image.

   i. Save your work.

5. Adjust the midpoint with levels.

   a. Take a moment to note the overall feel of the image, then relate that impression to the histogram on the Properties panel.

   b. Click the Create new fill or adjustment layer button on the Layers panel, then click Levels to add a second Levels adjustment layer.

   c. Drag the gray midpoint triangle left until the text box reads 1.30.

   d. Evaluate the appearance of the adjusted image.

   e. Drag the gray midpoint triangle right until the text box reads .80.

   f. Hide and show the new Levels 2 adjustment layer to see the midpoint adjustment. (*Hint*: Be sure the Levels 2 adjustment layer is showing when you're done.)

   g. Set the Foreground color to black, click the Brush tool, then on the Options bar, set the Size to 175 px and the Hardness to 0%.

   h. Click the Opacity list arrow on the Options bar, then set the opacity to 30%.

   i. Target the layer mask on the Levels 2 adjustment layer, then paint to lighten the center of the flower slightly.

   j. Compare your result to Figure D-24, save your work, then close levels skills_PS-D.psd.

FIGURE D-24

Skills Review (continued)

6. **Investigate an RGB image.**

   a. Open PS D-9.psd, then save it as **color balance skills_PS-D**. (*Hint*: The file has been saved in RGB Color mode.)

   b. Click Edit (Win) or Photoshop (Mac) on the Menu bar, point to Preferences, click Interface, click the Show Channels in Color check box to add a check mark, if necessary, then click OK.

   c. Verify that the two readouts on the Info panel are set to RGB Color, click the Eyedropper tool, then position it over different areas of the image.

   d. Click Window on the Menu bar, click Channels, then click the channel thumbnail on the Red channel.

   e. Click the Green channel thumbnail to see the Green channel, click the Blue channel thumbnail to see the Blue channel, then click the RGB channel thumbnail to see the composite image.

   f. Select the right half of the canvas, fill the selection with white, deselect, then position the Eyedropper tool to sample the white pixels.

   g. Click the Red channel thumbnail, fill the channel with black, then click the RGB channel thumbnail to see the composite image.

   h. Undo the fill to restore the Red channel, fill the Green channel with black, then click the RGB channel thumbnail.

   i. Undo the fill to restore the Green channel, fill the Blue channel with black, then click the RGB channel thumbnail.

   j. Click File on the Menu bar, then click Revert.

7. **Use the Color Balance adjustment.**

   a. Take a moment to look at the image and get a feel for what it looks like, and how you think it could be made better. (*Hint*: Elephants are usually gray, not brown.)

   b. Click the Eyedropper tool, sample different areas of the image, and note the RGB readouts on the Info panel. (*Hint*: Red dominates almost every pixel in the image.)

   c. Sample the whites in the tusk.

   d. Click the Create new fill or adjustment layer button on the Layers panel, then click Color Balance.

   e. Take some time to experiment with the sliders, noting the effect on the image, then click the Reset to adjustment defaults button on the panel.

   f. Verify that the Midtones option button is selected, then drag the Cyan/Red slider to –34.

   g. Drag the Magenta/Green slider to –6, then drag the Yellow/Blue slider to +20.

   h. Click the Tone list arrow on the Properties panel, click Highlights, drag the Cyan/Red slider to –25, then drag the Magenta/Green slider to –12.

   i. Close the Properties panel, hide and show the Color Balance 1 adjustment layer to see the before and after view of the image, then save your work. (*Hint*: Note how the yellow flowers in the background remain yellow and vibrant. Note too how the grass/brush behind the elephant has a more natural and realistic color.)

Skills Review (continued)

8. Use the Vibrance adjustment.

   a. Verify that the Color Balance 1 adjustment layer is targeted on the Layers panel, click the Create new fill or adjustment layer button, then click Vibrance.

   b. Drag the Saturation slider all the way to the left.

   c. Drag the Saturation slider all the way to the right.

   d. Click the Reset to adjustment defaults button, then drag the Vibrance slider to +40.

   e. Hide and show the Vibrance 1 adjustment layer on the Layers panel to see a before and after view of the image.

   f. Drag the Saturation slider gradually to +12.

   g. Hide and show the Vibrance 1 adjustment layer on the Layers panel to see a before and after view of the image.

FIGURE D-25

   h. Compare your result to Figure D-25. (*Hint*: The figure shows the image before and after all adjustments.)

   i. Save your work, then close color balance skills_PS-D.psd.

Independent Challenge 1

You're designing a brochure of photos from your hometown and want to adjust an image to make it look its best.

a. Open PS D-10.psd, then save it as **hay bale_PS-D**.

b. Create a Brightness/Contrast adjustment layer.

c. Drag the Brightness slider to +35, then sample the brightest cloud in the sky.

d. Drag the Contrast slider to +60.

e. Sample the bright cloud again and verify that its values are somewhere between 200 and 225. (*Hint*: Because the cloud is very distant, you shouldn't make it too bright.)

f. Sample the shadows in the hay bale and on the ground to be sure they haven't become too black.

g. Create a Vibrance adjustment layer.

h. Drag the Vibrance slider all the way to the right.

i. Drag the Vibrance slider to +86, then compare your result to Figure D-26.

j. Save your work, then close hay bale_PS-D.psd.

Independent Challenge 2

You work for a boating magazine and are working on a photo you're going to use in a layout. The creative director tells you that the foreground of the image is great but that she'd like you to give the sky and the mountains in the distance "more weight for detail."

a. Open PS D-11.psd, then save it as **sailboat_PS-D**.

b. Create a Levels adjustment layer.

c. Drag the midpoint triangle right to .64.

d. Click the Brush tool.

e. Use various brush sizes and hardness values to mask the adjustment so that it affects only the sky and the mountain in the distance.

f. Save your work, compare your screen to Figure D-27, then close sailboat_PS-D.psd.

FIGURE D-27

Independent Challenge 3

You're a designer for a greeting card company. You download an image from an online stock photography website and decide to improve it with some adjustments.

a. Open PS D-12.psd, then save it as **color flowers_PS-D**.

b. Create a Levels adjustment layer.

c. Drag the black slider toward the right to where the histogram starts, then drag the white triangle toward the left to where the histogram ends.

d. Create a Brightness/Contrast adjustment layer, then drag the Contrast slider to +35.

e. Create a Color Balance adjustment layer.

f. Drag the Cyan/Red slider to +6, drag the Magenta/Green slider to –12, then drag the Yellow/Blue slider to –26.

g. Click the Levels 1 adjustment layer, then drag the midpoint triangle left until the text box reads 1.16.

h. Drag the black triangle right until the text box reads 40.

i. Target the Color Balance 1 adjustment layer on the Layers panel, then create a Vibrance adjustment layer.

j. Drag the Saturation slider to +30.

k. Compare your results to Figure D-28.

Advanced Challenge Exercise

- Click the Levels 1 adjustment layer.
- Slowly drag the white triangle left to see the white petals begin to lose detail and "blow out."
- Keep dragging left until the petals are entirely white with no detail.
- Drag the white triangle right and sample with the Info panel to find the point where the pixels in the petals are their brightest but not at 255.

l. Hide/show the adjustment layers to see before and after.

m. Save your work, then close color flowers_PS-D.psd.

Real Life Independent Challenge

You're a talented amateur photographer. You use great equipment, and so your photos download from your camera looking good without any editing. You just returned from your trip out west and are using Photoshop to tweak your photos from looking good to looking great.

a. Open PS D-13.psd, then save it as **canyon_PS-D**.

b. Create a Levels adjustment layer.

c. Drag the black triangle right to 12, then drag the white triangle left to 212.

d. Drag the midpoint slider right to .90.

e. Create a Color Balance adjustment layer.

f. Drag the Cyan/Red slider to +5, then drag the Yellow/Blue slider to –10.

g. Create a Vibrance adjustment layer.

h. Drag the Vibrance slider to +62.

Advanced Challenge Exercise

- Open the History panel.
- Click the PS D-13 thumbnail at the top of the panel to see the image in its original state.
- Click the Modify Levels Layer state on the History panel.

i. Compare your results to Figure D-29, save your work, then close canyon_PS-D.psd.

Visual Workshop

Open PS D-14.psd, then save it as **visual solution_PS-D**. Apply adjustments to the image so that the canvas resembles Figure D-30.

FIGURE D-30

Working with Type and Gradients

Files You Will Need:

To view a list of files needed for this unit, see the Data Files Grid in the back of the book.

When people think of Photoshop, usually their first thought is of images, photographs, and special effects. But another great Photoshop feature is the ability to create sophisticated typographical effects. Photoshop makes it easy to create classic effects like beveled and embossed text, chiseled text, and text that shines as though it were made of chrome. Even better, you can combine type with photographic images to produce truly unique typographical designs. When you start working extensively with type, you often find yourself working with gradients as well. **Gradients** are blends between two or more colors, and they are very striking when applied to type and typography. A white-to-black gradient can add weight to a title, or a green-to-yellow gradient can make for a vibrant headline that appears to glow. Gradients offer so many more options than a simple solid color for filling type. Jon gives you a number of different Photoshop projects that all involve working with type.

OBJECTIVES

Set type

Lock transparent pixels

Create bevel and emboss effects on type

Apply gloss contours to layer styles

Create a double emboss effect

Apply a gradient

Create a new gradient

Clip a gradient into type

Clip imagery into type

Fade type

Setting Type

Adobe has outfitted Photoshop with all the text editing capabilities you'd expect from any top-notch word processing or layout package. When you create type in Photoshop, it is "live type" just like in any other application; you can select it, copy it, paste it, and so on. The Character panel is command central for formatting type in Photoshop. You can do all of the formatting you need to do—setting the typeface, the size, the tracking, the kerning, and so forth—on the Character panel. ▩▩▩ Jon tells you about a new web client that will be working with your agency. He tells you to be prepared to design lots of different headlines for the different areas of their website. He asks to you to start by setting a simple headline in Photoshop.

STEPS

1. Open PS E-1.psd, then save it as set type_PS-E

2. Click the workspace switcher on the Menu bar, then click Typography

3. Press [T] to access the Horizontal Type tool T , then click the cursor at the left of the canvas

   A blinking type cursor appears, prompting you to begin typing. A type layer appears on the Layers panel.

4. Type the word Typography

5. Click the Move tool ▶⊕

   The type layer is automatically named with the word(s) that you typed, as shown in Figure E-1.

6. On the Character panel, click the Set the font family list arrow, then choose Garamond (or a similar typeface)

7. Click the Set the font style list arrow, click Bold, click the Set the font size list arrow, then click 60 pt

8. Drag the type to center it on the canvas, then open the Swatches panel

9. Click the blue swatch in the top row named RGB Blue, then press [Alt][Delete] (Win) or [option][delete] (Mac) to fill the text on the Typography layer with the foreground color

   Pressing [Alt][Delete] (Win) or [option][delete] (Mac) fills text on a layer with the foreground color. When you fill a text layer, only the text is filled with the color, not the entire canvas.

10. Compare your canvas to Figure E-2

> **QUICK TIP**
> You can also choose a workspace by clicking Window on the Menu bar, pointing to Workspace, and then clicking one of the workspaces.

> **QUICK TIP**
> You cannot use the Fill command in the Edit menu to fill type.

FIGURE E-1: Type layer

Indicates a type layer ——
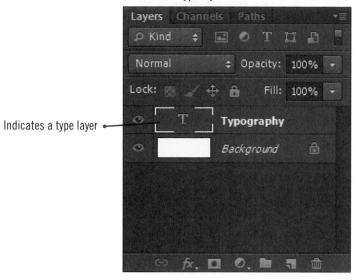

FIGURE E-2: Filling text with a color

FIGURE E-3: Character panel

Font size
Kerning
Vertical scale
Baseline shift

Font family
Font style
Leading
Tracking
Horizontal scale
Text color
Style buttons

Language setting   Anti-aliasing method

Working with the Character panel

Figure E-3 shows the Character panel and identifies the many options available to you when working with type. The Tracking and Kerning options are used to perfect the appearance of typography in terms of spacing. Tracking controls the overall spacing between letters in a given word or paragraph. Kerning controls the spacing between any two specific letters. The Horizontal and Vertical scale options resize selected text, making it wider or taller, respectively. Be sure to experiment with the style buttons at the bottom of the panel, which are very useful for making all caps, small caps, superscripts, and other classic examples of typographical formatting.

Locking Transparent Pixels

When you create a new layer in Photoshop, you'll see no changes to the artwork on your canvas. This is because each new layer is automatically a transparent layer; it's empty, because it has no artwork in it. You can apply color to any of the pixels on the layer—for example, you could fill the entire layer with color—but until you do, you can think of the pixels on the layer as being transparent, or "empty." This idea that a layer contains **transparency** is an important concept to understand, especially when working with type. On a type layer, the pixels on the layer that *aren't* used to render the type are transparent by default. To protect a pixel's transparency, you can lock the transparent pixels on a layer. Jon has asked you to create an interesting effect with type using black and red fill colors.

STEPS

1. **Verify that the Typography layer is targeted, click Layer on the Menu bar, point to Rasterize, then click Type**

   The term **rasterize** means "convert to pixels." When you rasterize a type layer, all of its contents are converted from type to pixels. The type icon disappears from the layer on the Layers panel, and the layer is no longer editable as type. To learn more about rasterizing type, read *What's the purpose of rasterizing type?* on the next page.

QUICK TIP

By default, transparent areas of a layer are displayed as a grid of gray and white squares. You can change the grid size and grid colors in the Transparency & Gamut category of the Preferences dialog box.

2. **Hide the Background layer**

   As shown in Figure E-4, many pixels on the Typography layer are transparent.

3. **Press [D] to access the default foreground and background colors**

4. **Press [Alt][Delete] (Win) or [option][delete] (Mac) to fill with the black foreground color**

   All the pixels on the layer—transparent and non-transparent—are filled with black.

5. **Undo the fill, then click the Lock transparent pixels icon ▨ on the Layers panel, as shown in Figure E-5**

   Locking the transparent pixels on the layer ensures that they will remain transparent when other pixels are being modified.

6. **Fill the layer with the black foreground color**

   The transparent pixels on the layer are not filled with black.

7. **Click the RGB Red swatch on the Swatches panel, click the Brush tool ✦, set the brush size to 50 px, set the Hardness to 100%, then set the Opacity to 100% if necessary on the Options bar**

8. **Paint different areas of the type red, then compare your result to Figure E-6**

   Because transparent pixels are locked, only the black pixels are affected by the Brush tool.

9. **Show the Background layer, save your work, then close set type_PS-E.psd**

FIGURE E-4: Identifying transparent pixels

Transparent pixels represented by gray and white checker-board

Typography

FIGURE E-5: Lock transparent pixels option activated

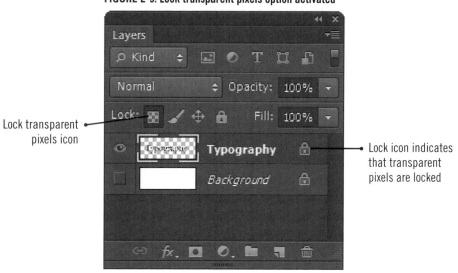

Lock transparent pixels icon

Lock icon indicates that transparent pixels are locked

FIGURE E-6: Painting in a layer with locked transparent pixels

Typography

What's the purpose of rasterizing type?

The term **rasterize** means to convert to pixels. When you rasterize a type layer, you convert it from "live" type—type that is selectable and editable—to pixels. Its appearance doesn't change, but functionally, it is really not live anymore. You can't select it or modify it.

Rasterizing type is a commitment. Once you do so, other than using the Undo command or reverting the file, you can never go back and convert the rasterized text back into live type. So why rasterize type in the first place? The biggest reason for rasterizing type is to avoid font issues. When you share a Photoshop file that includes font information, the person that opens your file will need the same font installed on their computer to render the type. When type is rasterized, you no longer need the font installed because it's not type anymore, it's just pixels.

Creating Bevel and Emboss Effects on Type

Prepare to fall in love with the Bevel & Emboss layer style, especially when you use it to design type. Bevel & Emboss is a layer style—a built-in effect that you can apply to layers—just like the Drop Shadow and Outer Glow layer styles you learned in Unit C. Bevel & Emboss is especially effective for type, because you can use it to create classic effects like raised text and chiseled text. And it's not just a one-trick pony layer style: the dialog box features a number of different styles and techniques that you can use to create all kinds of different bevel and emboss effects. It's a great place to experiment and play just to see the different looks you can achieve. ▰▰▰▰ Jon supplies you with type to use to create sample headline effects for your client's website. He asks that you start with the Bevel & Emboss layer style and asks that you experiment with a couple of different looks.

STEPS

1. **Open PS E-2.psd, save it as** bevel type_PS-E, **then click the** HEADLINE layer **on the Layers panel**

QUICK TIP
Double-click the layer to the right of the layer name to open the Layer Style dialog box.

2. **Click** Layer **on the Menu bar, point to** Layer Style, **then click** Bevel & Emboss
   The Layer Style dialog box opens with the default Bevel & Emboss settings selected.

3. **Set the Style to** Emboss, **set the Technique to** Smooth, **then set the Depth to** 100%

4. **Set the Size to 24 px, set the Soften value to 0 px, then click** OK
   Your canvas should resemble Figure E-7.

5. **Double-click the** Bevel & Emboss layer style **on the Layers panel to open the Layer Style dialog box**

6. **Set the Style to** Inner Bevel, **set the Technique to** Chisel Hard, **then set the Depth to** 120%

QUICK TIP
Note how the layer style creates the interesting effect on the letter J.

7. **Set the Size to 44, set the Soften value to 0, then click** OK
   As shown in Figure E-8, the modified settings produce an entirely different bevel and emboss effect.

8. **Save your work**

FIGURE E-7: Smooth Emboss effect

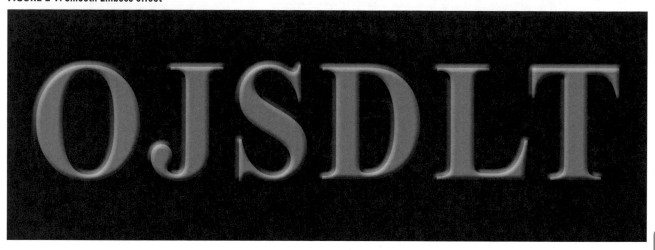

FIGURE E-8: Inner Bevel Chisel Hard effect

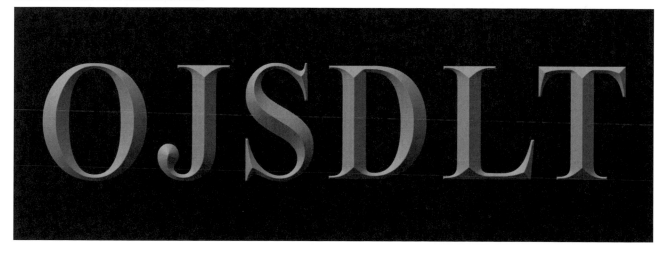

Using a Stroke Emboss layer style

A **stroke** is a basic artistic element that places an outline on an object or on type. For example, you can apply a black fill to type, then apply a colored stroke as an outline. In Photoshop, the best method for applying a stroke is to apply it as a layer style. This method allows you to apply the stroke, choose its color and its size, and—as with all layer styles—you can modify it or remove it at any time.

Once you've applied the Stroke layer style, you can then apply a Bevel & Emboss layer style to the stroke. To do this, click the Style list arrow in the Layer Style dialog box, then choose Stroke Emboss. As a result, only the stroke will be beveled and embossed.

Applying Gloss Contours to Layer Styles

Gloss contours are a set of 12 preset adjustments that affect the brightness and contrast of a layer style to create dramatic lighting effects. They are available for many different kinds of layer styles, not just Bevel & Emboss. Gloss contours fall into the "pick and choose" category of Photoshop features: you simply click through them to see what they do and how they affect the current artwork you're working with, and choose the one you like best. After a while, you'll get a sense of what to expect from each of them. However, the gloss contours will produce different results for different types of artwork. Jon tells you he likes the chiseled type effect you came up with for the type, but says he'd like to see you "jazz it up." He suggests you apply a gloss contour to the layer style.

STEPS

1. **Double-click the Bevel & Emboss layer style on the Layers panel to open the dialog box**

2. **Move the Layer Style dialog box out of the way, if necessary, so that you can see at least one of the letters on your canvas**

3. **Click the Gloss Contour list arrow, then position the mouse pointer over the third square in the second row: Ring – Double**

   As shown in Figure E-9, a tool tip appears, revealing the name of the gloss contour.

4. **Click Ring – Double to see the effect on the artwork, then click each of the remaining 11 gloss contours to see its effect on the type artwork**

5. **Click the gloss contour named Cone**

6. **Click the Anti-aliased check box beside the Gloss Contour list arrow, then click OK**

   Your artwork should resemble Figure E-10. You can use the Undo/Redo commands to see a before/after view of the change.

7. **Save your work**

FIGURE E-9: Gloss Contours in the Layer Style dialog box

Tool tip indicates name of gloss contour

FIGURE E-10: Cone gloss contour applied to artwork

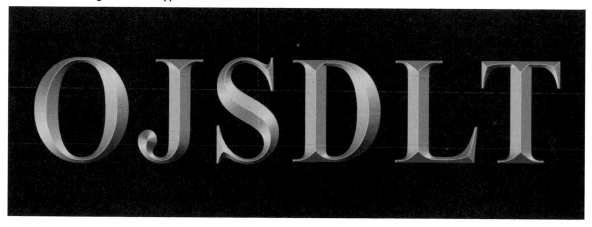

Understanding the Use Global Light option

Many layer styles produce their effects by adjusting the brightness and contrast of the artwork they're applied to. The effect is often created with a "light source," meaning that the artwork appears to be brightened from a certain direction. For example, if you apply a Bevel & Emboss layer style to chiseled text and set the light source to light the artwork from the right, you will create interesting shadows on the left side of the artwork.

You will find that you will apply multiple layer styles to multiple pieces of artwork when working in Photoshop. The Use Global Light option exists as a simple solution to help you maintain a consistent light source for multiple layer styles. With the Use Global Light option checked, all of your layer styles will create their individual effects using "light" from the same direction.

Consistency is great when you want it, and if you want a consistent light source, the Use Global Light feature is a great option. But don't think that you *must* have a consistent light source. Sometimes different layer styles applied to the same artwork look even more interesting when they strike the artwork from different angles or light sources. You can turn off the Use Global Light option and manually set the angle and the altitude of the light source by dragging the Direction of light source icon in the Shading section of the Layer Style dialog box. Always remember to experiment.

Creating a Double Emboss Effect

Layer styles are a lot of fun and they produce interesting and useful effects. But at some point, you're bound to feel that you're not really *creating* artwork with a layer style, because the result is something anyone could achieve by dragging the sliders to the same settings that you did. That is the truth about layer styles: they are canned effects, manufactured by Adobe Systems and packaged with the program. As a designer, it's your job to see past this built-in limitation of layer styles and figure out how to create *unique* artwork with these effects. The key to doing so is to work with *many* layer styles, combining them in inspired and insightful ways to produce artwork that is unexpected and brand-new. ▄▄▄ Jon tells you that he thinks your headline style is heading in the right direction, but that you need to take it to the next level and create a bevel and emboss headline that is unique, not just one layer style applied to one piece of artwork.

STEPS

1. **Verify that the Headline layer is targeted, then press [Ctrl][J] (Win) or ⌘ [J] (Mac) to duplicate the layer**

2. **Rename the new layer Inner Bevel, then hide it**

   In this exercise we are hiding the Inner Bevel layer style so that you can see the Outer Bevel layer style being built. However, if you were designing this type in a real-world project, you would probably want to show the Inner Bevel layer style to see the final effect of both layer styles together.

3. **Target the Headline layer, then rename it Outer Bevel**

4. **Drag the Indicates layer effects icon 🔲 on the Outer Bevel layer to the Delete layer button 🗑 on the Layers panel**

   The layer style is removed. Instead of deleting the layer style, we could have double-clicked it to open the dialog box and changed the Inner Bevel layer style to an Outer Bevel layer style. This method, however, allows you to see the outer bevel effect being built from scratch. Your Layers panel should resemble Figure E-11.

QUICK TIP
You must click to the right of the layer name to open the Layer Style dialog box.

5. **Double-click the right side of the Outer Bevel layer to open the Layer Style dialog box, then click the words Bevel & Emboss in the left column**

6. **Set the Style to Outer Bevel, set the Technique to Chisel Hard, then set the Depth to 100%**

7. **Set the Size to 13, then set the Soften value to 0**

8. **Apply the Cove – Deep gloss contour, then click the Anti-aliased check box**

   Your Layer Style dialog box should resemble Figure E-12.

9. **Click OK, then take a moment to view the effect**

10. **Show the Inner Bevel layer, then compare your canvas to Figure E-13**

11. **Save your work, then close bevel type_PS-E.psd**

FIGURE E-11: Viewing the Layers panel after deleting a layer style

Layer style removed

FIGURE E-12: Creating an Outer Bevel layer style

FIGURE E-13: Viewing the effect of combining layer styles

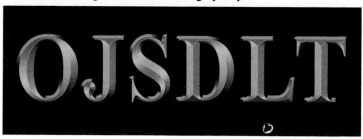

Applying a Gradient

A **gradient** is a blend between two or more colors. Often, a gradient between two colors creates a third distinct color. For example, any gradient between red and yellow will produce orange somewhere in between. Photoshop comes loaded with preset gradients of different colors that are available for you to apply with the Gradient tool. The Gradient tool is the single tool that you use to apply gradients; it determines the placement and the length of the gradient. The tool works by clicking, dragging, and releasing. Where you click determines where the gradient begins, where you drag determines the length of the gradient, and where you release determines where the gradient ends. In addition, the Gradient tool comes with options that allow you to determine the *type* of gradient you are applying. A **linear** gradient blends straight from one color to another in a linear fashion. A **radial** gradient blend radiates outward from one color to another, like a series of concentric circles. Jon tells you that the web client's headline graphics call for a number of gradient effects and asks you to experiment with some of Photoshop's default gradients.

STEPS

1. **Open PS E-3.psd, save it as** making the gradient_PS-E, **then click the** Default Foreground and Background Colors button ⬚ **on the Tools panel**

QUICK TIP
The Gradient tool might be hidden beneath the Paint Bucket tool.

2. **Click the** Gradient tool ▭, **then click the** Click to open Gradient picker list arrow **on the Options bar, shown in Figure E-14**

   A list of default gradient swatches becomes available.

3. **Click the** Blue, Yellow, Blue gradient swatch, **then click the** Linear Gradient button ▭ **on the Options bar**

   Table E-1 on the next page describes the five types of gradients.

4. **Position the mouse pointer at the left edge of the canvas, click and drag to the right edge of the canvas, then release the mouse button**

   As shown in Figure E-15, a linear gradient is created from the left edge of the canvas to the right edge of the canvas.

5. **Click and drag from the top of the canvas to the bottom of the canvas**

   The gradient is re-created from top to bottom.

6. **Click and drag from the upper-left to the lower-right corner of the canvas**

   The gradient is re-created diagonally from the upper-left to the lower-right corner of the canvas.

7. **Click anywhere on the canvas and drag from left to right for approximately one-half to one inch, then compare your result to Figure E-16**

   The length of the entire gradient is approximately one-half inch long. Any pixels outside of the one-half-inch range are filled with the solid start and end color, which in this case is blue.

8. **Click the** Radial Gradient button ▣ **on the Options bar**

9. **Repeat Step 7, then compare your result to Figure E-17**

   A radial gradient follows the same rules as a linear gradient: the gradient starts where you click and ends where you release. With a radial gradient, however, the gradient "radiates" out from a center point, like concentric circles.

10. **Save your work**

FIGURE E-14: Gradient swatches

Default gradient swatches

Radial Gradient

Linear Gradient

Click to open Gradient picker

Gradient tool

FIGURE E-15: Linear gradient across the canvas

FIGURE E-16: Shortened linear gradient

FIGURE E-17: Radial gradient

TABLE E-1: Five types of gradients

type of gradient	button icon	description
Linear		Blends from the starting point to the ending point in a straight line.
Radial		Blends from the starting point to the ending point in a circular pattern.
Angle		Blends in a counterclockwise sweep around the starting point. Think of an angle gradient as the big hand and the little hand being in the same place on a clock, like at midnight. The gradient is created from background to the foreground color from the big hand to the little hand in a counterclockwise direction.
Reflected		Blends using symmetric linear gradients on either side of the starting point. Think of a reflected gradient as a mirror. Click and drag from your foreground to background color and it creates a linear gradient *plus* a mirror image of that gradient at the point where you first clicked. Practically speaking, this type of gradient would be useful for making something that looks like a lead pipe or some other kind of metal tube.
Diamond		Blends from the starting point outward in a diamond pattern. The ending point defines one corner of the diamond. The result appears to be concentric squares, with the starting color being in the center. The result appears very three-dimensional and could be especially useful for web graphics.

Creating a New Gradient

In addition to the preset gradients that come with Photoshop, you can create your own customized gradients in the Gradient Editor dialog box. The colors that make up a gradient are called **color stops**. In the Gradient Editor dialog box, you create a customized gradient on the **gradient ramp** in the dialog box. You can create gradients between two color stops or between multiple color stops. You add color stops simply by clicking the gradient ramp, and you remove them by dragging them down and off of the gradient ramp. You determine the length of the gradient between color stops by moving color stops closer to or farther away from each other. The **Location** text box below the gradient ramp identifies a selected color stop's location, from left to right, on the gradient ramp. ▰▰▰▰ You tell Jon that you'd prefer to design the client's headline graphics with customized gradients rather than those that come prepackaged with Photoshop. He agrees and asks that you start by creating a simple three-color gradient.

STEPS

QUICK TIP
The gradient fill box on the Options bar is also called *Click to edit the gradient box.*

1. **Click the gradient fill box on the Options bar, as shown in Figure E-18**

   The gradient fill on the Options bar is the last gradient fill used. It appears when you select the Gradient tool. Clicking the gradient fill on the Options bar opens the Gradient Editor dialog box. The Blue, Yellow, Blue gradient appears in the gradient ramp in the dialog box. The color stops on the gradient ramp represent blue, yellow, and blue.

2. **Drag the first color stop all the way to the left, as shown in Figure E-19, then click the Color box below the gradient ramp to open the Color Picker**

   The name of the gradient in the Name text box changes to "Custom" once you begin to modify the existing gradient.

3. **Type 255 in the R text box, type 0 in the G and B text boxes, then click OK**

   The color stop on the gradient ramp has changed to red.

4. **Drag the last color stop all the way to the right, then change its color to 0R/255G/0B**

QUICK TIP
To delete a color stop, drag it straight down and off of the gradient ramp.

5. **Click right below the gradient ramp between the first and second color stops**

   A new color stop is added to the gradient ramp where you click.

6. **Drag the new color stop until the Location text box reads 25%**

   The Location text box indicates where a color stop is positioned on the gradient ramp, from left to right. For example, at 25%, the new color stop is exactly between the first stop at 0% and the middle stop at 50%.

7. **Change the color of the new color stop to 255R/150G/0B**

8. **Type Red, Orange, Yellow, Green in the Name text box, then click the New button**

   As shown in Figure E-20, the new gradient is added to the group of presets in the Gradient Editor.

9. **Click OK, save your work, then close making the gradient_PS-E.psd**

Applying an opacity setting to a gradient stop

When you apply color to a gradient stop, you can also reduce the opacity of the gradient stop. Simply drag the opacity stop at the top of the gradient ramp or drag the Opacity slider in the Stops section to choose a new value. You can add opacity stops by clicking the top of the gradient ramp and remove them by dragging them off of the gradient ramp. Having varying levels of opacity in a gradient can be very visually effective; the gradient will appear more transparent in some areas, more opaque in others. This can be especially effective when you want a gradient to fade in and out of specific areas of a layout.

FIGURE E-18: Clicking the active gradient fill

Last gradient fill used

When the Gradient tool is selected, the last gradient fill used appears on the Options bar

FIGURE E-19: Creating a new gradient

Name changes to Custom once you modify a gradient

Opacity stop

Gradient Ramp

First color stop

Click to change color of selected stop

Last color stop

Middle color stop

FIGURE E-20: Viewing the new gradient in the Gradient Editor

New gradient swatch

Working with Type and Gradients

Clipping a Gradient into Type

Clipping refers to using artwork on one layer to mask the artwork on a layer (or multiple layers) above it. The artwork that functions as the mask is referred to as a **clipping mask**. The simplest example of clipping and a clipping mask would be of a type layer with a layer above it filled with a gradient. If you target the gradient layer and then create a clipping mask, the gradient will be clipped into the type layer beneath it and will be visible only within the type. The transparent areas of the type layer will mask the gradient artwork. The layer functioning as the clipping mask—the type layer in the above example—is referred to as the **base layer**. For artwork to be clipped, it must be immediately above the base layer. Base layers can have multiple layers clipped into them, but all of those layers must be immediately above the base layer on the Layers panel. ▄▄▄▄▄ Jon asks that you clip a gradient into a type headline. You clip the Red, Orange, Yellow, Green gradient into the headline and then move it within the clipping mask to see different parts of the gradient.

STEPS

1. **Open PS E-4.psd, then save it as** clip layers_PS-E

2. **Hide the effects on the Inner Bevel layer, create a new layer above the Inner Bevel layer, then name the new layer** Gradient

3. **Click the** Gradient tool ▦, **then verify that the Red, Orange, Yellow, Green gradient is the active gradient on the Options bar**

4. **Click the** Linear Gradient button ▦ **on the Options bar**

5. **Verify that the Gradient layer is targeted on the Layers panel, position the mouse pointer at the top edge of the canvas, then create a linear gradient from the top to the bottom of the canvas**

   Your canvas should resemble Figure E-21.

6. **Click the** Layers panel menu button ▦, **then click** Create Clipping Mask

   As shown in Figure E-22, the Gradient layer is clipped into the Inner Bevel layer, indicated by the bent arrow on the Gradient layer. The gradient artwork is visible only where there is artwork on the Inner Bevel layer. The gradient artwork is not visible—it is masked—where there are transparent pixels on the Inner Bevel layer.

7. **Click the** Move tool ▦, **then, in one move, drag the gradient artwork straight down so more of the red in the gradient is visible**

   The gradient artwork moves but continues to be masked by the Inner Bevel layer.

8. **Undo the move, click** ▦, **then drag from the top of the letter T to the bottom of the letter T**

9. **Make the Effects layer visible on the Inner Bevel layer, then compare your canvas to Figure E-23**

   The gradient artwork is beveled and embossed. When a layer style is applied to a layer, any artwork that is clipped into the layer will take on the appearance of the layer style.

10. **Save your work**

Saving gradient presets

When you create a gradient in the Gradient Editor dialog box, it will remain available to you in every Photoshop file you open. However, it will not "travel" with the file. In other words, if you email a file with a gradient to a friend, your friend can open the file, but the gradient you created won't appear in his list of gradients. You can save gradients for use on other computers. Click the Save button in the Gradient Editor dialog box. This will save the gradient as a GRD file into the Presets folder in your Photoshop application folder. You can then email to the GRD file or copy it to an external drive and have your gradients with you wherever you go.

FIGURE E-21: Red, Orange, Yellow, Green gradient applied to the canvas

FIGURE E-22: Red, Orange, Yellow, Green gradient masked by the Inner Bevel layer

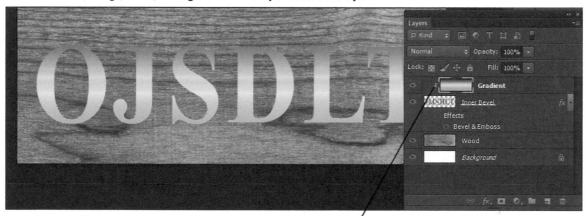

Bent arrow indicates layer is
being clipped into base layer

FIGURE E-23: Making the layer style effect visible

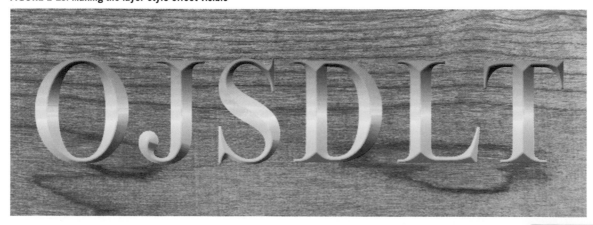

Clipping Imagery into Type

Clipping imagery into type works the same way as clipping a gradient into type, except that you are clipping a picture instead of a gradient fill. A good example of clipping a picture into type would be an old fashioned postcard with the word *FLORIDA* and different scenes of Floridian attractions inside the letters. Clipping an image into type is a classic type of design that is visually interesting and communicates an idea with strength and clarity. Remember, when you clip an image into text that has layer styles applied to it, the image takes on the effects of the layer style. Jon tells you that some of the client's headlines will involve a nature motif and asks that you clip an image of wood grain into the headline.

STEPS

1. **Hide the effects on the Inner Bevel layer**

2. **Drag the Wood layer to the top of the Layers panel**

3. **Click the Layers panel menu button ☰, then click Create Clipping Mask**

   As shown in Figure E-24, the wood artwork is clipped into the Inner Bevel artwork. It's important that you understand that the Wood layer is being clipped into the Inner Bevel layer, not into the Gradient layer immediately beneath it. The gradient artwork has no visual impact on the final artwork because the gradient artwork is beneath the wood artwork.

4. **Show the effects on the Inner Bevel layer, then compare your canvas to Figure E-25**

5. **Save your work, then close clip layers_PS-E.psd**

Clipping layers quickly

Rather than using the Create Clipping Mask command on the Layers panel menu to clip layers, you can use a quick and easy keyboard technique. Let's say you had two layers on the Layers panel—Layer A and Layer B—and you wanted to clip Layer B into Layer A. To do so, press and hold [Alt] (Win) or [option] (Mac), then float your cursor over the line between the two layers on the Layers panel. A square icon with a small black arrow will appear. Click the small black arrow on the line that separates the two layers and the top layer will be clipped into the layer beneath it.

FIGURE E-24: Clipping the Wood layer into the Inner Bevel layer

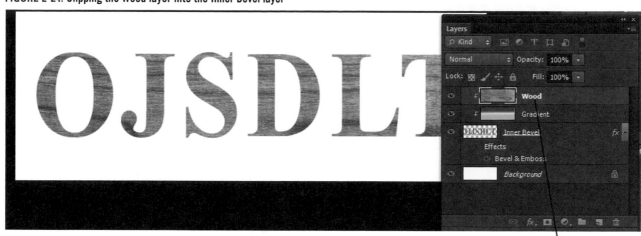

Wood layer is clipped
into Inner Bevel layer

FIGURE E-25: Viewing the artwork with the layer style visible

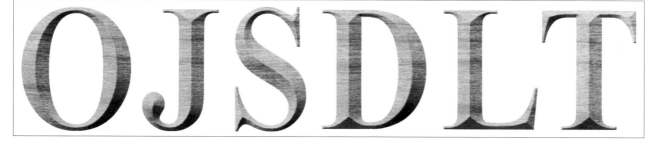

Fading Type

Gradients play an important visual and artistic role when they function as a color element in artwork. Gradients play an important *practical* role when used in layer masks. The fundamental rule of a layer mask is that white areas of the mask reveal 100% of the related artwork on the layer, and black areas of the mask hide or mask 100% of the related artwork on the layer. Therefore, it follows logically that gradients in a layer mask that blend from white to black affect the related artwork as a blend from "revealed" to "masked." Thus, a gradient in a layer mask becomes a powerful tool for gradually fading artwork on the layer. Jon provides you with a stylized headline for the client's website and asks that you use a layer mask to fade it gradually from top to bottom. He tells you to experiment with different fades and to be sure that the headline remains legible even with the fade.

STEPS

1. **Open PS E-5.psd, then save it as** fade type_PS-E

2. **Target the** FADE OUT **layer, then click the** Add layer mask button ▣ **on the Layers panel**
   An all-white layer mask is added to the layer.

3. **Verify that the foreground color is white and the background color is black**

4. **Click the** Gradient tool ▣ **, click the** Click to open Gradient picker list arrow **on the Options bar, then click the** Foreground to Background gradient swatch

5. **Verify that the layer mask is targeted on the Fade Out layer, create a gradient from the top of the type down to the bottom of the type, then compare your result to Figure E-26**
   Because the layer mask was targeted, you applied the gradient to the layer mask. The layer mask gradates from white to black from the top to the bottom of the type. Thus, the type is fully visible at its top edge, completely invisible at its bottom edge, and gradually fades from top to bottom.

6. **Create a gradient from the top of the type down to the bottom of the canvas, then compare your result to Figure E-27**

7. **Press and hold** [Alt] **(Win) or** [option] **(Mac), then click the** layer mask **to view the layer mask**
   The area of the mask that corresponds to the bottom of the type is dark gray, not black. Thus, the type does not fully disappear at its bottom edge.

8. **Press and hold** [Alt] **(Win) or** [option] **(Mac), then click the** layer thumbnail **to view the layer artwork**

9. **Save your work, then close fade type_PS-E.psd**

FIGURE E-26: Fading the type completely

FIGURE E-27: Fading the type, but not completely

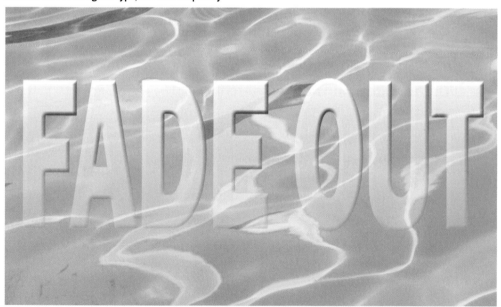

Practice

Concepts Review

Label the elements of the Photoshop screen shown in Figure E-28.

FIGURE E-28

Match each term with the statement that best describes it.

6. **Gradient**
7. **Gloss contour**
8. **Clipping**
9. **Foreground to Background**
10. **Radial gradient**

a. Color blend that radiates outward from its center
b. Name of a default gradient swatch
c. Using one layer's artwork as a mask for another layer's artwork
d. Preset color adjustment applied to layer style for a visual effect
e. Blend between one or more colors

Select the best answer from the list of choices.

11. **Which of the following is not an option in the Layer Style dialog box for formatting a Bevel & Emboss layer style?**
    a. Gloss contour
    b. Size
    c. Technique
    d. Create clipping mask
12. **Which of the following is a type of style available in the Bevel & Emboss layer style dialog box?**
    a. Chisel Hard
    b. Chisel Soft
    c. Inner Bevel
    d. Smooth

13. Which of the following is not true about gloss contours?

    a. They can be used with all styles of bevel and emboss effects.

    b. They can be used only with bevel and emboss layer styles.

    c. They are preset adjustments.

    d. They each have a name.

14. Which of the following is not true about gradients?

    a. All gradients are made with at least two colors.

    b. Some gradients are made with more than two colors.

    c. Radial gradients can gradate from left to right on the canvas.

    d. Linear gradients can move from top to bottom on the canvas.

Skills Review

1. Set type.

    a. Open PS E-6.psd, then save it as **set skills type_PS-E**.

    b. Click the workspace switcher on the Menu bar, then click Typography.

    c. Click the Type tool, then click on the left side of the canvas.

    d. Type the words **Type It**.

    e. Click the Move tool.

    f. On the Character panel, click the Set the font family list arrow, then choose Impact (or a similar typeface).

    g. Set the font size to 96 pt by typing **96** in the Set the font size text box.

    h. Center the type on the page, click the RGB Red swatch on the Swatches panel, then press [Alt][Delete] (Win) or [option][delete] (Mac) to fill the type.

    i. Save your work.

2. Lock transparent pixels.

    a. Verify that the Type It layer is targeted, click Layer on the Menu bar, point to Rasterize, then click Type.

    b. Hide the Background layer.

    c. Press [D] to access the default foreground and background colors.

    d. Press [Alt][Delete] (Win) or [option][delete] (Mac) to fill with the black foreground color.

    e. Undo the fill, then click the Lock transparent pixels icon on the Layers panel.

    f. Fill the layer with the black foreground color.

    g. Click the RGB Magenta swatch on the Swatches panel, click the Brush tool, set the Size to 50, then set the Hardness to 100%.

FIGURE E-29

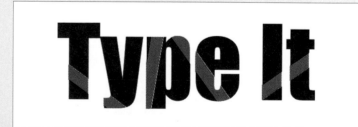

    h. Paint different areas of the type magenta, then compare your result to Figure E-29.

    i. Show the Background layer, save your work, then close set skills type_PS-E.psd.

3. Create bevel and emboss effects on type.

    a. Open PS E-7.psd, save it as **bevel skills type_PS-E**, then click the HEADLINE layer on the Layers panel.

    b. Click Layer on the Menu bar, point to Layer Style, then click Bevel & Emboss.

    c. Set the Style to Emboss, set the Technique to Smooth, then set the Depth to 100%.

    d. Set the Size to 24, set the Soften value to 0, then click OK.

    e. Double-click the Bevel & Emboss layer style on the Layers panel to reopen the dialog box.

    f. Set the Style to Inner Bevel, set the Technique to Chisel Hard, then set the Depth to 100%.

Skills Review (continued)

   g. Set the Size to 48, set the Soften value to 0, then click OK.

   h. Save your work.

4. Apply gloss contours to layer styles.

   a. Double-click the Bevel & Emboss layer style on the Layers panel to open the dialog box.

   b. Click the gloss contour named Cone.

   c. Click the Anti-aliased check box, then click OK.

   d. Save your work.

5. Create a double emboss effect.

   a. Duplicate the Headline layer, rename the new layer **Inner Bevel**, then hide it.

   b. Target the Headline layer, then rename it **Outer Bevel**.

   c. Drag the Indicates layer effects icon on the Outer Bevel layer to the Delete layer button on the Layers panel.

   d. Click Layer on the Menu bar, point to Layer Style, then click Bevel & Emboss.

   e. Set the Style to Outer Bevel, set the Technique to Chisel Hard, then set the Depth to 100%.

   f. Set the Size to 12, then set the Soften value to 0.

   g. Apply the Ring gloss contour, then click to activate the Anti-aliased check box, if necessary.

   h. Click OK, then show the Inner Bevel layer.

   i. Save your work, then close bevel skills type_PS-E.psd.

6. Apply a gradient.

   a. Open PS E-8.psd, then save it as **gradient skills_PS-E**.

   b. Click the Gradient tool, click the Linear Gradient button on the Options bar, then click the Click to open Gradient picker list arrow on the Options bar.

   c. Click the Copper swatch.

   d. Position the mouse pointer at the left edge of the canvas, click and drag to the right edge of the canvas, then release the mouse button.

   e. Click and drag from the top of the canvas to the bottom of the canvas.

   f. Click and drag from the upper-left to the lower-right corner of the canvas.

   g. Click approximately one-half inch in from the left edge of the canvas and drag left to right for approximately one inch.

   h. Click the Radial Gradient button on the Options bar.

   i. Repeat Step g, then save your work.

FIGURE E-30

Skills Review (continued)

7. **Create a new gradient.**

   a. Click the active gradient fill on the Options bar to open the Gradient Editor dialog box.

   b. Click the Blue, Red, Yellow swatch.

   c. Drag the left color stop all the way to the left (if necessary), then click the Color box below the gradient ramp.

   d. Type **0** in the R text box, **255** in the G text box, and **255** in the B text box, then click OK.

   e. Click the far right color stop, drag it all the way to the right, then change its color to **210R/0G/255B**.

   f. Click immediately below the gradient ramp between the first and second color stops.

   g. Drag the new color stop so that the Location text box reads 35%.

   h. Change the color of the new color stop to white.

   i. Name the new gradient **Cyan To Purple**, as shown in Figure E-30, then click the New button.

   j. Click OK, save your work, then close gradient skills_PS-E.psd.

8. **Clip a gradient into type.**

   a. Open PS E-9.psd then save it as **skills clip layers_PS-E**.

   b. Hide the effects on the Inner Bevel layer, create a new layer above the Inner Bevel layer, then name the new layer **Gradient**.

   c. Click the Gradient tool, then verify that the Cyan To Purple gradient is the active gradient.

   d. Verify that the new layer is targeted on the Layers panel, position the mouse pointer at the top edge of the letters, then create a linear gradient from the top to the bottom of the letters.

   e. Click the Layers panel menu button, then click Create Clipping Mask.

   f. Click the Move tool, then, in one move, click and drag the gradient artwork straight down so other areas of the gradient become visible.

   g. Undo the move.

   h. Make the effects visible on the Inner Bevel layer, then save your work.

9. **Clip imagery into type.**

   a. Hide the effects on the Inner Bevel layer.

   b. Move the Granite layer to the top of the Layers panel.

   c. Click the Layers panel menu button, then click Create Clipping Mask.

   d. Show the effects on the Inner Bevel layer, then compare your result to Figure E-31.

   e. Save your work, then close skills clip layers_PS-E.psd.

FIGURE E-31

Skills Review (continued)

10. Fade type.

    a. Open PS E-10.psd, then save it as **fade skills type_PS-E**.

    b. Target the FADE AWAY layer, then click the Add layer mask button on the Layers panel.

    c. Press [D] to access default foreground and background colors. (If necessary, click the Switch foreground and background colors button so that your foreground color is white and your background color is black.)

    d. Click the Gradient tool, click the Click to open Gradient picker list arrow, then click the Foreground to Background gradient swatch.

    e. Verify that the layer mask is targeted in the FADE AWAY layer, then create a gradient from the left edge of the letter F to the right edge of the letter Y.

    f. Create a gradient from the middle of the letter D to the right edge of the canvas, then compare your result to Figure E-32.

    g. Press and hold [Alt] (Win) or [option] (Mac), then click the layer mask to view the layer mask.

    h. Press and hold [Alt] (Win) or [option] (Mac), then click the layer thumbnail to view the layer artwork.

    i. Save your work, then close fade skills type_PS-E.psd.

FIGURE E-32

Independent Challenge 1

A clothing line named Black On Blue has asked your company to design a simple sign for them to use at a trade show. The client asks that you use just a "basic" typeface and to do something with color to "make it a little bit more interesting" than just black type on a white background.

    a. Open PS E-11.psd, then save it as **black on blue_PS-E**.

    b. Press [D] to access the default foreground and background colors.

    c. Click the Type tool, then type the words **BLACK ON BLUE** in all uppercase letters.

    d. Click the Move tool, then open the Character panel.

    e. Apply the Impact font or a similar bold font.

    f. Change the font size to 60 pts, then fill the type with the RGB Blue swatch.

    g. Click the Move tool, then center the text on the canvas.

    h. Rasterize the type.

    i. Click the Rectangle Marquee tool, then create a rectangular marquee around the entire top half of the rasterized type.

    j. Press [D] to access the default foreground and background colors.

    k. Lock the transparent pixels, then fill the selection with the black foreground color.

    l. Deselect, then compare your result to Figure E-33.

    m. Save your work, close black on blue_PS-E.psd, then exit Photoshop.

FIGURE E-33

BLACK ON BLUE

Independent Challenge 2

One of your luxury hotel clients has asked your firm to design a postcard for one of their daily evening events. The only design advice that they give you is that they want something "eye-catching."

a. Open PS E-12.psd, then save it as **sunset gradient_PS-E**.

b. Fill the Background layer with black, then lock transparent pixels on both of the type layers.

c. Fill the type on the two type layers with white.

d. Open the Gradient Editor dialog box.

e. Click the Red, Green gradient swatch.

f. Change the color of the left color stop to 255R/228G/0B.

g. Change the color of the right color stop to 0R/0G/0B.

h. Add a third color stop between the first and second color stops.

i. Change the color of the new color stop to 255R/0G/0B, then change its location to 75%.

j. Add a new color stop between the first color stop and the new color stop.

k. Change the color of the new color stop to 255R/132G/0B, change its location to 50%.

l. Name the new gradient **Sunset Gradient**, click New, then click OK.

m. Create a new layer above the Sunset type layer, then name the new layer **Sunset Gradient**.

FIGURE E-34

n. Click the Gradient tool, then verify that Sunset Gradient is the active gradient on the Options bar.

o. Position your cursor at the top edge of the SUNSET type, then create a linear gradient from the top of the SUNSET type to the bottom of the SUNSET type.

p. Click the Layers panel menu button, then click Create Clipping Mask.

q. Compare your canvas to Figure E-34.

r. Save your work, close sunset gradient_PS-E.psd, then exit Photoshop.

Independent Challenge 3

Your firm's hotel client calls and says that he would like you to make changes to a postcard you previously designed. He requests that you define the type a little better by adding a stroke. He asks for "something interesting," not just a "boring white stroke."

   a. Open PS E-13.psd, then save it as **sunset stroke emboss_PS-E**.

   b. Click the SUNSET layer on the Layers panel.

   c. Click Layer on the Menu bar, point to Layer Style, then click Stroke.

   d. Click the Set color of stroke swatch, type **128** in the R, G, and B text boxes, then click OK.

   e. Set the Size to 10, then set the Position to Center.

   f. In the Styles column at the left of the dialog box, click the words Bevel & Emboss.

FIGURE E-35

   g. Set the Style to Stroke Emboss, set the Technique to Chisel Hard, then set the Depth to 110%.

   h. Set the Size to 2, then set the Soften value to 0.

   i. Click the Gloss Contour list arrow, click the Gaussian gloss contour, then verify that the Anti-aliased check box is checked.

   j. Click OK, then compare your result to Figure E-35.

Advanced Challenge Exercise

- Double-click the Bevel & Emboss layer style on the Layers panel.
- Drag the Highlight Mode opacity slider to 100%.
- Click the Set color for highlight swatch, type **255R/255G/0B**, then click OK.
- Click OK to close the Layer Style dialog box.

   k. Save your work, then close sunset stroke emboss_PS-E.psd.

Real Life Independent Challenge

Your best friend is getting married and has planned many activities during the weekend leading up to the wedding ceremony. He asks you to help him create an invitation for a special bonfire on the beach two nights before the wedding. You choose an image of a beach scene, duplicate it to create a sunset scene, then clip the sunset artwork into type.

    a. Open PS E-14.psd, then save it as **sunset clipped_PS-E**.

    b. Verify that only the Background and Original layers are showing on the Layers panel.

    c. Show, then hide the Sunset layer, comparing the artwork to the Original artwork. (*Hint*: The Sunset artwork is a duplicate of the Original artwork. It has been colorized orange, and sunset artwork has been added at the center.)

    d. Show all layers, then drag the Sunset layer above the HEADLINE layer.

    e. Clip the Sunset layer into the HEADLINE layer.

    f. Add a white layer mask to the Sunset layer.

    g. Set the foreground and background colors to white and black.

    h. Click the Gradient tool, then click the Foreground to Background gradient swatch.

    i. Position the mouse pointer halfway up from the base of the letter N.

    j. Drag down, releasing the mouse button at the base of the letter N, to create a linear gradient in the mask.

    k. Duplicate the Original layer.

    l. Drag the Original copy layer above the HEADLINE layer.

    m. Duplicate the Sunset layer, then drag the Sunset copy layer to the top of the Layers panel.

    n. Delete the layer mask on the Sunset copy layer without applying the mask.

    o. Clip the Sunset copy layer into the type layer beneath it.

    p. With the Sunset copy layer still targeted, drag the Opacity slider on the Layers panel to 70%.

    q. Compare your Layers panel and your artwork to Figure E-36.

FIGURE E-36

Advanced Challenge Exercise

- Double-click the Bevel & Emboss layer style on the Layers panel.
- Click the Use Global Light check box to remove the check mark.
- Change the Angle to 180°.
- Click OK to close the Layer Style dialog box.

    r. Save your work, then close sunset clipped_PS-E.psd.

Visual Workshop

Open PS E-15.psd, then save it as **radial gradient_PS-E**. Create and apply a gradient so that your canvas resembles Figure E-37.

FIGURE E-37

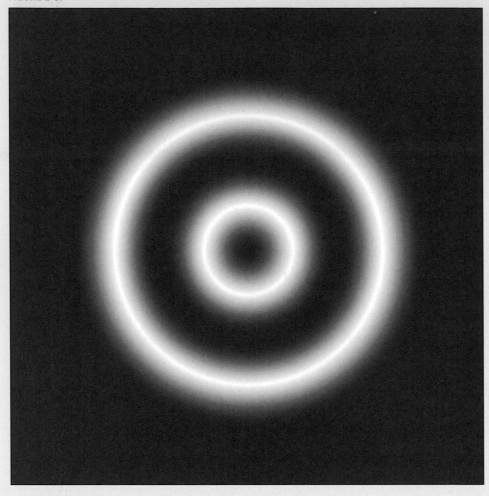

Working with Brushes and Color Effects

Manipulating color in Photoshop tends to take on two different roles: improving realistic color to make a better image or creating special effects with color. In Unit D, you used adjustment layers to improve color in color images. In this unit, you will use a variety of techniques to create color effects. These techniques include adjustment layers, layer masks, and color adjustment utilities.

Because many color effects involve using layer masks with adjustments, working effectively with the Brush tool and the Brush panel becomes an important set of skills. You use brushes for both practical and artistic painting effects. Of all the Photoshop panels, the Brush panel is arguably the most multi-faceted and complex. In many ways, you never stop learning about brushes and using them effectively. Jon assigns you many different projects, all of which need improvements in color.

OBJECTIVES

Create custom brushes

Paint with automatic brush strokes

Paint a complex mask

Understand the Color Picker

Modify color with the Hue/Saturation adjustment

Use the Replace Color dialog box

Use the Black & White adjustment

"Colorize" a Black & White adjustment

Creating Custom Brushes

Photoshop comes with hundreds of brushes on the Brush panel, but many designers like to create their own set of brushes with specific characteristics. You can save the brushes you create as custom brushes. The two most basic characteristics of a brush are the size (the diameter of the brush) and the hardness (how hard or soft the edge of the brush is). ▓▓▓ Jon asks you to create two medium-sized brushes—one hard-edged, one soft—to use for future projects.

STEPS

1. Open PS F-1.psd, then save it as connect the dots_PS-F

2. Target the Hard Brush layer on the Layers panel

3. Click the Brush tool ✎, click Window on the Menu bar, then click Brush to open the Brush panel

TROUBLE
If your Brush panel has the Shape Dynamics check box checked, click the check box to remove the check mark.

4. Scroll to the top of the Brush panel, then click the brush named Hard Round 30 or a similar sized hard brush

   As shown in Figure F-1, the Brush panel shows a preview of the Hard Round 30 brush stroke. The Smoothing check box is checked on the Brush panel. The Smoothing option produces smoother curves when you make brush strokes. This option is most effective when you are using a stylus pen rather than a mouse.

5. Drag the Size slider on the Brush panel to 31 px

6. Drag the Hardness slider to 0%

7. Click the Brush panel menu button ▼ then click New Brush Preset

   The Brush Name dialog box opens. The name given to the new brush is Soft Round 31 1.

8. Click OK

   The new brush is added to the Brush panel and is automatically selected.

9. Drag the Hardness slider to 100%, click ▼, click New Brush Preset, then click OK

   A new brush named Hard Round 31 1 is selected on the Brush panel.

Turning off Shape Dynamics

The Shape Dynamics option, when activated, offers you greater control for painting, such as using a brush that fades or a brush that responds to the pressure you apply when painting. Shape Dynamics are essentially programmed for people using a pressure-sensitive stylus pen instead of a mouse. For this entire chapter, be sure that the Shape Dynamics option is not checked when you select a brush. This is not as simple as it sounds, because many brushes on the Brush panel have been designed with Shape Dynamics as their default setting, and therefore Shape Dynamics could be activated automatically when you select a brush.

FIGURE F-1: Brush panel

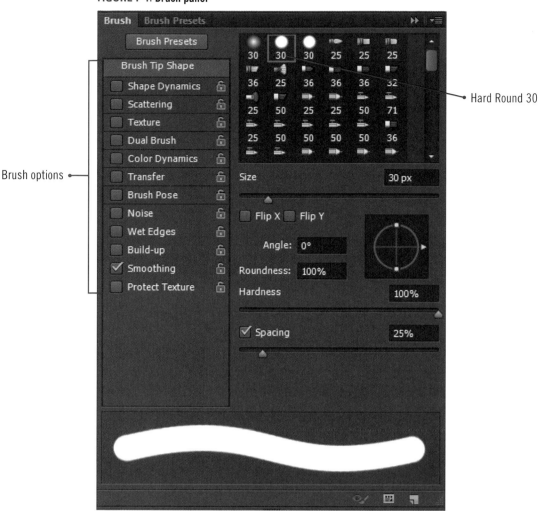

Brush options •

Hard Round 30

Setting preferences for brushes

The paintbrush cursor for the Brush tool does not change when you change the size of the brush you are using. However, you can change the preference settings for painting cursors in the Cursors section of the Preferences dialog box, as shown in Figure F-2. Notice that the Normal Brush Tip is the default option. To change this option, click Edit (Win) or Photoshop (Mac) on the Menu bar, point to Preferences, click Cursors, then choose a new option, such as Full Size Brush Tip. The Full Size Brush Tip setting displays the Brush tool icon as a circle representing the size and shape of the Brush tool.

FIGURE F-2: Preferences for painting cursors

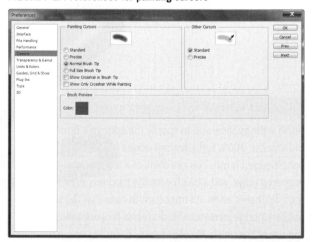

Working with Brushes and Color Effects

"Colorizing" a Black & White Adjustment

There are many techniques for adding color to a black and white image to create a "colorized" effect. One of the simplest is to use the layer mask on a Black & White adjustment layer to introduce the black and white adjustment in different strengths to different areas of the image. Jon emails you a color image with a Black & White adjustment layer. He asks that you create a "colorized" effect by gradually fading in color to one area of the image.

STEPS

1. **Open PS F-6.psd, then save it as** colorize_PS-F

2. **Hide and show the Black & White adjustment layer**

3. **Target the** layer mask, **click** Edit **on the Menu bar, then click** Fill

4. **Enter the settings shown in Figure F-15, then click** OK
   A small amount of color shows in the image.

5. **Undo the fill, select all, click** Edit **on the Menu bar, then click** Copy Merged
   The composite image (the image as it appears) is copied.

6. **With the entire canvas still selected, press and hold** [Alt] **(Win) or** [option] **(Mac) then click the** layer mask thumbnail
   You are now viewing the layer mask.

7. **Click** Edit **on the Menu bar, point to** Paste Special, **click** Paste Into, **then deselect**
   The black and white image is pasted into the layer mask.

8. **Click the** Black & White adjustment thumbnail **to view the image, then compare your result to Figure F-16**

9. **Hide and Show the adjustment to see a before and after view of the image**
   The effect is subtle and effective.

10. **Save your work, then close colorize_PS-F.psd**
    Be sure the Black & White adjustment layer is showing when you are done.

Working with Brushes and Color Effects

FIGURE F-15: Fill dialog box

FIGURE F-16: Colorize effect

Working with Brushes and Color Effects

Practice

Concepts Review

Label the elements of the Photoshop screen shown in Figure F-17.

FIGURE F-17

1. _____   4. _____

2. _____   5. _____

3. _____

Match each term with the statement that best describes it.

6. **Hue**   a. Brush setting that defines a brush's diameter

7. **Saturation**   b. Modifies color based on sampling

8. **Replace Color**   c. Photoshop panel

9. **Brush**   d. Photoshop adjustment

10. **Black & White**   e. Defines a brush's edge

11. **[Shift]**   f. Intensity of a color

12. **Hardness**   g. Name of a color

13. **Size**   h. Used when creating automatic brush strokes

Select the best answer from the list of choices.

14. **Which of the following is not a Photoshop color adjustment?**
    a. Hue/Saturation
    b. Black & White
    c. Replace Color
    d. Color Balance

15. **Which of the following cannot be used to make a color file appear as black and white?**
    a. Black & White adjustment
    b. Hue/Saturation adjustment
    c. Convert to Grayscale
    d. Vibrancy adjustment

16. **Which key is involved in making automatic brush strokes?**
    a. Alt/option
    b. Shift
    c. Ctrl
    d. Spacebar

17. **Which of the following is not an option for defining a brush?**
    a. Length
    b. Size
    c. Hardness
    d. Shape Dynamics

18. **Which of the following is a component of the Replace Color dialog box?**
    a. Brightness/Contrast
    b. Levels
    c. Color Balance
    d. Hue/Saturation

Skills Review

1. **Create custom brushes.**
    a. Open PS F-7.psd, then save it as **dots_PS-F**.
    b. Click the Brush tool, then on the Brush panel, click the brush named Hard Round 30 pixels or a similar size hard brush.
    c. Remove the check mark in the Shape Dynamics check box, if necessary.
    d. Drag the Size slider on the Brush panel to 37, drag the Hardness slider to 0%, click the Brush panel menu button, then click New Brush Preset.
    e. Accept the name Soft Round 37 1 in the Name text box, then click OK.
    f. Drag the Hardness slider to 100%, click the Brush panel menu button, click the New Brush Preset command, accept the name Hard Round 37 1 in the Name text box, then click OK.

2. **Paint with automatic brush strokes.**
    a. Verify that the Hard Round 37 brush is selected on the Brush panel and that the Foreground color is set to black.
    b. Press [ ] multiple times to enlarge the size of the brush to 80 pixels.
    c. Target the Hard Brush layer, then click point #1 on the canvas.
    d. Press and hold [Shift], then click point #2.
    e. Using the same method, click each point through point #6, then target the Soft Brush layer on the Layers panel.
    f. Click the Soft Round 37 brush on the Brush panel, then change the Foreground color to white.
    g. Click where point #1 would be if it were visible, press and hold [Shift], then click point #2.
    h. Using the same method, click each point through point #6.
    i. Save your work, then close dots_PS-F.psd.

3. **Paint a complex mask.**
    a. Open PS F-8.psd, save it as **heels_PS-F**, then hide and show the adjustment layer to see the effect of the color adjustment.
    b. Zoom in to 400% to get a sense of the hardness of the edge pixels where the shoe meets the satin background.
    c. Zoom out to 300%, click the Brush tool, click the Hard Round 37 brush on the Brush panel, set the Hardness to 55%, then verify that the Foreground color is set to black.
    d. Using the automatic brush strokes technique, paint in the layer mask completely around the striped upper part of the shoe (not the wooden sole or heel). (*Hint*: Reduce and enlarge the size of the brush as you see fit.)
    e. Paint to mask the satin background within the ankle strap.

Skills Review (continued)

f. Press [Alt] (Win) or [option] (Mac), click the layer mask to view it, click the Magic Wand tool, set the Tolerance to 8, then verify that the Contiguous check box is checked.

g. Click the white background to select it, click Select on the Menu bar, point to Modify, then click Expand.

h. Type **8** in the Expand By text box, click OK, then fill the selection with black.

i. Click the adjustment layer thumbnail to view the artwork, then deselect the black selection.

j. Click to activate the layer mask, then mask the metal buckle and the white interior of the shoe from the adjustment.

k. Save your work, and keep the file open.

4. Understand the Color Picker.

a. Click the Foreground color button on the Tools panel to open the Color Picker, verify that the H option button is activated, then drag the Hue slider up and down, noting the changes to the H value.

b. Drag the slider until the H value reads 185.

c. Click and drag in the large color box to the left of the Hue slider, and note the changes to the new box as you drag.

d. Continue clicking and dragging and note the changes to the H, S, and B text boxes.

e. Drag the circle all the way to the upper-right corner of the color box.

f. Drag down along the right edge of the color box.

g. Click the upper-left corner, then drag down along the left edge of the color box.

h. Click near the center of the color box, then drag the circle right and left, noting the changes to the S text box and the new box.

i. Click near the center, then drag slowly toward the upper-right corner.

j. Click Cancel to close the Color Picker dialog box.

5. Modify color with the Hue/Saturation adjustment.

a. On the Info panel, click the eyedropper icon on the first readout, then click HSB Color to change the display to HSB (if necessary).

b. Double-click the layer thumbnail (not the mask thumbnail) on the Layers panel to show the Hue/Saturation adjustment layer.

c. Drag the Hue slider right to +69, then sample the canvas to see the before and after values on the Info panel.

FIGURE F-18

d. Drag the Hue slider left to –56.

e. Drag the Saturation slider right to +30.

f. Drag the Saturation slider left to –100.

g. Hide and show the Hue/Saturation adjustment layer.

h. Save your work, compare your screen to Figure F-18, then close heels_PS-F.psd.

6. Use the Replace Color dialog box.

a. Open PS F-9.psd, then save it as **replace color skills_PS-F**.

b. Duplicate the Background layer, rename the duplicate **Replace Color**, click Image on the Menu bar, point to Adjustments, then click Replace Color.

c. Drag the Fuzziness slider to 36, click the Eyedropper tool in the Replace Color dialog box, then click a light green area on the sandal.

d. Drag the Fuzziness slider to 70.

e. Drag the Hue slider left to –139.

f. Click the Add to Sample tool, then click in the dark green shadow area created by the sandal strap.

g. Use the Add to Sample tool to click a remaining green pixel in the sandal, if you can see one.

h. Click OK, then hide and show the Replace Color layer, if you can see one.

i. Add a layer mask and quickly mask any part of the Replace Color layer that may have affected the background.

j. Save your work, then close replace color skills_PS-F.psd.

Skills Review (continued)

7. Use the Black & White adjustment.

   a. Open PS F-10.psd, save it as **b & w skills_PS-F**, duplicate the Background layer, then rename it **Desaturate**.

   b. Press [Ctrl][U] (Win) or ⌘[U] (Mac) to open the Hue/Saturation dialog box, drag the Saturation slider all the way left to –100, then click OK.

   c. Hide the Desaturate layer, then target the Background layer.

   d. Click the Create new fill or adjustment layer button on the Layers panel, then click Black & White.

   e. Drag sliders in different directions to experiment with various results.

   f. Click the Reset to adjustment defaults button on the Properties panel.

   g. Drag the Blues slider to –14, then drag the Cyans slider to 20.

   h. Drag the Reds slider to 50, then drag the Yellows slider to 85.

   i. Show and hide the Desaturate layer to compare the quality of the two different results.

   j. Save your work.

8. "Colorize" a Black & White adjustment.

   a. Verify that the Desaturate layer is hidden.

   b. Target the layer mask on the B&W adjustment layer, click Edit on the Menu bar, then click Fill.

   c. Click the Use arrow, click Black, change the Opacity to 10%, then click OK.

   d. Click the Brush tool, set the Size to 1500, set the Hardness to 0%, then set the Opacity to 20%.

   e. Position the brush at the center of the girl's face, then click two times. (*Hint:* Click additional times if necessary.)

   f. Press [three times to reduce the brush size to 1200, then click the image twice.

   g. Press [three times, then click the image twice.

   h. Repeat Step g until your result resembles Figure F-19.

   i. Save your work, then close b & w skills_PS-F.psd.

FIGURE F-19

Independent Challenge 1

You need an image of a stop sign for a website, so you snap a picture with your digital camera, copy it into Photoshop, then use a layer mask to isolate the sign from the background.

   a. Open PS F-11.psd, then save it as **stop sign_PS-F**.

   b. Duplicate the Background layer, name the new layer **Stop Sign**, then fill the Background layer with black.

   c. Add a layer mask to the Stop Sign layer, then click the Brush tool.

   d. Choose a brush size of 27 px, then set the Hardness to what you think is best to outline an image of a stop sign.

   e. Use the automatic brushes technique to mask the outline of the sign quickly.

FIGURE F-20

   f. Switch to view the layer mask itself.

   g. Select the white background of the layer mask—*outside* of the strokes you painted—with the Magic Wand tool.

   h. Expand the selection by 6 pixels so that the selection of the white background overlaps slightly the black strokes you painted.

   i. Fill the selection with black.

   j. Deselect the mask, click the Stop Sign layer thumbnail, then compare your result to Figure F-20.

   k. Save your work, then close stop sign_PS-F.psd.

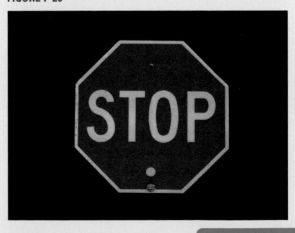

Independent Challenge 2

You're designing a catalogue for a children's clothing company. Your client emails you a photo to use but tells you that they would prefer to show the dress in green rather than blue. You decide that using the Replace Color dialog box will be the best method for making a color change on such non-selectable areas.

a. Open PS F-12.psd, then save it as **green dress_PS-F**.

b. Duplicate the Background layer, rename the duplicate **Green Dress**, click Image on the Menu bar, point to Adjustments, then click Replace Color.

c. Drag the Fuzziness slider to 36, click the Eyedropper tool in the Replace Color dialog box, then click a light blue area on the left sleeve of the dress.

d. Click the Add to Sample tool, then click in a darker blue area inside the same sleeve.

e. Drag the Fuzziness slider to 70.

f. Drag the Hue slider left to –55.

FIGURE F-21

g. With the Add to Sample tool, click in the dark blue shadow area underneath the camera.

h. Use the Add to Sample tool to click any noticeable blue area (if necessary).

i. Click OK, then hide and show the Green Dress layer.

j. Add a layer mask and quickly mask any part of the Green Dress layer that may have affected the background, especially above the hat. (*Hint*: In this case, it would be a smart idea to mask the face and hair whether or not you see any changes—just to be sure.)

k. Save your work, compare your screen to Figure F-21, then close green dress_PS-F.psd.

Independent Challenge 3

You design a monthly newsletter, and you've run into a tricky problem. The newsletter is printed in black and white, but your client has given you a *very* colorful image to include in this month's edition. You decide to use a few different methods to create black and white from color so you'll have options for picking the best result.

a. Open PS F-13.psd, save it as **newsletter_PS-F**, duplicate the Background layer, then rename it **Desaturate**.

b. Open the Hue/Saturation dialog box, then drag the Saturation slider all the way left to –100.

c. Hide the Desaturate layer, then target the Background layer.

d. Create a new Black & White adjustment layer.

e. Drag sliders in different directions to experiment with various results. (*Hint*: An interesting situation with this image is that the actual colors are not really important once adjusted. It doesn't really matter, for example, if the original yellows get darker than the original reds. Now that this is a black and white image, all that matters is that the result is black and white with many grays—a full range of grays.)

f. Click the Reset to adjustment defaults button on the Properties panel.

g. Drag the Yellows slider to 28, drag the Reds slider to 28, then drag the Greens slider to 44.

h. Drag the Cyans slider to 43, drag the Blues slider to 101, then drag the Magentas slider to 77.

i. Hide and show the Desaturate layer to compare the quality of the two different results, then hide the Desaturate layer.

Independent Challenge 3 (continued)

Advanced Challenge Exercise

- Target the Background layer.
- Click Image on the Menu bar, point to Mode, then click Grayscale.
- Click OK in the warning box about the adjustment layer being discarded, then click Discard when you are asked to confirm the conversion.
- Compare the Grayscale conversion on the Background layer to the artwork on the Desaturate layer.

j. Compare your results to Figure F-22, save your work, then close newsletter_PS-F.psd.

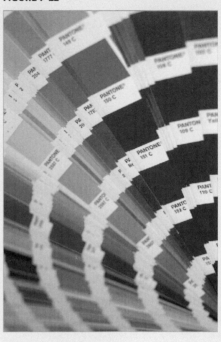

Real Life Independent Challenge

You're a graphic designer, and you're creating icons for a website. The theme is adding multiple colors to random, everyday items, items that are known for being just a single color. To apply different colors to different areas of the image, you need to use layer masks and layers creatively.

a. Open PS F-14.psd, then save it as **pylon_PS-F**.
b. Duplicate the Background layer, name the new layer **Pylon**, then fill the Background layer with white.
c. Add a layer mask to the Pylon layer, then click the Brush tool.
d. Set the Hardness to what you think is best to outline an image of a pylon.
e. Use your best brush techniques to mask the background—without a shadow—completely.
f. Duplicate the Pylon layer, then name then new layer **Shadow**.
g. Drag the Shadow layer down below the Pylon layer.
h. Hide the Pylon layer.
i. Fill the layer mask on the Shadow layer with white.
j. Using a large soft brush, mask everything except the base of the pylon and the shadow beneath the base.
k. Show the Pylon layer.

Advanced Challenge Exercise

- Click the Foreground Color button on the Tools panel.
- Drag the Hue slider up approximately half way until you see green in the color box.
- Click and drag in the large color box, then note the HSB values and the RGB values.
- Click Cancel to close the Color Picker dialog box.

l. Save your work, compare your screen to Figure F-23, then close pylon_PS-F.psd.

FIGURE F-23

Visual Workshop

Open PS F-15.psd, then save it as **snow cones_PS-F**. Duplicate the original cone and its shadow to produce two more cones. Position the two new cones on either side of the original cone, then reduce their sizes so that they appear to be behind the center cone. Apply adjustment layers to change the colors of the cones so that your result resembles Figure F-24.

FIGURE F-24

Creating Special Effects

Files You Will Need:

To view a list of files needed for this unit, see the Data Files Grid in the back of the book.

When you study Photoshop, you learn one thing at a time. When you practice Photoshop, you practice one thing at a time. But when you work in Photoshop—really work on a full-scale project—you must use *many* skills in tandem to achieve your goal. This unit will be a good opportunity for you to make a shift in consciousness and really start looking at Photoshop in a "big picture" sense. You can learn exactly what all the tools and commands and panels in Photoshop do, but it's up to you and your own artistic sense to decide *when* to use them, and to what effect. Photoshop does not make "art" any more than a paintbrush or a palette knife does. Photoshop is simply a collection of tools, commands, and layers that are available to you, the artist, to create your own designs. Photoshop doesn't make art—you do. Jon tells you about a new client that is well known for their cutting-edge graphics. To prepare you for working with them, he asks you to test out various special effects using blending modes, filters, and transformations.

OBJECTIVES

Use the Color blending mode

Use the Multiply blending mode

Add noise with the Overlay blending mode

Sharpen with the High Pass filter

Apply the Lens Flare filter with Screen mode

Apply the Motion Blur filter

Apply non-destructive filters

Distort images

Using the Color Blending Mode

Blending modes are mathematical algorithms that define how pixels affect pixels beneath them to create a specific effect. You can apply blending modes throughout many Photoshop features—like layer styles—but they are most prominent on the Layers panel and as options with specific tools, like the Brush tool. The best way to think of blending modes is to think about three colors: the **base color** is the color of the original pixel; the **blend color** is the color being applied; and the **result color** is the color produced by combining the first two colors using the blending mode. The Color blending mode is very useful for colorizing monochromatic images. It applies the hue of the blend pixel to the base pixel and automatically affects the saturation of the base pixel so that the base pixel beneath it takes on the color of the blend pixel. █████ A new client at MegaPixel delivers an image to you and asks you to colorize it for them to use on their website. Jon tells you to do the work using the Color blending mode.

STEPS

1. **Open PS G-1.psd, save it as** colorize with color mode_PS-G, **click the** Create new fill or adjustment layer button 🔳, **on the Layers panel, then click** Solid Color
   The Color Picker dialog box opens.

2. **Change the color to** 134R/154G/174B, **click OK, click the** blending mode list arrow **on the Layers panel, click** Color, **then compare your Layers panel and image to Figure G-1**
   The hues of all the base pixels take on the hue of the blend layer. The saturation of the base pixels is automatically adjusted. The brightness values of the base pixels are not affected.

3. **Using the** Brush tool 🖌️, **paint black in the layer mask so that the change in color affects only the background area of the image, not the woman**

4. **Create a new layer above the Color Fill 1 layer, name the layer** Sweater, **then set the blending mode to** Color

5. **Set the foreground color to** 196R/223G/155B, **then paint the sweater green**
   Because the blending mode of the layer is set to Color, any color you paint on the layer will be transparent and will affect the color of the artwork on layers beneath.

6. **Create a new Hue/Saturation adjustment layer, then set the blending mode for the layer to** Color

7. **Click the** Colorize check box **on the Properties panel, set the Hue to** 35, **then set the Saturation to** 30
   The adjustment affects the entire image. The Colorize option is necessary to apply color to a black-and-white image. You can read more about the Colorize option on the next page.

8. **Name the layer** Face, **then use a layer mask so that the Hue/Saturation adjustment affects the face and the lips, but not the eyes, as shown in Figure G-2**

9. **Using the same method you used in Steps 6 through 8, create three more Hue/Saturation adjustment layers with different values for Hue and Saturation, to finish colorizing other areas of the image, like the eyes, lips and hair**
   Figure G-3 shows one potential result.

10. **Save your work, then close the file**

FIGURE G-1: Solid color blended over the image

FIGURE G-2: Painting in a layer set to Color mode

FIGURE G-3: Colorized image

Using the Colorize option on the Hue/Saturation Properties panel

The Colorize option on the Hue/Saturation Properties panel is necessary to colorize a black-and-white image. Normally, moving the Hue and Saturation sliders on the Hue/Saturation Properties panel modifies the existing hue and saturation values of selected pixels. In a black-and-white image, however, all of the pixels have a saturation value of 0. Therefore, any adjustments you make in the Hue/Saturation-adjustment to black-and-white base art will have no effect; you can't modify color where there is no color in the first place. The Colorize option overrides the 0% saturation of the base art and allows you to apply Hue/Saturation color adjustments to the base pixels. Remember, whenever you want to use the Hue/Saturation dialog box to apply color to black-and-white art, you must also activate the Colorize option.

Using the Multiply Blending Mode

Imagine you had a black–and-white printed image, and you placed a sheet of red transparent film over that image. If you can imagine what the image would look like through the red film, that's a great analogy for the Multiply blending mode. Multiply is perhaps the most common blending mode. It makes the blend pixels transparent, and any base art will be seen *through* that color. That's why Multiply mode is always used when creating shadows and drop shadows: shadows in nature are always transparent. Two important things to remember about Multiply mode: when you multiply black, the result is always black, and when you multiply white, white always becomes 100% transparent. ▰▰ Jon mentions a project you worked on a long time ago. The client has asked that the art be more "eye-catching." Jon suggests you use Multiply blending effects for the layered artwork.

STEPS

1. **Open PS G-2.psd, then save it as** final roman holiday_PS-G

2. **Show the Understand Multiply layer, then study it a bit**

3. **Set the Understand Multiply layer blending mode to** Multiply, **then hide and show the Understand Multiply layer to see its effect**

   As shown in Figure G-4, everything becomes transparent, but the black area behind the letter M still appears black because the result of multiplying any color with black is black. The white M becomes completely invisible because white always becomes 100% transparent when multiplied. The black-to-white gradient on the left transitions from black on the top to completely transparent on the bottom.

4. **Hide the Understand Multiply layer, target the** Roses Shadow layer, **then set its blending mode to** Multiply

   The artwork on this layer is a simple gray fill with a feathered edge. When multiplied, it becomes transparent and looks like a realistic shadow.

5. **Change the blending mode of the Couple Shadow layer to** Multiply

   When working with black or very dark colors, the Multiply blending mode effect is not so noticeable. Nevertheless, you should always set the blending mode of any artwork that is functioning as a shadow to Multiply.

6. **Set the blending mode of the Colosseum and Bottom Coin layers to** Multiply

   The images themselves become transparent, creating the effect of seeing the passport background through the images.

7. **Target the hidden** Understand Multiply layer, **click the** Create new fill or adjustment layer button ▣▾ **on the Layers panel, then click** Solid Color

8. **Set the color to** 255R/225G/0B, **click** OK, **then change the blending mode to** Multiply

9. **Reduce the Opacity to 60%, compare your result to Figure G-5, then save your work**

Brightness and the Color blending mode

It's important to understand the Color blending mode does not in any way affect the brightness value of base pixels; it affects only hue and saturation. This is a critical component of what makes the Color blending mode so effective. Because brightness is not affected, the integrity of the tonal grayscale range from black to white is maintained. Thus, the image changes color, but it continues to appear realistic.

FIGURE G-4: Understanding the Multiply blending mode

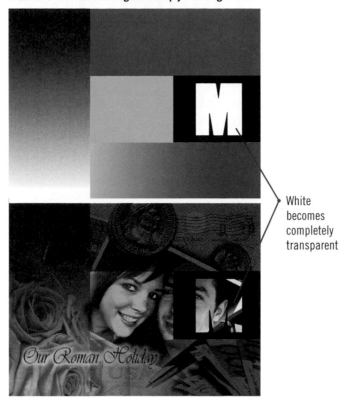

White
becomes
completely
transparent

FIGURE G-5: Multiplying a solid color

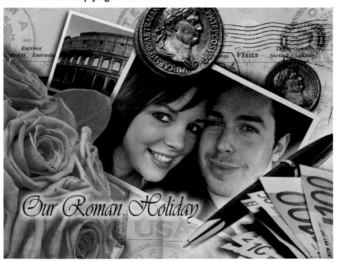

Working with the Color Burn and Linear Burn blending modes

Color Burn and Linear Burn are two effective blending modes that are similar to the Multiply blending mode but produce effects that are subtly different. Both use an algorithm that is far more complex than Multiply, but you can think of Color Burn as the Multiply blending mode with increased contrast. Often, if you use the Multiply blending mode on a lighter color over dark shadows, the shadows brighten slightly and become weak. Color Burn can be a smart alternative, because it increases contrast. Linear Burn creates a multiply effect by decreasing brightness. Of the three, it's probably the least used, but in the right circumstance, it can be the best choice. When you apply a multiply effect with a solid color, take a moment to experiment with Color Burn and Linear Burn. You might like the results even more.

Creating Special Effects

Adding Noise with the Overlay Blending Mode

Noise is a term used to describe a blanket of high-contrast pixels that produce a grainy effect over an image. Sometimes, noise is a problem. You've probably seen noise as what you'd call "grain" in low-quality images online or especially in photos you download from a cell phone. On the other hand, adding noise to an image is a technique that designers often use to "finish" a design. A layer of noise over an image can add a heightened sense of sharpness and focus to an image. Noise is especially effective with multiple images used in a montage. Often, in a montage of images from different sources, the challenge is to make the final montage appear to be one piece of artwork, not a composite of different pictures. A layer of noise adds a consistent texture across the artwork and can be very effective in achieving this goal. ░░░░ Jon tells you that, at MegaPixel, it is standard procedure to add noise to any artwork that involves a montage to help unify the artwork as one complete piece and to add a sense of artificial sharpness or "crunchiness" to the montage. He tells you that MegaPixel always adds noise using a technique with the Overlay blending mode, which he wants you to try.

STEPS

1. **Hide the Color Fill 1 layer, show the Understand Overlay layer, rename it** Noise, **then set its blending mode to** Overlay

   As shown in Figure G-6, the Overlay blending mode uses the blend colors to increase the contrast of the base art. Darker blend colors will have a different effect than lighter blend colors. The figure shows the black blend color drastically darkens the shadow point of the base art, while the white blend color dramatically brightens the highlight point of the base art. Note an important fact: The gray middle blend color becomes transparent in Overlay mode.

2. **Change the blending mode to** Normal, **click** Edit **on the Menu bar, then click** Fill

3. **Click the** Use list arrow, **click** 50% Gray, **verify that the Opacity is set to 100%, then click** OK

   The layer is filled with gray. Note that it is solid gray. The term *50% Gray* refers to the layer's color—exactly between black and white—not its opacity.

4. **Click** Filter **on the Menu bar, point to** Noise, **then click** Add Noise

5. **Enter the settings shown in the Add Noise dialog box shown in Figure G-7, then click** OK

   QUICK TIP
   To evaluate a noise effect, you must be viewing the image at a minimum of 100%.

6. **Change the blending mode to** Overlay, **zoom in on the image if necessary so that you are viewing it at 100%, then compare your result to Figure G-8**

   Since this artwork is a montage of various images, the noise effect creates a consistent texture across the image, adding a sense that it is one unified image. It also adds a sense of sharpness to the artwork.

7. **Reduce the Opacity to** 50%

8. **Save your work**

FIGURE G-6: Understanding the Overlay blending mode

FIGURE G-7: Add Noise dialog box

FIGURE G-8: Viewing results of the Noise filter

Understanding the Noise Overlay technique

The technique you used in this lesson for adding noise started by filling a layer with gray pixels. This was necessary because you cannot add noise to an empty layer; Photoshop creates noise from existing pixels. Thus, we added the gray fill to add noise then set the blending mode to Overlay, knowing that gray becomes transparent with the Overlay blending mode. The result is that we're left with only the noise being visible.

There is another technique for adding noise, one worth examining for the way in which it fails. Create a single copy/merge layer of the entire image at the top of the layer stack. Then, add noise to that layer. The issue is that it's not editable. With the Noise Overlay technique, you can continue to edit the layers beneath the noise layer; the noise is on its own layer, independent of the others. With the copy/merge technique, if you edit the image, you need to recreate the noise layer to reflect the changes.

Sharpening with the High Pass Filter

In order to understand sharpness in Photoshop, you first need to understand edges. **Edges** are any areas in an image where highly contrasting pixels meet. For example, if you had an image of a yellow leaf on dark blue velvet, the point where the bright yellow pixels at the very edge of the leaf meet the dark pixels of the blue background would be defined as an edge. High Pass is a filter that is very effective at finding and isolating edges. It finds edges using a mathematical algorithm to identify where in the image pixels of high contrast abut. It then fills the layer with solid gray everywhere except in the edge areas. Essentially, High Pass isolates edge areas. Edges are mostly involved in blurring and sharpening an image. When you blur edges, Photoshop reduces the contrast where edge pixels meet. When you sharpen an image, Photoshop finds edge areas and increases the contrast. The result is a sense of heightened focus to the image. Jon likes the noise you've added to the montage and asks you to finish the piece by sharpening it. He tells you that MegaPixel always sharpens using a technique that combines the High Pass filter with the Overlay blending mode.

STEPS

1. **Target the Noise layer, then hide it**

   Whenever you sharpen a file (using this or any other method) turn off any noise layers; you seldom want to sharpen noise.

2. **Select all, click Edit on the Menu bar, click Copy Merged, click Edit on the Menu bar, then click Paste**

   A merged copy of all the layers is pasted onto one layer.

3. **Name the new layer High Pass**

4. **Click Filter on the Menu bar, point to Other, then click High Pass**

   The image is filled with gray. Edge pixels—places where highly contrasting pixels meet—are visible through the gray.

5. **Enter the setting shown in Figure G-9, then click OK**

6. **Set the blending mode to Overlay, then zoom in so that you are viewing the image at 100%**

   With the High Pass filter, most of the image is filled with gray. Only edge pixels are visible. With the Overlay blending mode applied, the edge pixels are overlayed over the image. Thus, contrast is increased in edge areas, creating the effect of sharpness and focus.

7. **Hide and show the High Pass layer**

   Many areas are improved. Some areas—like the sharp highlight on the man's tooth and the glints in the eyes—are too sharp.

8. **Reduce the Opacity on the layer to 70%, add a layer mask, then mask any areas that are too sharp**

9. **Show the Noise layer, then compare your artwork to Figure G-10**

10. **Save your work, then close final roman holiday_PS-G.psd**

FIGURE G-9: Applying the High Pass filter

FIGURE G-10: Viewing the sharpened file

Understanding how the Overlay/High Pass technique works

Whenever you use the Overlay blending mode, it increases contrast in the base art. When you duplicate an image and use the duplicate in Overlay mode, it dramatically increases contrast, especially at the edges. The Overlay/High Pass technique essentially does just that—overlays an image on top of itself—but only at the edges. The filter works by filling the layer with 50% gray, which will become transparent when overlayed. The only areas that aren't filled with gray are edge areas. The more you increase the Radius value, the greater the area of the image that Photoshop will define as an edge area. When you apply the Overlay mode to the filtered artwork, most of the filtered artwork becomes transparent, because it's been filled with gray. The edge areas—which aren't filled with gray— are overlayed, thus increasing the contrast dramatically.

Creating Special Effects

Applying the Lens Flare Filter with Screen Mode

A **lens flare** is a bright spot often captured in the glass of a camera lens, especially when the camera is pointed at a bright light source. You have probably noticed lens flares in photos of the sun or photos of a bright sunny day. Photoshop offers the Lens Flare filter, which is very useful for adding glints or bright spots to artwork, especially artwork that involves metallic textures, like swords or chrome. The Lens Flare filter can't be created in an empty layer; it needs to be applied to already existing pixels. However, you often will want just the lens flare itself as part of your artwork, so a good technique to use is to fill a layer with black, apply the Lens Flare filter, then use the Screen blending mode to make the black areas transparent, leaving just the flare. **Figure** Jon tells you that the client has approved one of your typography compositions and has asked that you "liven it up" a bit for their website. He suggests that you start by adding a lens flare.

STEPS

1. **Open PS G-3.psd, then save it as silver streak_PS-G**

   The file has been saved in RGB Color mode. The Lens Flare filter is available in RGB Color mode but not in CMYK Color mode.

2. **Create a new layer at the top of the Layers panel, fill it with black, then name the new layer Lens Flare**

3. **Click Filter on the Menu bar, point to Render, then click Lens Flare**

4. **Click each option button in the Lens Type section of the Lens Flare dialog box to sample them, click the 50–300mm Zoom option button, drag the Brightness slider to 110, then click OK**

5. **Click Image on the Menu bar, point to Adjustments, then click Desaturate**

   The goal is to have the flare reflect the silver metallic texture of the letters.

6. **Change the blending mode of the Lens Flare layer to Screen**

   In Screen blending mode, white pixels show and black pixels become invisible. Thus, the black background of the layer becomes 100% transparent, allowing you to see only the lens flare effect on the layer and the type artwork on the layers beneath.

7. **Move the center of the white flare over the letter S, so that your screen resembles Figure G-11, click Edit on the Menu bar, point to Transform, click Scale, then scale the lens flare 80% so that your screen resembles Figure G-12**

   When you scale the lens flare, the rectangular edge of the flare artwork becomes visible, which is an obvious problem. However, we want only the flare to be visible, not the midtones, so we can remove the midtones from the equation.

8. **Press and hold [Alt] (Win) or [option] (Mac), click the Create new fill or adjustment layer button ⊘ on the Layers panel, then drag to Levels**

9. **Click the Use Previous Layer to Create Clipping Mask check box in the New Layer dialog box, click OK, then drag the black triangle immediately below the histogram on the Properties panel to the right until the text box reads 45**

   The midtones disappear.

10. **Compare your result to Figure G-13, then save your work**

FIGURE G-11: Positioning the screened lens flare

Hard edge visible

FIGURE G-12: Scaling down the size of the flare

Hard edge visible

FIGURE G-13: The final effect

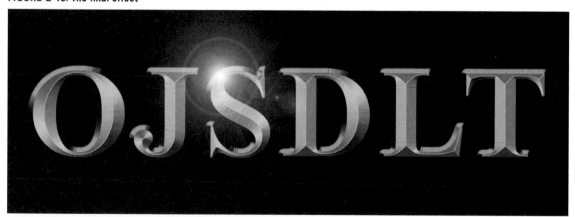

Screen blending mode vs. Multiply blending mode

Make it a point to remember that the Screen blending mode functions as the exact opposite of the Multiply blending mode. In the Screen blending mode, white pixels remain white and black pixels become invisible. However, Screen mode is similar to Multiply mode in that if you screen a color, the color becomes transparent. In Screen mode, though, a screened color always brightens the base color.

Because it makes black pixels invisible, Screen mode is very useful for superimposing bright pixels over an image: for

example, smoke. Smoke is a great design element, but how do you capture a photograph in a way that you can access just the smoke? Screen mode makes this possible. Photograph the smoke against a black background. When you bring the file into Photoshop, use the Levels adjustment to brighten the smoke and darken the black background so that it is actually black. Then, when you apply the Screen blending mode, the black pixels disappear and voila: you've got smoke—and just smoke—to work with.

Applying the Motion Blur Filter

Photoshop offers a number of blur filters. The Motion Blur filter dialog box allows you to specify a distance and an angle for blurring pixels. The result is a blur that can be used to create the appearance of motion. Think of watching a race car flying by you in real life. If you had a photo of that car, you could use the Motion Blur filter to create the effect of the car moving so fast, there's a blur of colors trailing it. The Motion Blur filter can also be used very effectively on text and headlines to create a sense of movement and action. ▄▄▗▄ Jon likes the lens flare you applied to the headline and tells you to finish the piece by applying a motion blur to the text. He tells you to "make it visually not too simplistic." With that in mind, you decide to use multiple blurs in conjunction with each other to create the effect.

STEPS

1. **Duplicate both the Inner Bevel and Outer Bevel layers, select both duplicate layers, click the Layers panel menu button ▣, then click Merge Layers**

2. **Name the merged layer Motion Blur, then drag it down below the Outer Bevel layer**

3. **Duplicate the Motion Blur layer, then rename the new layer Motion Blur Top**

4. **With the Motion Blur Top layer still targeted, click Filter on the Menu bar, point to Blur, then click Motion Blur**

   The Motion Blur dialog box opens.

5. **Set the Angle to 0, set the Distance to 50, then click OK**

   Your screen should resemble Figure G-14.

6. **Target the Motion Blur layer, open the Motion Blur dialog box, verify that the Angle is set to 0, set the Distance to 100 pixels, then click OK**

7. **Reduce the Opacity of the Motion Blur layer to 70%**

8. **Set the blending mode on the Motion Blur Top layer to Screen**

9. **Compare your result to Figure G-15, save your work, then close silver streak_PS-G.psd**

Grouping blending modes on the Layers panel

On the Layers panel, note how the blending modes have been grouped into six sections. This grouping is intentional and specific. Though each blending mode is programmed to produce a different effect, the effects themselves fall into similar behaviors. The blending modes are grouped based on those similarities.

　Moving from the top of the menu down:
- The blending modes in the second section all darken the base art when applied. White pixels become transparent with these blending modes.

- Blending modes in the third section all lighten the base art when applied. Black pixels become transparent with these blending modes.
- The blending modes in the fourth section all increase contrast in the base art when applied. Gray pixels become transparent with these blending modes.

As you work through this book, refer back to this bulleted list. Once you get a sense of the similarity of blending modes, it opens the door to experimenting with different but similar blending modes to find the best effect.

FIGURE G-14: Viewing the first motion blur applied

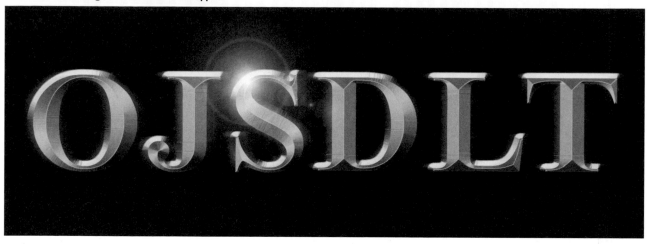

FIGURE G-15: Viewing the final effect with two motion blurs applied

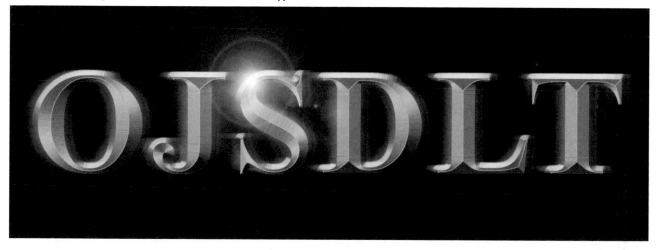

Applying Non-Destructive Filters

Throughout this book, you've learned about "non-destructive" editing, even though you might not have referred to it as such. When you apply a Levels adjustment layer, for example, that's a non-destructive edit. It's called "non-destructive" because the adjustment is not applied directly to the artwork. Instead, the adjustment exists on a separate layer that can be shown, hidden, edited, or even deleted. In any case, the original artwork is not permanently altered. A layer style is another example of a non-destructive edit; it doesn't permanently alter the artwork to achieve the effect. Photoshop also offers you the ability to create non-destructive filter layers, allowing you to create filters on a layer that can be shown, hidden, edited, or deleted. These so-called "smart filters" even come with a layer mask and can be altered with an opacity adjustment or with a blending mode. Non-destructive filters are great because they allow you to experiment with different filters without permanently altering the original artwork. A client wants you to apply some filters to an image to make it more interesting. However, the client wants to be able to manipulate the filters you apply to customize the effect. Jon tells you to use smart filters.

STEPS

1. **Open PS G-4.psd, save it as** non-destructive filters_PS-G, **then target the** Plaza layer

2. **Click** Filter **on the Menu bar, click** Convert for Smart Filters, **then click** OK **in the warning dialog box**

   The artwork on the layer is converted to a smart object, signified by the Smart Object thumbnail icon. Smart objects preserve artwork's original characteristics while allowing you to perform non-destructive editing to the layer.

3. **Click** Filter **on the Menu bar, then click** Filter Gallery

4. **Expand the** Texture folder, **then click** Grain

5. **Click the** Grain Type list arrow, **click** Speckle, **then set both the Intensity and the Contrast settings to** 25

6. **Click** OK, **then compare your Layers panel to Figure G-16**

   The Grain filter is applied as a layer beneath the Plaza layer. It has a default white layer mask, and it is visible.

7. **Click the** Toggle all smart filter visibilities button 👁 **to hide the filter, then click again to show the filter**

8. **Double-click the** ≣ **button on the Grain filter on the Plaza layer on the Layers panel**

   The Blending Options (Filter Gallery) dialog box opens.

9. **Drag the** Opacity slider to 80%, **then click** OK

10. **Double-click** Filter Gallery **on the Plaza layer to open the Grain dialog box, increase both the Intensity and the Contrast settings to** 35, **then click** OK

11. **Compare your artwork to Figure G-17, save your work, then close non-destructive filters_PS-G.psd**

FIGURE G-16: The Grain filter as a layer on the Layers panel

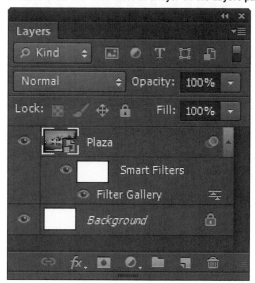

FIGURE G-17: Viewing the filter applied with 80% opacity

Courtesy of Chris Botello

Masking filters

One of the extra great benefits of working with non-destructive filters, as we did in this lesson, is that they are created with a mask—call it a **filter mask**—which functions and which you can use exactly like a layer mask. That means that you can subtly mask or show non-destructive filters using the filter mask in conjunction with the Brush tool, a gradient, etc. One catch, though: if you apply multiple filters, there's still just one mask available, and that mask will hide or show all of the applied filters. You can't mask just one of many filters applied to the same artwork.

Distorting Images

Earlier in this book, you learned about transforming images; specifically, you learned how to scale and rotate images, and how to flip them horizontally or vertically. Often, you'll want to distort images, sometimes for an artistic effect and sometimes for a practical effect, like creating a sense of three-dimensional artwork. In Photoshop, the Distort command is another type of transformation, just like scaling or rotating. The methodology is similar, but the results can be very dramatic and eye-catching. ▰▰▰ MegaPixel has been working with a Hollywood movie studio on an outdoor campaign for a theatrical release. The client likes your design of a billboard, and Jon asks you to "put it in an environment" to give the client a sense of how it will appear on a billboard in the real world.

STEPS

1. **Open PS G-5.psd, save it as distort_PS-G, then hide and show the Background layer**
   The billboard was duplicated and exists alone on its own layer.

2. **Open charlie billboard_PS-G.psd, select all, click Edit on the Menu bar, click Copy, then close the file**

3. **Target the Billboard layer, paste, then name the new layer Charlie**

4. **Press [Alt] (Win) or [option] (Mac), then click between the Charlie layer and the Billboard layer to clip the Charlie layer into the Billboard layer**

5. **Click Edit on the Menu bar, point to Transform, then click Distort**
   The Distort command allows you to move all the handles on the transform bounding box independently, thus distorting the artwork.

QUICK TIP
You may have to zoom out to view all four handles.

6. **Move the four handles of the bounding box to the four corners of the Billboard artwork, as shown in Figure G-18**

7. **Press [Enter] (Win) or [return] (Mac) to execute the transformation**

8. **Compare your artwork to Figure G-19**

9. **Save your work, then close distort_PS-G.psd**

Removing smart filters

Because they are non-destructive by definition, smart filters can be removed from layered artwork at any time. You can simply hide the filter or, if you want to remove it permanently, drag it to the Delete layer button on the Layers panel. All smart filters will be deleted from a layer if you convert the layer from a smart object back to a normal layer. To do so, target a layer containing smart filters, click Layer on the Menu bar, point to Smart Filter, then click Clear Smart Filters. The filters are removed from the layer.

FIGURE G-18: Distorting the artwork by moving the handles

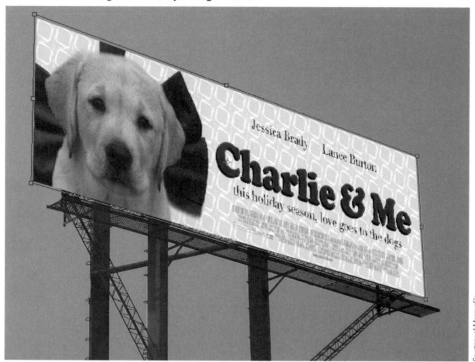

FIGURE G-19: Viewing the final distorted artwork

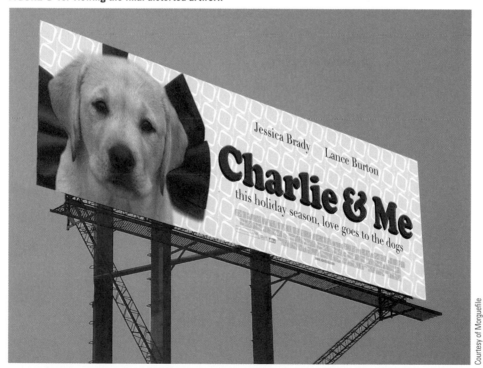

Understanding the Skew and Perspective transformations

In addition to the Distort transformation, you can transform with the Skew and Perspective commands. Skew will transform the art as though it were positioned on an angle. With the Skew transformation, the opposite sides of the bounding box always remain parallel. The Perspective command transforms art with a forced perspective toward an unspecified vanishing point. With the Perspective command, one set of opposite sides of the bounding box remains parallel, while the other set is pulled apart to create a perspective effect. You can look at the Distort command as being the extreme version of these transformations: only with Distort can you move the four handles of the bounding box independently of one another.

Practice

Concepts Review

Label the elements of the Photoshop screen shown in Figure G-20.

FIGURE G-20

Match each term with the statement that best describes it.

6. **Color blending mode**
7. **Black**
8. **White**
9. **Gray**
10. **Multiply blending mode**
11. **Screen blending mode**
12. **High Pass**
13. **Render**

a. Always invisible in Screen mode
b. Filter that can be used to sharpen an image
c. Always lightens base art
d. Modifies both hue and saturation of base color
e. Always invisible in Overlay mode
f. Category of a collection of filters
g. Always darkens base art
h. Always invisible in Multiply mode

Select the best answer from the list of choices.

14. **Which of the following is not a Photoshop blending mode?**
    - **a.** Color Burn
    - **b.** Hue
    - **c.** High Pass
    - **d.** Linear Light

15. **When working with colors and blending modes, what is the color of the original pixel called?**
    - **a.** Result color
    - **b.** Base color
    - **c.** Blend color
    - **d.** Hue color

16. **The Distort command is an example of what type of Photoshop operation?**
    - **a.** Transformation
    - **b.** Saturation
    - **c.** Calibration
    - **d.** Resolution

17. **Which of the following is not true of the Multiply blending mode?**
    - **a.** A multiplied color is transparent.
    - **b.** Multiplying always darkens the base art (except if the base pixel is already black).
    - **c.** Fifty percent gray pixels become invisible when multiplied.
    - **d.** When multiplied, anything black remains black.

18. **The Colorize option is included in which adjustment?**
    - **a.** Levels
    - **b.** Brightness/Contrast
    - **c.** Color Balance
    - **d.** Hue/Saturation

Skills Review

1. **Use the Color blending mode.**
   - **a.** Open PS G-6.psd, save it as **colorize skills_PS-G**, click the Create new adjustment or fill layer button on the Layers panel, then click Solid Color.
   - **b.** Change the color to 195R/207G/221B, click OK, click the blending mode list arrow, then click Color.
   - **c.** Mask the Color Fill 1 layer so that it affects only the background area of the image. (*Hint*: Because the background is mostly white and white can't be colorized with Color mode, painting the background will affect only the top right corner of the background.)
   - **d.** Create a new layer above the Color Fill 1 layer, name the layer **T-Shirt**, then set the blending mode to Color.
   - **e.** Set the foreground color to 172R/211G/115B, click the Brush tool, then paint the t-shirt green.
   - **f.** Create a new Hue/Saturation adjustment layer, then set the blending mode for the layer to Color.
   - **g.** Click the Colorize check box in the Properties panel, set the Hue to 28, then set the Saturation to 43.
   - **h.** Name the layer **Face**, then use a layer mask so that the Hue/Saturation adjustment affects the face, neck and the lips, but not the eyes.
   - **i.** Use the same method you used in Steps f–h, with different values for Hue and Saturation, to finish colorizing the image.
   - **j.** Save your work and keep the file open.

2. **Use the Multiply blending mode.**
   - **a.** Click Image on the Menu bar, then click Duplicate.
   - **b.** Type **multiply skills_PS-G** in the As text box in the Duplicate Image dialog box, then click OK.
   - **c.** Click the T-Shirt layer on the Layers panel, then change the blending mode from Color to Multiply.
   - **d.** Click the Face layer, change its blending mode to Multiply, then reduce its Opacity to 70%.
   - **e.** Click the Color Fill 1 layer, then change its blending mode to Multiply. (*Hint*: The white areas of the background can be colorized with Multiply mode.)
   - **f.** Paint white in the Color Fill 1 layer mask to colorize the entire background and the man's hair.

Skills Review (continued)

   g. Position the two open files side by side, then compare your results to Figure G-21.

   h. Save your work, then close both files.

FIGURE G-21

3. Add noise with the Overlay blending mode.

   a. Open PS G-7.psd, then save it as **shining future skills_PS-G**.

   b. Target the Type layer, create a new layer above it, then name the new layer **Noise**.

   c. Click Edit on the Menu bar, then click Fill.

   d. Click the Use list arrow, click 50% Gray, verify that Mode is set to Normal and Opacity is set to 100%, then click OK.

   e. Change the blending mode on the Noise layer to Overlay so that the gray fill becomes transparent.

   f. Click Filter on the Menu bar, point to Noise, then click Add Noise.

   g. Set the Amount to 3, set the Distribution to Gaussian, if necessary click the Monochromatic check box to activate it, then click OK.

   h. Zoom in on the image, if necessary, so that you are viewing it at 200%.

   i. Hide and show the Noise layer so that you can see the effect.

   j. Change the blending mode on the three different "moon" layers to Overlay.

   k. Save your work.

4. Sharpen with the High Pass filter.

   a. Target then hide the Noise layer.

   b. Select all, click Edit on the Menu bar, click Copy Merged, click Edit again, then click Paste.

   c. Name the new layer **High Pass**.

   d. Click Filter on the Menu bar, point to Other, then click High Pass.

   e. Type **2** in the Radius text box, then click OK.

   f. Set the blending mode to Overlay, then zoom in so that you are viewing the purple globe at the center of the flower at 200%.

   g. Hide and show the High Pass layer.

   h. Add a layer mask, then mask any areas that are too sharp.

   i. Show the Noise layer.

   j. Save your work.

Skills Review (continued)

5. Apply the Lens Flare filter with Screen mode.

   a. Create a new layer at the top of the layer stack, fill it with black, then name the new layer **Lens Flare**.

   b. Click Filter on the Menu bar, point to Render, then click Lens Flare.

   c. Click each option button in the Lens Type section of the Lens Flare dialog box to sample them, click the 105mm Prime flare option button, drag the Brightness slider to 100, then click OK.

   d. Click Image on the Menu bar, point to Adjustments, then click Desaturate.

   e. Change the blending mode on the Lens Flare layer to Screen.

   f. Move the center of the white flare to the 10 o'clock position at the edge of the purple globe.

   g. Add a clipped Levels adjustment layer above the Lens Flare layer, then, on the Properties panel, drag the black triangle immediately below the histogram right until the text box reads 32.

   h. Save your work.

6. Apply the Motion Blur filter.

   a. Duplicate the Type layer, name the new layer **Type Blur**, drag the new layer beneath the Type layer, then hide the Drop Shadow layer style.

   b. Click Filter on the Menu bar, point to Blur, then click Motion Blur.

   c. Set the Angle to 0, set the Distance to 166, then click OK.

   d. Show the Drop Shadow layer style.

   e. Save your work.

7. Apply non-destructive filters.

   a. Duplicate the Flower layer, name the new layer **Flower Blur**, then drag the new layer beneath the Flower layer.

   b. If it's not already targeted, click the Flower Blur layer, click Filter on the Menu bar, click Convert for Smart Filters, then click OK.

   c. Click Filter on the Menu bar, point to Blur, then click Motion Blur.

   d. Set the Angle to 0, set the Distance to 200, then click OK.

   e. Double-click the ▦ button at the right of the Motion Blur filter on the Flower Blur layer on the Layers panel.

   f. Drag the Opacity slider to 90%, then click OK.

   g. Double-click the words Motion Blur on the Motion Blur filter on the Flower Blur layer to open the Motion Blur dialog box, reduce the Distance value to 150, then click OK.

   h. Save your work.

Skills Review (continued)

8. Distort images.

a. Target the Child layer, create a new layer above it, then name the new layer **Flower Shadow**.

b. Target the Flower layer.

c. Press and hold [Ctrl] (Win) or ⌘ (Mac), then click the Flower layer thumbnail to load it as a selection.

d. Click Select on the Menu bar, point to Modify, click Feather, type **5** in the Feather Radius text box, then click OK.

e. Target the Flower Shadow layer, fill the selection with black, then deselect.

f. Click Edit on the Menu bar, point to Transform, then click Flip Vertical.

g. Move the Flower shadow artwork down so that your screen resembles Figure G-22.

h. Click Edit on the Menu bar, point to Transform, then click Distort. (*Hint*: You may need to reduce the view of the canvas substantially to see all four handles of the Distort bounding box.)

i. Move the bottom two handles of the bounding box so that your screen resembles Figure G-23.

j. Press [Enter] (Win) or [return] (Mac) to execute the transformation.

k. Change the blending mode of the layer to Multiply, then reduce the Opacity to 65%.

l. Duplicate the Background layer, change the blending mode on the duplicate layer to Multiply, reduce its Opacity to 60%, then compare your artwork to Figure G-24.

m. Save your work, then close shining future skills_PS-G.psd.

FIGURE G-22

FIGURE G-23

Distort bounding box

FIGURE G-24

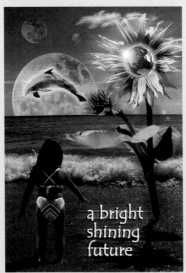

Independent Challenge 1

Your creative director comes to you with an image she wants to use for a website. She tells you that the image was "damaged." There's a green field over the image, and the image has been flattened. She tells you she needs you to make a "quick fix." You look at the image and decide that, rather than try to mask the damaged area, it would be faster and most effective to use the Color blending mode to fix the image.

a. Open PS G-8.psd, then save it as **color mode correction_PS-G**.
b. Create a new layer, name it **Correct**, then set its blending mode to Color.
c. Click the Brush tool, set the Hardness to 0, then set the Size to 60.
d. Sample a gray pixel in the jacket's lapel, adjacent to the green discoloration.
e. Use the Brush tool to paint the green area.
f. Sample a darker gray from the lapel, then repaint the area or parts of the area to see if it improves the correction.
g. Reduce the Opacity of the Brush tool to 50%, then paint over adjacent "non-damaged" areas to help transition from the correction to the original areas.
h. Compare your results to Figure G-25.
i. Save your work, then close color mode correction_PS-G.psd.

Independent Challenge 2

You're designing point-of-purchase displays for a Hollywood movie studio. The client has sent you low-resolution, flattened artwork to use in the layout for the display. You decide to add noise to the artwork and sharpen it for the best display.

a. Open PS G-9.psd, then save it as **key art_PS-G**.
b. Hide and then show the All Type folder on the Layers panel to see how the file is built.
c. Target the Background layer, then create a new layer above it named **Noise**.
d. Fill the Noise layer with 50% Gray.
e. Click Filter on the Menu bar, point to Noise, then click Add Noise.

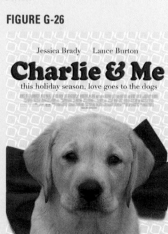

f. Type **4** in the Amount text box, then, if necessary, click the Gaussian option button and the Monochromatic check box.
g. Click OK, then set the blending mode to Overlay.
h. Hide the All Type folder and the Noise layer.
i. Duplicate the Background layer, then rename the new layer **High Pass 2.0**.
j. Click Filter on the Menu bar, point to Other, then click High Pass.
k. Type **2.0** in the Radius text box, then click OK.
l. Set the blending mode to Overlay.
m. Show all layers, then compare your results to Figure G-26.
n. Save your work, then close key art_PS-G.psd.

Independent Challenge 3

The art director at the point-of-purchase display company you're working for asks you to "skin" the key art into a table display template to give the client a sense of the final piece.

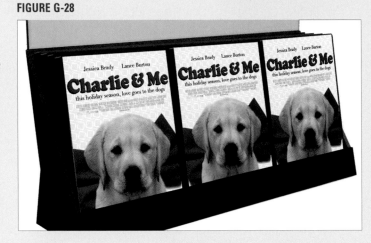

   a. Open PS G-10.psd, then save it as **12 count_PS-G**.

   b. Open the file named charlie key art_PS-G.psd, select all, apply the Copy Merged command, then close charlie key art_PS-G.psd.

   c. Return to the 12 count_PS-G.psd file, target the Videos layer, then paste.

   d. Name the new layer **Left Video**, then clip it into the Videos layer.

   e. Click Edit on the Menu bar, point to Transform, then click Distort.

   f. Move the four handles of the bounding box so that your screen resembles Figure G-27.

   g. Using the same methods, paste and distort the artwork into the remaining two video covers. (*Hint*: Name the new layers **Center Video** and **Right Video**.)

   h. Compare your artwork to Figure G-28.

Advanced Challenge Exercise

FIGURE G-28

- Open backer_PS-G.psd, select all, click Edit on the Menu bar, then click Copy Merged.
- In the 12 count_PS-G.psd file, target the Blue layer, then paste.
- Name the new layer **Backer**, then clip it into the Blue layer.
- Click Edit on the Menu bar, point to Transform, then click Perspective.
- Move the handles on the bounding box to position the artwork in perspective.
- Click [Enter] (Win) or [return] (Mac) to execute the transformation.

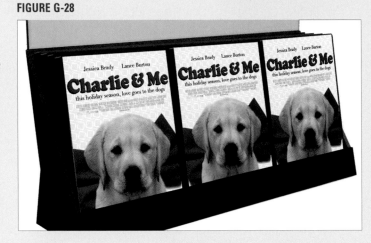

   i. Save your work, close all open files, then exit Photoshop.

Real Life Independent Challenge

Just back from vacation, you snapped a great photo of your daughter jumping off of a dock. You decide that it will make a great postcard and use layer masks to capture the image of your daughter on a separate layer. You then decide to put a motion blur on the image to give it some action and energy.

a. Open PS G-11.psd, then save it as **diver_PS-G**.

b. Turn the layers on and off to get an understanding of how the file was built.

c. Verify that all the layers are visible, duplicate the Julie layer, then rename the duplicate **Julie Blur**.

d. Click Filter on the Menu bar, point to Blur, then click Motion Blur.

e. Set the Angle to 0, set the Distance to 100, then click OK.

f. Drag the Julie Blur layer down beneath the Julie layer.

g. Add a layer mask to the Julie Blur layer, then mask the blur entirely on the screen-left edge of the Julie artwork, as shown in Figure G-29.

h. Click the Julie layer, click Filter on the Menu bar, then click Convert for Smart Filters.

i. Open the Motion Blur dialog box, reduce the Distance value to 17, then click OK.

Advanced Challenge Exercise

- Click the filter mask on the Julie layer to target it.
- Click the Brush tool, set the Size to 70, then set the Hardness to 0%.
- Reduce the Opacity of the Brush tool to 20%.
- Gradually mask the blur on the girl's face and other areas that you want to keep in better focus.

j. Save your work, compare your results to Figure G-30, then close diver_PS-G.psd.

FIGURE G-29

FIGURE G-30

Visual Workshop

Open PS G-12.psd, then save it as **two motion blurs_PS-G**. Create horizontal and vertical motion blurs of the artwork. Reduce the opacity of the blurred letters so that your result resembles Figure G-31.

FIGURE G-31

Improving Productivity

Photoshop is not only about design and photography. In fact, Photoshop plays many roles in a graphics environment, including roles that don't necessarily incorporate any kind of design or photography skills. For example, at a web design and development company, you'd find that a number of job descriptions are dedicated to managing assets, processing images, uploading content, and other types of non-design work. Recognizing this, Adobe has designed Photoshop to be something of a workhorse, with many built-in modules dedicated to making Photoshop very effective as an image processor in a graphics workflow environment. MegaPixel has contracted with a new client to produce a series of international websites. Jon tells you to expect to be working with a large number of images, all of which will need to be managed and processed daily to maintain the websites. He asks that you explore various options for automating workflow to make the best use of the department's time.

OBJECTIVES

Use the Image Processor

Create and run an action

Batch process an action

Use the History panel

Create a snapshot and use the History Brush tool

Clone with the Clone Stamp tool

Clone with the Healing Brush tool

Experiment with cloning options

Using the Image Processor

Certain types of workflows call for repetitive tasks. You'll tend to see this especially in a web environment. For example, it's often the case when maintaining a client's website that the client will send folders full of images that need to be converted to the same file format. They might all be PSD files that need to be saved as JPEGs, or as both JPEGs and TIFFs. Photoshop's Image Processor feature is great for quickly converting groups of files to other file formats. Jon gives you a CD with seven PSD files and asks that you make two copies of each, one set saved as JPEGs for the website and one set saved as TIFFs for archiving. You decide to use the Image Processor.

STEPS

1. **Open the seven files in the** Automation folder **located in the folder where your Data Files are stored**

   The files are all PSD (Photoshop Document) files, with the .psd extension.

2. **Click** File **on the Menu bar, point to** Scripts, **then click** Image Processor

3. **In Section 1, click the** Use Open Images **option button**

4. **In Section 2, click the** Save in Same Location **option button**

5. **In Section 3, click the** Save as JPEG **check box if it is not already checked, then type** 12 **in the Quality text box**

6. **In Section 3, click the** Save as TIFF **check box**

7. **Verify that nothing is checked in Section 4, then compare your Image Processor dialog box to Figure H-1**

8. **Click** Run

   The Image Processor saves the two sets of files. The seven original PSD files remain open after the Image Processor is done.

9. **Navigate to the Automation folder, then open the Automation folder**

   The Automation folder now contains a folder named JPEG and a folder named TIFF. These two folders contain the JPEG and TIFF copies generated by the Image Processor.

10. **Keep all the files open**

Investigating other options with the Image Processor

Take some time to note some other options available to you in the Image Processor dialog box. Section 1 allows you the option of not having to open the files you want to process; you can simply direct the Image Processor to a folder of files that you want to process. Section 2 allows you to save to a folder other than the one that contains your original files.

And don't forget this one: Section 3 will convert CMYK files to RGB files if you are saving them as JPEGs. It's often the case that you will have CMYK print files that someone will want to use on a web page, which is always an RGB environment. The Image Processor will instantly convert those files for you as it processes.

FIGURE H-1: Image Processor dialog box

Photoshop CS6

Creating and Running an Action

Actions are about repetition. Photoshop is also about repetition. If you're a designer, you're going to soon find—if you haven't already—that you do some of the same things over and over and over again. This is where actions come into play. Since you'll be executing the same operations repeatedly, it's a smart idea to save those steps as an action, thereby avoiding time consuming repetition of efforts. Actions are created, stored, and automatically saved on the Actions panel. Once you create an action, it will be available on the Actions panel for all files you open in the future. Jon asks you to execute the same operation on a series of images. He tells you to work smart and save time by creating an action on the Actions panel.

STEPS

1. **Click the flowers_PS-H.psd document tab, click Window on the Menu bar, then click Actions**
   The Actions panel appears.

2. **Click the Actions panel menu button ▾, click New Action, type Invert in the Name text box, then click Record**
   As shown in Figure H-2, a new action named Invert appears on the Actions panel. The red Begin recording button on the panel is activated.

3. **Click Image on the Menu bar, point to Adjustments, then click Invert**
   The file is inverted.

4. **Click File on the Menu bar, click Save, click File on the Menu bar, then click Close**
   As shown in Figure H-3, the three commands that were executed—Invert, Save, and Close—are listed as commands under the Invert action.

5. **Click the Stop playing/recording button ■ on the Actions panel**
   When you click the Stop playing/recording button, Photoshop stops recording the steps you execute as part of the given action.

6. **Click the marble_PS-H.psd document tab, then click the Invert action on the Actions panel to highlight it**

7. **Click the Play selection button ▶ on the Actions panel**
   The marble_PS-H.psd file was inverted, saved, and then closed, because Close was the last command in the Invert action. Note that after you ran the Invert action, Invert is automatically highlighted again on the Actions panel.

8. **Apply the Invert action to the remaining open files**
   When you are done, all the files will be closed.

9. **Open all seven PSD files in the Automation folder**
   All seven images have been inverted.

10. **Close all the files**

FIGURE H-2: New action added to the Actions panel

Play selection button

Begin recording button

Stop playing/ recording

Invert action

Create new action button

FIGURE H-3: Three commands added to the Invert action

Three commands added

Understanding what it means to invert

In this lesson, you used the Invert command for the first time. What is it? If you apply the Invert command to a black and white image, it will make the image look just like an X-ray photograph. Black areas become white, white areas become black; that's the key to the Invert command. From a grayscale perspective, it's easy to understand how Photoshop creates the invert effect: it changes a pixel's grayscale value to its opposite on the grayscale. For example, any pixel that has a grayscale value of 0 (black) changes to 255 (white); a grayscale value of 1 becomes 254; a grayscale value of 253 becomes 2; and so on. Invert is seldom used as a visual effect—how many times do you need an X-ray effect in a design? However, the Invert command has a great practical use. When you create an adjustment layer—let's say you use Levels to dramatically brighten an image—a layer mask is automatically created with the adjustment and is automatically targeted. Simply press [Ctrl][I] (Win) or ⌘ [I] (Mac) to invert the mask from white to black. That completely masks the adjustment, and you can use the Brush tool with a white foreground color to gradually "brush the adjustment in" to affect the artwork. Give it a try—it's a great way to work with adjustments.

Batch Processing an Action

Imagine that you had an action that you wanted to apply to a folder of images—an action more complicated than something like converting a PSD file to a JPEG or TIFF, which you could do with the Image Processor. For example, you want to change the image size of a file to 72 ppi, then convert it to Grayscale. You could create an action with those commands, then batch process an entire folder with that action. Batch process means, rather than opening each image in the folder and executing the action by hand, you can simply tell Photoshop to apply the action to a folder of images. Jon gives you a disk containing seven files and tells you he wants you to invert all the files. You decide to batch process an action to do this quickly.

STEPS

1. **Click File on the Menu bar, point to Automate, then click Batch**

2. **In the Play section, click the Action list arrow to see all the actions available, then click Invert**

   All of the actions on the Actions panel are listed in the Action list.

3. **In the Source section, verify that Folder is chosen, then click the Choose button**

4. **In the Browse for Folder dialog box, navigate to and select the Automation folder, then click OK (Win) or Choose (Mac)**

5. **Verify that none of the four check boxes in the Source section is checked**

   Because of the work we did with the Image Processor in the first lesson of this unit, the Automation folder contains two subfolders—JPEG and TIFF. We do not want to apply the action to the contents of those folders.

6. **In the Destination section, verify that None is chosen**

   No destination means that we want to affect the targeted images in the folder and for those images to be saved with the change(s). If we wanted to save the affected images as copies, then we'd need to specify a destination for the copies, which we'd do in the Destination section.

7. **In the Errors section, verify that Stop for Errors is chosen, then compare your Batch dialog box to Figure H-4**

8. **Click OK**

   The seven images are opened, affected by the action, then closed.

9. **Open all seven PSD files from the Automation folder**

   All seven files are inverted again and appear as they did originally.

10. **Close all the open files**

FIGURE H-4: Batch dialog box

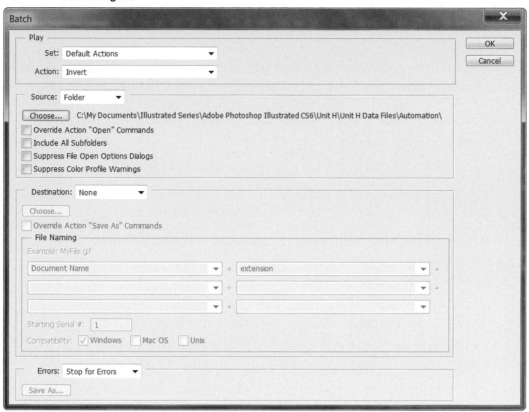

Exporting an action

Let's say you're a freelance designer and you work at a number of different locations for a number of different clients. One of the skills that make a designer valuable is the ability to work fast, and having a smart set of actions to rely upon can be a big plus for getting your work done quickly. If you work on different computers, you can save a set of actions to a portable drive or simply email the actions to yourself so they're available wherever you are. Actions that you want to save must be first placed in a set (folder) which you create by clicking the Create new set button on the Actions panel. To export a set of actions, click the folder on the Actions panel that you want to export, click the Actions panel menu button, then click Save Actions. The saved file will have an ATN extension. When you want to access your actions, click the Actions panel menu button, click Load Actions, then load the .atn file you saved. Voilà—actions to go!

Using the History Panel

The History panel offers lots of great features; one of them is the ability to quickly revert a file to its state when you first opened it, then bring it back to its current state. As you work, the History panel records your steps and lists the last twenty of them, called states, in the panel. The last state in the list represents the last change you made to the file. You can click a state in the list to go back to that point of your work, and then continue working from that state. ▓▓▓▓ Jon asks you to execute a series of commands then note how they are listed on the History panel.

STEPS

Note: This lesson and the next lesson must be done in one sitting. If you close the file after this lesson, you will not be able to do the next lesson.

1. **Open PS H-1.psd, save it as** it's history_PS-H, **click** Window **on the Menu bar, then click** History

   The History panel opens, showing one state: Open.

2. **Click** Image **on the Menu bar, point to** Adjustments, **then click** Desaturate

   The Desaturate command is listed as a state on the History panel.

3. **Click** Filter **on the Menu bar, point to** Stylize, **then click** Solarize

   Solarize is listed as a state on the History panel.

4. **Click** Image **on the Menu bar, point to** Adjustments, **click** Brightness/Contrast, **set the Brightness to** 100, **set the Contrast to** 50, **verify that Use Legacy check box is not checked, then click** OK

   Your canvas and History panel should resemble Figure H-5.

5. **Click** Desaturate **on the History panel**

   The file is reverted back to the state it was in after you applied the Desaturate command.

6. **Click** Brightness/Contrast **on the History panel**

   The file is reverted to the state it was in after you applied the Brightness/Contrast command.

7. **Note the thumbnail at the top of the History panel**

   Whenever you open a file, the History panel creates a thumbnail at the top of the panel representing the status of the file at the time it was opened. In this case, the thumbnail's name is listed as PS H-1.psd because that was the name of the file when it was opened. You might need to use the scroll bar on the History panel to see the thumbnail.

8. **Click the** PS H-1.psd thumbnail **at the top of the History panel**

   The file is returned to its state when you first opened it. This valuable option is available to you if the Automatically Create First Snapshot check box is checked in the History Options dialog box. You can access the History Options dialog box by clicking the History panel menu button, then clicking History Options.

9. **Click** Brightness/Contrast **on the History panel, and keep the file open for the next exercise without saving**

Setting the number of states on the History panel

As you work, the History panel logs each command that is performed as a new state. However, it will log only a specific number of states. That number is determined as a preference. To specify that preference, go to the Performance window of the Preferences dialog box. In the History & Cache section, the History States text box allows you to enter the number of states the History panel will list. Twenty is the default setting. The higher the number you enter, the more memory Photoshop will require to keep those states active.

FIGURE H-5: Viewing states on the History panel

Revert vs. "super" revert

It's important to understand the difference between using the Revert command and reverting a file using the History panel. Let's say you're working on a file for an hour, and over the course of the hour, you save the file three times. The Revert command, on the File menu, will return you to the state of the file the *last time you saved*.

Clicking the default thumbnail at the top of the History panel will take you back to the state of the file *when it was opened*. That's why you can think of it as a "super" revert. Remember though, that the default thumbnail is available only as long as you keep the file open. Once you close it, that status is lost.

Creating a Snapshot and Using the History Brush Tool

The History panel allows you to create a snapshot of your work at any given state. Creating a snapshot saves the current status of your work as a new thumbnail at the top of the History panel. The History Brush tool is a "revert" brush—it paints using any one of the snapshots at the top of the History panel as its source. You use it by clicking the icon beside the thumbnail that you want the History Brush tool to paint from. The icon is called the "Sets the source for the history brush." The History brush tool can function as a practical tool: use it to paint in artwork from a saved state. It can also function artistically. For example, you can set it to a low opacity and gradually "paint in" artwork from a saved state. Jon tells you to create a snapshot of the artwork you are working on, then to use the History Brush tool at different opacities to create a mixed-effect on the artwork.

STEPS

1. **On the History panel, verify that Brightness/Contrast is highlighted, then click the Create new snapshot button on the panel**

   As shown in Figure H-6, a new thumbnail named Snapshot 1 is added to the History panel below the default thumbnail. Snapshot 1 represents the status of the file when you created the snapshot.

2. **Look at the icon beside the PS H-1.psd thumbnail on the History panel**

   The icon identifies which thumbnail Photoshop regards as the "active" history status.

3. **Click the History Brush tool, click the Brush Preset picker list arrow on the Options bar, set the Hardness to 0%, set the Size to 70 pixels, then set the Opacity to 20%**

4. **Paint overlapping strokes over the image, starting with the boy's face, then compare your results to Figure H-7**

   The History Brush tool paints using the artwork from the PS H-1.psd status. Essentially, you are painting with the file as it was when it was first opened.

5. **On the History panel, click the gray square to the left of Snapshot 1 to change the source for the History Brush tool, as shown in Figure H-8**

   The next time you use the History Brush tool, it will use this state—Snapshot 1—as its source.

6. **Set the Opacity of the History Brush tool to 50%, then paint overlapping strokes only in the background of the image—not the boy**

7. **Save your work, then close it's history_PS-H.psd**

Saving a snapshot automatically

Some of the projects you work on in Photoshop won't last for hours or for days—they'll last for weeks. When working on complex projects, you'll find that you hit "landmark" points along the way. For example, you might get to a point where you're happy with the background of an image and start to work on a foreground element. This would be a good time to create a snapshot. That way, you can return to a point when you were happy with the status of the work.

A smart way to work is to have the History panel automatically save a snapshot every time you save. To do so, click the History panel menu button, click History Options, then click Automatically Create New Snapshot When Saving. Think of it as an insurance policy: if you mess up some good work you've saved, you can always click the snapshot to return to that state.

Remember though, that the insurance policy does not guard against catastrophe. If your computer crashes, all the snapshots you create automatically or by hand will be lost. Also, once you save and close the file, the snapshots from your previous work session will be gone.

FIGURE H-6: Viewing the snapshot added to the History panel

Sets the source for the history brush icon

Default thumbnail

New snapshot

Create new snapshot button

FIGURE H-7: Applying the History brush tool to the artwork

FIGURE H-8: Setting Snapshot 1 as the source for the History Brush tool

Sets the source for the History brush tool

Using "Fill from History"

Another great way to work with the History panel can be found in the Fill dialog box. Click Edit on the Menu bar, then click Fill. Click the Use list arrow, then click History, and the targeted layer on the Layers panel will be filled with the artwork from the targeted state on the History panel. When you fill using History, the other options in the Fill dialog box remain available to you. So you can fill from History with a specified opacity or blending mode.

Cloning with the Clone Stamp Tool

Cloning is the process of copying pixels from one area to another. Cloning has two parts: the sample and the clone. The sample is the area of the original image you clone from. The clone is the selection of pixels you copy from the sample. The Clone Stamp tool is used to clone pixels, and allows you to choose the brush size, hardness, and opacity. Each of these options affects the appearance of the clone you create. Current & Below is one of three sampling options that you can use with the Clone Stamp tool. The Current & Below option means that the Clone Stamp tool will sample artwork from the current layer and all the layers below it. Jon sends you a photo for a client's website. He tells you that the client is "allergic to even numbers" and wants to have five geese in the image, not four. Jon asks you to clone one of the geese. He also tells you to create the clone on a separate layer so that it can be moved around if the client wants to make changes.

STEPS

1. Open PS H-2.psd, save it as five geese_PS-H, create a new layer above the Background layer, then name the new layer Clone

2. Click the Clone Stamp tool 🔲, click the Brush Preset picker list arrow on the Options bar, set the Size to 150, then set the Hardness to 0%

3. Verify that the Aligned check box on the Options bar is checked

4. On the Options bar, click the Sample list arrow, then click Current & Below

   The Current & Below option is used often because it allows you to create a clone on a layer separate from the artwork you are sampling.

QUICK TIP
To turn this preview off, open the Clone Source panel, click the panel menu button, then click Show Overlay to remove the check mark.

5. Press and hold [Alt] (Win) or [option] (Mac), click the beak of the third goose from the left, then release [Alt] (Win) or [option] (Mac)

   This behavior is called sampling. When you sample, you set the source for the Clone Stamp tool, The Clone Stamp tool will now paint using this sample as its point of origin. A preview of what you have cloned appears with the pointer.

6. Position the mouse pointer over the upper-left area of the canvas

7. Click and drag to "paint" a clone of the goose in that area

   Your canvas should resemble Figure H-9.

8. Click Edit on the Menu bar, point to Transform, click Scale, then reduce the clone to 80% so that it's not an obvious duplicate

9. Add a layer mask to the Clone layer, then mask the darker clouds around the clone so that they blend with the lighter clouds behind them

10. Compare your results to Figure H-10, save your work, then close five geese_PS-H.psd

FIGURE H-9: Viewing the cloned bird

Cloned bird

FIGURE H-10: Viewing the finished artwork

Cloning on a separate layer

As you've learned throughout this book, the best way to work in Photoshop is "non-destructively." That goes for cloning, too. When you do anything with the Clone Stamp tool, you usually want to work in a way that doesn't permanently affect the original artwork. For example, let's say that you were using the Clone Stamp tool to remove a scar from someone's face. You wouldn't clone out the scar on the original artwork; you'd hide the scar with a clone of clear skin on a separate layer. This way, if the results aren't satisfactory, you haven't irrevocably altered the original artwork.

The Current & Below option is key to this concept, which is why it is the most commonly used option. Regardless of how many layers your artwork contains, when you need to clone, create an empty layer above the artwork for the clone. Then use the Current & Below option. Current & Below allows you to sample all the artwork below the empty layer; then you can clone safely onto the empty layer, protecting the original artwork from the changes.

Cloning with the Healing Brush Tool

Like the Clone Stamp tool, the Healing Brush tool is a cloning tool. But the Healing Brush tool is more complex and plays a different role. As with the Clone Stamp tool, you use the Healing Brush tool to sample from one area and clone to another. However, the Healing Brush tool matches the clone to the texture, lighting, and shading of the area you are cloning to. Practically speaking, the Healing Brush tool is useful for cloning large areas of non-specific data, like the sky or a shirt. If you tried to use the Healing Brush tool to clone an area of a brick wall onto another area, the results wouldn't be satisfying, because the many lines and textures involved would be too specific for the Healing Brush tool to blur and blend together. Your travel client sends you a disk with an image they want to use on the cover of their summer brochure. They tell you ahead of time that it's damaged, and when you open it, you see the damage right away. Jon tells you this challenge is a good example of the difference between using the Clone Stamp tool and the Healing Brush tool. He tells you that of the two, only the Healing Brush tool will solve the problem.

STEPS

1. Open PS H-3.psd, save it as sailboat scratches_PS-H, create a new layer above the Background layer, then name the new layer Remove Scratches

2. **Analyze the problems with the image**
   The Clone Stamp tool would not be very useful on this image because there's no "clean" place to sample from. Note that the sky at the top of the image is dark blue and gradually fades down to a lighter blue. As shown in Figure H-11, all of the dark blue area at the top is marred by the black scratches. This exercise is a great example of how the Healing Brush tool can solve a problem that the Clone Stamp tool can't. The key here is that the Healing brush tool lets you sample the undamaged light blue sky and clone it into the dark blue sky. Incredibly, the tool is sophisticated enough that it adjusts the tone of the light blue sample to match the dark blue sky at the top of the image.

QUICK TIP
The Healing Brush tool might be hidden behind the Spot Healing Brush tool.

3. **Click the Healing Brush tool** ✎, **click the Brush Preset picker list arrow on the Options bar, set the Size to 150, set the Hardness to 0%, click the Sample list arrow on the Options bar, then click Current & Below**

4. **Press and hold [Alt] (Win) or [option] (Mac), click the sky on the left side of the image in the light blue area above the clouds but below the bird, then release [Alt] (Win) or [option] (Mac)**

5. **Click and drag to "paint" a clone of the clear sky in the upper-left corner**
   The clear sky is cloned into the upper-left corner, and the color of the clone is automatically modified to match the darker blue area.

6. **Using the same method, continue sampling from the clear light blue sky and cloning into the darker damaged sky at the top until the image is repaired**

7. **Compare your results to Figure H-12, save your work, then close sailboat scratches_PS-H.psd**

Understanding aligned vs. nonaligned clones

All of the cloning tools—including the Clone Stamp tool—have an Aligned option that is available on the Options bar when you select the tool. Here's the key to understanding the Aligned option: It's all about what happens after you stop cloning. Imagine you start cloning a face in your document, and you stop cloning before you're done. With the Aligned option checked, and without resampling, if you continue cloning, the Clone Stamp tool will pick up where you left off and finish the face. That's an aligned clone.

Using the same example, if you do not activate the Aligned option and stop cloning, then start again, the Clone Stamp tool will automatically start the new clone from the original sample spot.

FIGURE H-11: Original image

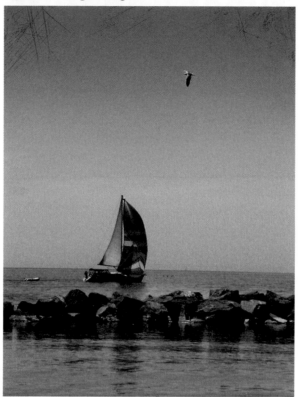

FIGURE H-12: Viewing the finished artwork

Improving Productivity

Experimenting with Cloning Options

Both the Clone Stamp tool and the Healing Brush tool share the same sampling options, and it's important to understand the difference between each to work effectively with the cloning tools. First, note the options for these tools fall under the title of "Sample". That's key to what these options do: they control how the cloning tool samples the artwork. The three sampling options are:

- **Current Layer:** The tool samples artwork only on the targeted layer. Artwork or adjustments on layers above or below the targeted layer will not be involved in the sample.
- **Current & Below:** The tool samples the *appearance* of the artwork as a composite of the current layer and all the layers beneath it. Artwork or adjustments on layers *above* the targeted layer are not involved in the sample.
- **All Layers:** The tool samples the appearance of the artwork as the result of all layers in the image.

You're training an assistant to help you with your work, and you receive a file from a client that provides a good example of how the cloning options you use—and the layer you clone on—will affect the clone.

STEPS

1. **Open PS H-4.psd, save it as** clone options_PS-H, **then hide and show the Levels adjustment layer**

   The Levels adjustment layer adds much-needed contrast to the image.

2. **Target the** Clone layer **on the Layers panel**

   The Clone layer is completely empty.

3. **Click the** Clone Stamp tool 🔲, **click the** Sample list arrow **on the Options bar, then click** Current Layer

4. **Sample an area from the boy's face and try to clone it in another location**

   Nothing will happen. Because the Clone layer is empty and the brush preference is set to Current Layer, you are sampling from the Clone layer only. There's nothing to sample from, so nothing can be cloned.

5. **Click the** Sample list arrow, **then choose** Current & Below

6. **Sample the boy's nose, then clone the entire face in the space to the left of the boy**

   As shown in Figure H-13, the boy's face is cloned. Because the brush preference is set to Current & Below, the brush sampled the current layer—the Clone layer—*and* all layers below it. In this case, that includes the artwork on the Background layer.

7. **Click the** Sample list arrow, **then choose** All Layers

8. **Sample the boy's nose, clone the entire face in the space in the upper-right corner of the canvas, then compare your result to Figure H-14**

   The clone is noticeably higher in contrast than the original. Because the brush preference is set to All Layers, the brush sampled all the layers, including the Levels adjustment layer above it. That means that the cloned area reflects the adjustment twice—in the sample and as a result of the Levels adjustment layer above it.

9. **Hide the Levels adjustment layer**

   The second clone still does not match the original. However, the first clone still matches the original, because it was sampled without the Levels adjustment being involved in the sample.

10. **Save your work, then close** clone options_PS-H.psd

FIGURE H-13: Viewing the first clone

FIGURE H-14: Viewing the second clone

Clone has increased contrast

Improving Productivity

Practice

Concepts Review

Label the elements of the Photoshop screen shown in Figure H-15.

FIGURE H-15

1. _____   4. _____
2. _____   5. _____
3. _____   6. _____

Match each term with the statement that best describes it.

7. **Healing Brush tool**	**a.** Saves current status
8. **History panel**	**b.** Useful for converting file formats of multiple files
9. **Action**	**c.** Sample option for a cloning tool
10. **Sample**	**d.** Origin of a clone
11. **Snapshot**	**e.** Can be used to revert to a previous status of a file
12. **Image Processor**	**f.** Cloning tool
13. **Current & Below**	**g.** Recording of a series of steps or commands

Select the best answer from the list of choices.

14. **Which of the following is not a sample option for a cloning tool?**
    - **a.** Current Layer
    - **b.** Current Source
    - **c.** Current & Below
    - **d.** All Layers

15. **Which of the following is not an automated process in Photoshop?**
    - **a.** Using the Image Processor
    - **b.** Batch processing an action
    - **c.** Executing an action
    - **d.** Creating an action

16. **Which of the following cannot be done using the History panel?**
    - **a.** Save a file
    - **b.** Revert a file
    - **c.** Capture a status
    - **d.** Undo a move

17. **Which one of the following actions best describes what the History Brush tool does?**
    - **a.** Clones
    - **b.** Samples
    - **c.** Automates
    - **d.** Reverts

18. **Which of the following best describes the result of using the Clone Stamp tool?**
    - **a.** Paint
    - **b.** Sample
    - **c.** Duplicate
    - **d.** Transform

Skills Review

1. **Use the Image Processor.**
    a. Open the seven files in the Skills Automation folder located in your Data Files folder. (*Hint*: The files are all PSD files.)
    b. Click File on the Menu bar, point to Scripts, then click Image Processor.
    c. In Section 1, click the Use Open Images option button.
    d. In Section 2, click the Save in Same Location option button.
    e. In Section 3, click the Save as JPEG check box, if necessary, then type **12** in the Quality text box.
    f. In Section 3, check the Save as TIFF check box, if necessary.
    g. Verify that nothing is checked in Section 4.
    h. Click Run.
    i. Navigate to the Skills Automation folder, then open the Skills Automation folder.
    j. Return to Photoshop and keep all files open.

2. **Create and run an action.**
    a. Click the girl_PS-H.psd document tab, click Window on the Menu bar, then click Actions to open the Actions panel, if necessary.
    b. Click the Actions panel menu button, click New Action, type **Invert Background** in the Name text box, then click Record.
    c. Click Image on the Menu bar, point to Adjustments, then click Invert.
    d. Click File on the Menu bar, click Save, click File on the Menu bar, then click Close.
    e. Click the Stop playing/recording button on the Actions panel.
    f. Click the petals_PS-H.psd document tab, then click the phrase Invert Background on the Actions panel to highlight it.
    g. Click the Play selection button on the Actions panel.
    h. Apply the Invert Background action to the remaining open files.
    i. Open all seven PSD files in the Skills Automation folder.
    j. Close all the files.

3. **Batch process an action.**
    a. Click File on the Menu bar, point to Automate, then click Batch.
    b. In the Play section, click the Action list arrow to see all the actions available, then click Invert Background.
    c. In the Source section, verify that Folder is chosen, then click the Choose button.

Skills Review (continued)

  d. Navigate to and select the Skills Automation folder, then click OK (Win) or Choose (Mac).

  e. Verify that none of the four check boxes in the Source section is checked.

  f. In the Destination section, verify that None is chosen.

  g. In the Errors section, verify that Stop for Errors is chosen.

  h. Click OK.

  i. Open all seven PSD files from the Skills Automation folder. (*Hint*: All seven files' backgrounds are inverted again and appear as they did originally.)

  j. Close all the open files.

4. Use the History panel.

  Note: Sections 4 and 5 must be done in one sitting. If you close the file after Section 4, you will not be able to do Section 5.

  a. Open PS H-5, save it as **history skills_PS-H**, then verify that the History panel is open.

  b. Press [Ctrl][L] (Win) or ⌘[L] (Mac) to open the Levels dialog box.

  c. Drag the black triangle immediately below the histogram to the right until the shadow text box reads 29, then click OK. (*Hint*: You've modified the layer directly, not with a Levels adjustment layer.)

  d. Press [Ctrl][U] (Win) or ⌘[U] (Mac) to open the Hue/Saturation dialog box.

  e. Click the Colorize check box, drag the Saturation slider all the way to the left to 0%, then click OK.

  f. Click Filter on the Menu bar, point to Stylize, then click Solarize.

  g. Click the Levels state on the History panel.

  h. Click the Hue/Saturation state on the History panel.

  i. Click the PS H-5.psd thumbnail at the top of the History panel.

  j. Click the Levels state on the History panel.

  k. Save the file.

5. Create a snapshot and use the History Brush tool.

  a. On the History panel, verify that Levels is highlighted.

  b. Click the Create new snapshot button on the panel.

  c. Click Solarize on the History panel.

  d. Click the gray square to the left of Snapshot 1 to set the source for the History Brush tool.

  e. Click the History Brush tool, set the Hardness to 0%, then set the Opacity to 100%.

  f. Paint just the boy so that your canvas resembles Figure H-16.

  g. Save your work, then close history skills_PS-H.psd.

6. Clone with the Clone Stamp tool.

  a. Open PS H-6.psd, then save it as **skills clone_PS-H**.

  b. Create a new layer above the Background layer, then name the new layer **Clone**.

  c. Zoom in on the flying bird and its shadow immediately above the swimming duck.

  d. Click the Clone Stamp tool, set the Size to 70, then set the Hardness to 0%. (*Hint*: Verify that the Aligned check box on the Options bar is checked.)

  e. On the Options bar, click the Sample list arrow, then click Current & Below.

  f. Press and hold [Alt] (Win) or [option] (Mac), click approximately ½ inch directly to the left of the bird, then release [Alt] (Win) or [option] (Mac).

  g. Click and drag to remove the bird and its shadow.

  h. Using the same method, remove the two birds to the left so that the only birds remaining in the image are the duck and the two birds flying in the reflection of the tree.

  i. Save your work.

FIGURE H-16

Skills Review (continued)

7. Clone with the Healing Brush tool.

FIGURE H-17

   a. Click the Healing Brush tool, set the Size to 70, set the Hardness to 0%, then verify that Current & Below is selected on the Options bar for the Clone layer.

   b. Press and hold [Alt] (Win) or [option] (Mac), click in the reflection of the tree in the water approximately ½ inch to the left of the leftmost bird, then release [Alt] (Win) or [option] (Mac).

   c. Click and drag to remove the far left bird and its shadow.

   d. Using the same method, remove the remaining flying bird and its shadow.

   e. Compare your results to Figure H-17, save your work, then close skills clone_PS-H.psd.

8. Experiment with cloning options.

   a. Open PS H-7.psd, save it as **blue birds_PS-H**, then hide and show the Hue/Saturation 1 adjustment layer.

   b. Target the Clone layer on the Layers panel. (*Hint*: The Clone layer is completely empty.)

   c. Click the Clone Stamp tool, then choose a large soft brush.

FIGURE H-18

   d. Click the Sample list arrow on the Options bar, then click Current Layer.

   e. Sample the beak of the third bird from the left, and try to clone it to another location. (*Hint*: Nothing will happen.)

   f. Click the Sample list arrow, then choose Current & Below.

   g. Paint in the upper-left corner of the canvas to clone the bird.

   h. Click the Sample list arrow, then choose All Layers.

   i. Sample the beak of the same bird, then clone the entire bird and some of the surrounding sky in the space in the upper-right corner of the canvas.

   j. Compare your result to Figure H-18.

   k. Save your work, then close blue birds_PS-H.psd.

Independent Challenge 1

You have some downtime at work. Your creative director suggests that you use the time to create an action for the noise technique that you use repeatedly when finishing layered artwork.

FIGURE H-19

   a. Open PS H-8.psd, then save it as **noise action_PS-H**.

   b. Click the Actions panel menu button, click New Action, type **Noise 2 Pixels** in the Name text box, then click Record.

   c. Create a new layer on the Layers panel, then name the new layer **Noise 2.0**.

   d. Click Edit on the Menu bar, click Fill, click the Use list arrow, click 50% Gray, verify that Mode is set to Normal and Opacity is set to 100%, then click OK.

   e. Click Filter on the Menu bar, point to Noise, then click Add Noise.

Independent Challenge 1 (continued)

f. Type **2** in the Amount text box, then verify that both the Gaussian option button and the Monochromatic check box are activated.

g. Click OK.

h. Change the blending mode on the Noise 2.0 layer to Overlay.

i. Click the Stop playing/recording button on the Actions panel.

j. Your Actions panel should resemble Figure H-19.

k. Save your work, then close noise action_PS-H.psd.

Independent Challenge 2

Your creative director gives you a folder of seven images. He asks that you apply noise to all seven images. To get the work done quickly, you decide to batch process an action.

(*Note*: **You must first have completed Independent Challenge 1 to have this action listed on the Actions panel.**)

a. Click File on the Menu bar, point to Automate, then click Batch.

b. In the Play section, click the Action list arrow to see all the actions available, then click Noise 2 Pixels.

c. In the Source section, verify that Folder is chosen, then click the Choose button.

d. Navigate to the location where you store your Data Files, select the folder named Noise Files, then click OK (Win) or Choose (Mac).

e. Verify that none of the four check boxes in the Source section is checked.

FIGURE H-20

f. Click the Destination list arrow, then click Folder.

g. Click the Choose button under the Destination section, navigate to the location where you store your Data Files, then click OK (Win) or Choose (Mac).

h. In the Errors section, verify that Stop for Errors is chosen.

i. Click OK. (*Hint*: Photoshop will run the Noise action on the seven files. If you are prompted, click OK to verify saving options.)

j. Open the family_PS-H.psd file, then compare your Layers panel to Figure H-20.

k. Close family_PS-H.psd.

Independent Challenge 3

Your client has sent you a close-up image of a flower and asks that you create "an interesting special effect" that involves some amount of a blur and desaturation. Your creative director suggests that you work from saved history on the History panel to create the effect.

a. Open PS H-9.psd, then save it as **flowering_PS-H**.

b. Click Image on the Menu bar, point to Adjustments, then click Posterize.

c. Type **4** in the Levels text box, then click OK.

d. Click Filter on the Menu bar, point to Blur, then click Gaussian Blur.

e. Type **2.4** in the Radius text box, then click OK.

f. Click Image on the Menu bar, point to Adjustments, then click Desaturate.

g. Click Posterize on the History panel.

Independent Challenge 3 (continued)

h. Click Gaussian Blur on the History panel.

i. Click Desaturate on the History panel.

FIGURE H-21

Advanced Challenge Exercise

- Click Edit on the Menu bar, then click Fill.
- Click the Use list arrow, then click History.
- Click the Mode list arrow, then click Overlay.
- Type **50** in the Opacity text box.
- Click OK.
- Click the PS H-9.psd thumbnail on the History panel to see the original image.
- Click the Desaturate command on the History panel.

j. Verify you can see the entire image in the window.

k. Click the History Brush tool on the Tools panel.

l. On the Options bar, set the Size to 800 px, set the Mode to Overlay, set the Opacity to 50%, then verify that the Flow is set to 100%.

m. In one move, paint the entire canvas with the History Brush tool.

n. Compare your results to Figure H-21.

o. Save your work, then close flowering_PS-H.psd.

Real Life Independent Challenge

Just back from vacation, you snapped some great photos that you want to upload to a stock photography website. You go through your photos and circle areas that you want to retouch. You decide on an image of a sailboat to work on. You open it to retouch it and improve its color balance.

FIGURE H-22

a. Open PS H-10.psd, then save it as **sailboat cleanup_PS-H**.

b. Review the circled and numbered areas on the image and then hide the Fixes layer.

c. Create a new layer named **Clone** above the Background layer.

d. Click the Clone Stamp tool, then clone out the bird in the sky.

e. Sample the horizon, then clone out the faint boat on the horizon.

f. Clone out the birds in the water to the right of the boat.

g. Clone out the dinghy to the left of the boat.

h. Compare your results to Figure H-22.

Advanced Challenge Exercise

- Click the Create a new fill or adjustment layer on the Layers panel, then click Levels.
- Drag the gray midtone slider to the right until the text box reads .60.
- Press [Ctrl][I] (Win) or [⌘][I] (Mac) to fill the layer mask with black.
- Click the Brush tool, then set the Opacity to 40%.
- Painting with white, gradually "brush in" the Levels adjustment.

i. Save your work, then close sailboat cleanup_PS-H.psd.

Visual Workshop

Open PS H-11.psd, then save it as **dog balloon_PS-H**. Compare using the Clone Stamp tool and the Healing Brush tool for cloning out the wires. Use a separate layer for cloning. Compare your final result to Figure H-23. (*Hint*: Use the automatic brush strokes technique with the Clone Stamp tool and Healing Brush tool when cloning out the long straight wires.)

FIGURE H-23

Data Files for Photoshop CS6 Illustrated

Data File Supplied	Student Creates File	Used In
UNIT A		
Lessons		
PS A-1.psd	birdie_PS-A.psd	Lessons 3- 4
	birdie_PS-A.tif	
	birdie_PS-A.jpg	
PS A-2.psd	birdie resize_PS-A.psd	Lesson 5
PS A-3.psd	birdie magazine_PS-A.psd	Lesson 6
	birdie web graphic_PS-A.psd	
	new document_PS-A.psd	Lesson 7
PS A-4.psd	parrots_PS-A.psd	Lesson 8
PS A-5.psd		
PS A-6.psd	estonia house_PS-A.psd	Lesson 9
PS A-7.psd	hotel postcard_PS-A.psd	Lesson 10
Skills Review		
PS A-8.psd	tallinn_PS-A.psd	
PS A-9.psd	eagle resize_PS-A.psd	
	skills new_PS-A.psd	Skills Review
PS A-10.psd	title_PS-A.psd	
PS A-11.psd	email postcard_PS-A.psd	
PS A-12.psd	san francisco_PS-A.psd	
IC1		
PS A-13.psd	web graphic 1_PS-A.jpg	
PS A-14.psd	web graphic 2_PS-A.jpg	Independent Challenge 1
PS A-15.psd	web graphic 3_PS-A.jpg	
IC2		
PS A-16.psd	triptych_PS-A.psd	
	triptych_PS-A.jpg	Independent Challenge 2
PS A-17.psd		
PS A-18.psd		
IC3		
PS A-19.psd	bookmark_PS-A.psd	Independent Challenge 3
Real Life IC		
PS A-20.psd	mother's love_PS-A.psd	Real Life IC
	mother's love_PS-A.jpg	
Visual Workshop		
PS A-21.psd	visual solution_PS-A.psd	Visual Workshop

Data File Supplied	Student Creates File	Used In
UNIT B		
Lessons		
PS B-1.psd	selections puzzle_PS_B.psd	Lessons 1-3
PS B-2.psd	air balloon_PS-B.psd	Lesson 3
PS B-3.psd	save selections_PS-B.psd	Lessons 4-5
PS B-4.psd	apple edges_PS-B.psd	Lesson 6
PS B-5.psd	vignette_PS-B.psd	Lesson 7
PS B-6.psd	eagle silhouette_PS-B.psd	Lesson 8
Skills Review		
PS B-7.psd	shapes_PS-B.psd	
PS B-8.psd	clown posterize_PS-B.psd	
PS B-9.psd	skills edges_PS-B.psd	Skills Review
PS B-10.psd	apple silhouette_PS-B.psd	
IC1		
PS B-11.psd	magic wand mask_PS-B.psd	Independent Challenge 1
IC2		
PS B-12.psd	orange balloons_PS-B.psd	Independent Challenge 2
IC3		
PS B-13.psd	iq test_PS-B.psd	Independent Challenge 3
PS B-14.psd		
Real Life IC		
PS B-15.psd	posterized woman_PS-B.psd	Real Life IC
Visual Workshop		
PS B-16.psd	visual solutions_PS-B.psd	Visual Workshop
UNIT C		
Lessons		
PS C-1.psd	roman holiday 1_PS-C.psd	Lessons 1-2
PS C-2.psd	roman holiday 2_PS-C.psd	Lessons 3-8
Colosseum.psd		
Skills Review		
PS C-3.psd	shining future 1_PS-C.psd	
PS C-4.psd	shining future 2_PS-C.psd	Skills Review
PS C-5.psd	bright shining future_PS-C.psd	
Globe.psd		
IC1		
PS C-6.psd	roman numerals_PS-C.psd	Independent Challenge 1
IC2		
PS C-7.psd	dolphin moon_PS-C.psd	Independent Challenge 2
Dolphin Sky.psd		
IC3		
PS C-8.psd	double dolphins_PS-C.psd	Independent Challenge 3
Real Life IC		
PS C-9.psd	sisters postcard_PS-C.psd	Real Life IC
Annie.tif		
Jenny.tif		
Visual Workshop		
PS C-10.psd	three glowing globes_PS-C.psd	Visual Workshop

Data File Supplied	Student Creates File	Used In
UNIT D		
Lessons		
PS D-1.psd	grayscale_PS-D.psd	Lessons 1-2
PS D-2.psd	adjust brightness contrast_PS-D.psd	Lesson 3
PS D-3.psd	adjust white and black points_PS-D.psd	Lessons 4-5
PS D-4.psd	rgb_PS-D.psd	Lesson 6
PS D-5.psd	color balance_PS-D.psd	Lessons 7-8
Skills Review		
PS D-6.psd	grayscale skills_PS-D.psd	
PS D-7.psd	brightness contrast skills_PS-D.psd	
PS D-8.psd	levels skills_PS-D.psd	Skills Review
PS D-9.psd	color balance skills_PS-D.psd	
IC1		
PS D-10.psd	hay bale_PS-D.psd	Independent Challenge 1
IC2		
PS D-11.psd	sailboat_PS-D.psd	Independent Challenge 2
IC3		
PS D-12.psd	color flowers_PS-D.psd	Independent Challenge 3
Real Life IC		
PS D-13.psd	canyon_PS-D.psd	Real Life IC
Visual Workshop		
PS D-14.psd	visual solution_PS-D.psd	Visual Workshop
UNIT E		
Lessons		
PS E-1.psd	set type_PS-E.psd	Lessons 1-2
PS E-2.psd	bevel type_PS-E.psd	Lessons 3-5
PS E-3.psd	making the gradient_PS-E.psd	Lessons 6-7
PS E-4.psd	clip layers_PS-E.psd	Lessons 8-9
PS E-5.psd	fade type_PS-E.psd	Lesson 10
Skills Review		
PS E-6.psd	set skills type_PS-E.psd	
PS E-7.psd	bevel skills type_PS-E.psd	Skills Review
PS E-8.psd	gradient skills_PS-E.psd	
PS E-9.psd	skills clip layers_PS-E.psd	
PS E-10.psd	fade skills type_PS-E.psd	
IC1		
PS E-11.psd	black on blue_PS-E.psd	Independent Challenge 1
IC2		
PS E-12.psd	sunset gradient_PS-E.psd	Independent Challenge 2
IC3		
PS E-13.psd	sunset stroke emboss_PS-E.psd	Independent Challenge 3
Real Life IC		
PS E-14.psd	sunset clipped_PS-E.psd	Real Life IC
Visual Workshop		
PS E-15.psd	radial gradient_PS-E.psd	Visual Workshop

Data File Supplied	Student Creates File	Used In
UNIT F		
Lessons		
PS F-1.psd	connect the dots_PS-F.psd	Lessons 1-2
PS F-2.psd	flip flops_PS-F.psd	Lesson 3
PS F-3.psd	hsb_PS-F.psd	Lessons 4-5
PS F-4.psd	replace color_PS-F.psd	Lesson 6
PS F-5.psd	color fan_PS-F.psd	Lesson 7
PS F-6.psd	colorize_PS-F.psd	Lesson 8
Skills Review		
PS F-7.psd	dots_PS-F.psd	Skills Review
PS F-8.psd	heels_PS-F.psd	
PS F-9.psd	replace color skills_PS-F.psd	
PS F-10.psd	b&w skills_PS-F.psd	
IC1		
PS F-11.psd	stop sign_PS-F.psd	Independent Challenge 1
IC2		
PS F-12.psd	green dress_PS-F.psd	Independent Challenge 2
IC3		
PS F-13.psd	newsletter_PS-F.psd	Independent Challenge 3
Real Life IC		
PS F-14.psd	pylon_PS-F.psd	Real Life IC
Visual Workshop		
PS F-15.psd	snow cones_PS-F.psd	Visual Workshop
UNIT G		
Lessons		
PS G-1.psd	colorize with color mode_PS-G.psd	Lesson 1
PS G-2.psd	final roman holiday_PS-G.psd	Lessons 2-4
PS G-3.psd	silver streak_PS-G.psd	Lessons 5-6
PS G-4.psd	non-destructive filters_PS-G.psd	Lesson 7
PS G-5.psd	distort_PS-G.psd	Lesson 8
charlie billboard_PS-G.psd		
Skills Review		
PS G-6.psd	colorize skills_PS-G.psd	Skills Review
PS G-7.psd	shining future skills_PS-G.psd	
IC1		
PS G-8.psd	color mode correction_PS-G.psd	Independent Challenge 1
IC2		
PS G-9.psd	key art_PS-G.psd	Independent Challenge 2
IC3		
PS G-10.psd	12 count_PS-G.psd	Independent Challenge 3
charlie key art_PS-G.psd		
backer_PS-G.psd		
Real Life IC		
PS G-11.psd	diver_PS-G.psd	Real Life IC
Visual Workshop		
PS G-12.psd	two motion blurs_PS-G.psd	Visual Workshop

Data File Supplied	Student Creates File	Used In
UNIT H		
Lessons		
Automation folder	TIFF folder	Lessons 1-3
bricks_PS-H.psd	bricks_PS-H.tif	
flowers_PS-H.psd	flowers_PS-H.tif	
marble_PS-H.psd	marble_PS-H.tif	
rice paper_PS-H.psd	rice paper_PS-H.tif	
water_PS-H.psd	water_PS-H.tif	
wood_PS-H.psd	wood_PS-H.tif	
woodchip paper_PS-H.psd	woodchip paper_PS-H.tif	
	JPEG folder	
	bricks_PS-H.jpg	
	flowers_PS-H.jpg	
	marble_PS-H.jpg	
	rice paper_PS-H.jpg	
	water_PS-H.jpg	
	wood_PS-H.jpg	
PS H-1.psd	woodchip paper_PS-H.jpg	
PS H-2.psd	it's history_PS-H.psd	Lessons 4-5
PS H-3.psd	five geese_PS-H.psd	Lesson 6
PS H-4.psd	sailboat scratches_PS-H.psd	Lesson 7
	clone options_PS-H.psd	Lesson 8
Skills Review		Skills Review
Skills Automation Folder	TIFF folder	
family_PS-H.psd	family_PS-H.tif	
girl_PS-H.psd	girl_PS-H.tif	
grit_PS-H.psd	grit_PS-H.tif	
lake_PS-H.psd	lake_PS-H.tif	
petals_PS-H.psd	petals_PS-H.tif	
raindrops_PS-H.psd	raindrops_PS-H.tif	
vegas_PS-H.psd	vegas_PS-H.tif	
	JPEG folder	
	family_PS-H.jpg	
	girl_PS-H.jpg	
	grit_PS-H.jpg	
	lake_PS-H.jpg	
	petals_PS-H.jpg	
	raindrops_PS-H.jpg	
	vegas_PS-H.jpg	
PS H-5.psd	history skills_PS-H.psd	
PS H-6.psd	skills clone_PS-H.psd	
PS H-7.psd	blue birds_PS-H.psd	
IC1 and IC2		
PS H-8.psd	noise action_PS-H.psd	Independent Challenge 1
Noise Files folder		Independent Challenge 2
family_PS-H.psd		
girl_PS-H.psd		
grit_PS-H.psd		
lake_PS-H.psd		
petals_PS-H.psd		
raindrops_PS-H.psd		
vegas_PS-H.psd		

Data File Supplied	Student Creates File	Used In
IC3 PS H-9.psd	flowering_PS-H.psd	Independent Challenge 3
Real Life IC PS H-10.psd	sailboat cleanup_PS-H.psd	Real Life IC
Visual Workshop PS H-11.psd	dog balloon_PS-H.psd	Visual Workshop

Glossary

Actions Created, stored, and automatically saved in the Actions panel, actions execute specific procedures automatically.

adjustment layers Adjustments that exist as layers on the Layers panel.

adjustments Operations that affect the appearance of an image, such as manipulating brightness and contrast.

aliased edge A hard selection edge in which the "stair-stepped" pixels are obvious and the edge is noticeably blunt.

alpha channels Saved selections stored in the Channels panel.

anti-aliased edge A crisp but smooth selection edge.

Bitmap graphic A graphic composed of pixels. All Photoshop images are bitmap graphics.

black point The darkest pixel in an image.

blending modes Mathematical algorithms that define how pixels affect pixels beneath them to create a specific effect.

brightness Defined by a pixel's grayscale value: the higher the number, the brighter the pixel.

Canvas The bed of pixels that make up an image.

clipping Term that refers to using artwork on one layer to mask the artwork on a layer or layers above it.

cloning Copying pixels from one area to another.

CMYK Cyan, magenta, yellow, and black; a color model in Photoshop; the subtractive primary colors; the four process colors central to conventional offset printing.

color model Defines the colors we see and work with in digital images. RGB (red, green, blue), CMYK (cyan, magenta, yellow, black), and HSB (hue, saturation, brightness) are all color models and each uses a different method for describing color.

color profile A group of preset settings for controlling how color will appear on your monitor and in a printed document.

color stops Specified colors that make up a gradient.

contiguous Term referring to pixels that border other pixels.

continuous tone A smooth transition from shadows to midtones to highlights.

contrast Represented by the relationship between highlights and shadows.

cropping A basic task in which you define an area of an image that you want to keep and then discard the remainder of the image.

Digital image Image that you get from a digital camera, from scanning a photograph or a slide, or that you create from scratch in Adobe Photoshop.

drop shadow Commonly used effect and/or layer style where artwork appears to cast a shadow.

Feathered edge A soft selection edge created by blending selected pixels and the background image.

flipping Transformation that creates a mirror image of the artwork, vertically or horizontally.

Gloss contours A set of 12 preset adjustments that affect the brightness and contrast of a layer style to create dramatic lighting effects.

gradient Blend between two or more colors.

grayscale image A digital image in which each pixel can be one—and only one—of 256 shades of gray.

Highlights The lightest areas of an image, represented by pixels whose value falls in the upper third of the grayscale range.

high-res A shortened form of "high-resolution"; usually refers to images with a minimum of 300 pixels per inch.

histogram A graph that represents the distribution of pixels in the image across the grayscale. The histogram appears on the Properties panel when a Levels or Curves adjustment layer is created.

HSB Hue, saturation, and brightness; a color model in Photoshop.

hue The name of a color: red, orange, and blue are all hues.

Image size Refers to the physical dimensions (width/height) of the Photoshop file.

interpolation Process used when an image is enlarged in which new pixels are created based on color information from existing pixels.

Layer mask Used to define which areas of artwork on a single layer are visible, not visible, or partly visible.

linear gradient Blend that progresses straight from one color to another in a linear fashion.

Marquee zoom Dragging the Zoom tool on the image to magnify a specific area.

midtones Pixels whose color falls into the middle range of the grayscale.

montage Multiple art components overlapping to create a single composition.

Noise A blanket of high-contrast pixels that produce a grainy effect over an image.

Opacity Refers to how opaque pixels on a layer are. A layer with 0% opacity is completely transparent and not visible.

Pixel Smallest component of a bitmap graphic; derived from the words picture and element.

posterize A special effect that is created by reducing the number of colors available for the image.

Radial gradient Blend that radiates outward from one color to another, like a series of concentric circles.

rasterize Term that means "convert to pixels." Type elements, for example, can be rasterized from vector type to pixels.

resampling Changing the total pixel count of an image when resizing an image.

resolution The number of pixels per inch (ppi) in a bitmap graphic.

revert A Photoshop command that restores the file to its status when you last saved.

RGB Red, green, and blue; the most-used color model in Photoshop; the additive primary colors of light; red, green, and blue light can combine to produce all the other colors in the spectrum; colors you see on your monitor are created by mixing varying strengths and combinations of red, green, and blue.

rotating A transformation that moves an object clockwise or counterclockwise around a given point.

Saturation The intensity of a color: how close it is to a pure hue; interchangeable with the term vibrance.

scaling A term for resizing artwork.

selection edge The outermost pixels in a selection.

shadows The darkest areas of an image, represented by pixels in the lowest third of the grayscale range.

sharpness An effect created when edge pixels are high in contrast.

smart filters Non-destructive filter layers that can be shown, hidden, edited, or deleted without permanently affecting artwork.

Tolerance A tool setting and dialog box setting that determines which pixels will be affected based upon their similarity in color.

transform Operations that change the location of pixels; Photoshop transformations include scaling, rotating, skewing, and distorting pixels.

Vibrance Intensity of a color; interchangeable with the term saturation.

vignette A visual effect in which the edge of an image gradually fades away; usually created with a feathered selection.

White point The brightest pixel in the image.

workspace The application interface; includes the Menu bar, the Tools panel, the dock of panels on the right of the screen, and the document.

Index